09/08
31.25

Joan Blondell

Hollywood Legends Series
Ronald L. Davis, General Editor

Joan Blondell

A Life between Takes

Matthew Kennedy

UNIVERSITY PRESS OF MISSISSIPPI • JACKSON

www.upress.state.ms.us

The University Press of Mississippi is a member of the Association of American
University Presses.

Library of Congress Cataloging-in-Publication Data
Kennedy, Matthew, 1957–
  Joan Blondell : a life between takes / Matthew Kennedy.
    p. cm. — (Hollywood legends series)
  Filmography: p.
  Includes bibliographical references and index.
  ISBN-13: 978-1-57806-961-3 (cloth : alk. paper)
  ISBN-10: 1-57806-961-0 (cloth : alk. paper)
1. Blondell, Joan. 2. Motion picture actors and actresses—United States—
Biography. I. Title.
  PN2287.B458K46 2007
  791.4302′8092—dc22
  [B]
                                                            2007011137

British Library Cataloging-in-Publication Data available

For Norman, who first had the idea, and Ellen,
who lived much of this

CONTENTS

ACKNOWLEDGMENTS

Joan Blondell's stature as a person and actress was reflected in the enthusiasm and affection of interviewees in recalling the movie, stage play, or television series they shared. My thanks to directors Norman Jewison and Curtis Harrington, producer Nancy Malone, camera operator Michael Ferris, agent Hillard Elkins, dolly grip Chico Anzures, and actors Theodore Bikel, Alice Ghostley, and Anthony Franciosa. Actor Gloria Manon offered invaluable comments on Blondell at the end of her career, and special mention must be paid to the witty testimony of the *Here Come the Brides* crowd: actors Robert Brown, Bridget Hanley, and Susan Tolsky, and story consultant William Blinn. Jill Jackson and Rose Lundin, two who knew Blondell but did not work with her, provided additional keen perceptions. Thanks, also, for responses from actors Lauren Bacall, Joan Fontaine, Karl Malden, Elizabeth Taylor, Vera Miles, James Garner, Gigi Perreau, Elliott Reid, Kay Armen, John Saxon, and Jean Simmons, and director Robert Wise.

Good advice and support came from entertainment writers, critics, editors, and historians, including Cari Beauchamp, John Kern, Gary Morris, Miles Kreuger, Karen McHale, Thomas Gladysz, André Soares, Leonard Maltin, Rex Reed, Roberto Friedman, Sam Staggs, and Mark Vieira. Ronald L. Bowers and David Martin were gracious in sharing their writings that pertain to Blondell. James Robert Parish has bestowed more wisdom and friendly guidance than I could possibly summarize. Without collectors, I would not have been able to see many of Blondell's rare movies and television. For loaning hours of video, appreciation goes to Randy Deucus, Eric Chadbourne, Marc Kagan, Martin McQuade, Tom Kleinschmidt, and

Sidney Bloomberg. Nick Davis and Eleanor Knowles Dugan came through like champions in the rare film search. Amazing Larry Chadbourne lent dozens of films to me from his vast collection, and what he didn't have he found elsewhere.

Archivist and librarians who unearthed brittle clippings and little known facts, and who have my thanks, include Charles Silver of the Museum of Modern Art, Julie Graham and Lauren Buisson of the Special Arts Collection at UCLA, Mark Quigley of the Research and Study Center at the UCLA Film and Television Archive, Mark Swartz of the Shubert Archive, Caroline Sisneros of the American Film Institute's Louis B. Mayer Library, Jane Klain and Richard Holbrook of the Museum of Television and Radio in New York, Anne Coco and Barbara Hall of the Margaret Herrick Library of the Academy of Motion Picture Arts and Sciences, and Kim Cupit of the Denton County Historical Commission. Researching at the Warner Bros. Archives is always a pleasure thanks to the thoughtful oversight of director Randi Hokett and curator Haden Guest. Ned Comstock found what appeared to be every published reference to Joan Blondell in the entire Cinema-Television Library at USC.

Thanks, also, to those who provided well-timed help with referrals and suggestions: Susan White, Yannek Aga Khan, publicist Larry Bloustein, Kim Briggs, Nick Langdon, Marge Meisinger, Henry Traub, Allan Taylor, and the ever-supportive Casey Searcy. I remain beholden to those friends who offer salient quips, subtle perceptions, and good-humored rapport: Mike Blubaugh, David Bowman, Eddie Hosey, Ralph Cole Jr., Stan Godin, Vi Klaseen, Joanna Pace, David Perry, Eric Lynxwiler, and Phil McKinley. Mark Cromwell does more than amuse and enlighten. For him and me, archives offer a peculiar comfort, and the benefits of his research are immeasurable. Abiding thanks to family for varied and valuable contributions, be it editing from sister Anne Peterson, research in New York from niece Elliott Kennedy, or "accidental" editing from cousin Walter Kennedy. My mother did not live to see this book published, but her love is on every page.

I am humbled and thankful that Joan Blondell's family has been so generous with time, history, memory, ephemera, and feelings. They, more than any print sources or film footage, help me understand the singular person that was their "Matey." My sincerest thanks to grandchildren Sandra Powell Espe, Scott Powell, and Stephanie Powell Murphy, niece Kathy Blondell, and former daughter-in-law Ann McDowell Traub. Granddaughter Joan Hayward Krooms recalled loving details, many of which are in the book. Daughter-in-law Ellen Levine was a source of referrals, scrapbooks, mementos, photos, and careful editing. Norman Powell's taped accounts of his mother's life were a blessing of clear-eyed and loving recollections. Daughter Ellen Powell's contributions are inestimable. She read each page with an eagle's eye for detail and meaning, but more importantly she helped me to see the large themes of her mother's life. Ellen's spirit, strength, courage, and talent have been inspiring.

Director Seetha Srinivasan, assistant editor Walter Biggins, and the entire staff at the University Press of Mississippi were a true pleasure to work with, as was copy editor Karen Johnson. Thanks as ever to my agent, Stuart Bernstein, who shepherds this writer with uncommon finesse. Finally, to my partner, Jeffrey Reid, who had a gentle and loving hand in the creation of this book. Errors found herein must not be attributed to any of the above-named good people, but to the author alone.

Joan Blondell

Introduction

Without work, what is life?
—Joan Blondell

Joan Blondell has always been an enigma. As a beloved actress, she was in front of the cameras for five decades, yet was adamant in her priorities to family and home life. She made good money due to an exhausting schedule, yet was never far ahead of the bill collectors. She was one of the most reliably good actresses Hollywood has ever seen, yet she was rarely showcased and never won a major award. She was a most steadfast friend to many, yet her three marriages ended badly.

Blondell's multiple contractions drew me to her as an irresistible subject of biography. If stereotypes of early and mid-twentieth-century womanhood are dominated by unremunerated domesticity, then that fact was lost on her, who began in show business in 1909 when she was three and didn't stop until her death in 1979. In writing this book, I wanted to recreate what it means to be always gazed upon, and how public expectation might vie with self-doubt in the life and mind of an actor. Work was always a performance but never the same performance. And what did it mean to be just short of major stardom, yet always in some degree of demand?

3

Joan Blondell, it turns out, is the perfect subject for pursuing these questions. As a child of vaudevillians, she was introduced to show business in the womb, and she never knew anything else. In examining her life, one fact stands above all others: She worked hard, really and truly hard, for over seventy years. Looking back more than a century after her birth, the reasons for her astonishing survival are not hard to define. Throughout her career, she was fun-loving, warm, and assertive without ever sacrificing her femininity. If she was typecast, she was a type we welcomed again and again. Perhaps it was her voice that first took you in. "Her voice was low-pitched, nasal, and gave the impression that there was a marble rolling around in her mouth somewhere," noted film historian James Robert Parish. Even with that distinctively husky tone, her line readings were a wonder of effortless precision. Her diction was flawless, and her rapid-fire delivery could give even Rosalind Russell a run for her money.

She came with many natural gifts. The architecture of her mouth, simultaneously sharp and soft, suggested Cupid. She had a radiant smile, straight white teeth, pillowy lips, and easy curls in her gamboge blonde hair. Two beauty marks to the east of her nose attractively punctuated her fair complexion, though they were often covered with pancake. Her figure was voluptuous, at one time measuring 37–21½–36.

Her translucent, saucer eyes merit special attention. Whether in black and white or color, they were spellbinding on screen, and apparently more so in person. Granddaughter Joan Hayward Krooms described them as "martini olive green with a coffee bean perimeter. Her pupils were encircled by a flaming light brown that glistened in the light. One eye had what looked like a freckle, which later was found to be caused by her near death from scarlet fever and diphtheria. Once you looked into her eyes, you were drawn to her like a moth to a flame." Actress Susan Tolsky remembered that they "always sparkled, no matter what time of day or night, no matter how tired she was. It was her soul, that pure, wonderful soul that bubbled up and popped out of her eyes."

Due to family demands, idling was rarely an option, and time and again Blondell found ways to enliven and dignify questionable material. Producers and audiences knew this and responded by keeping her working. The sheer volume of her output is impressive, but there is ample quality, and many of her films survive as classics: *The Public Enemy, Gold Diggers of 1933, A Tree Grows in Brooklyn, Nightmare Alley, Desk Set, The Cincinnati Kid, Opening Night,* and *Grease.* Other titles (*Blonde Crazy, Bullets or Ballots, Blondie Johnson, Stand-In,* and *Three Girls about Town*) remain lesser-known worthwhile gems on her resume.

Time has confirmed what a fine and underappreciated actress she was. Hers was the three-dimensional face on a two-dimensional screen. She was full of surprises, one moment as tough as Joan Crawford, the next as fragile as Margaret Sullavan, and the next as saucy as Mae West. Her powers of empathy were magnificent, as when she urged her niece to unleash a torrent of cathartic tears in a memorable scene in *A Tree Grows in Brooklyn.* She could even cry on cue, a talent sorely envied by Bette Davis. She excelled in a wide variety of genre pictures, including mysteries, romantic comedy, film noir, musicals, westerns, screwball comedies, family dramas, and satire.

Joan's career took her from Warner Bros. to MGM, Columbia, Fox, RKO, Goldwyn, Paramount, United Artists, and Universal. Her work at each offers a tapestry of studio system politics and creativity at its best and worst, but her Warner Bros. tenure in the 1930s stands out. During the Great Depression, she appeared in no less than fifty-two films over an eight year period while supporting her parents and younger brother and sister. Her naturally lighthearted disposition was most often used for comedic roles, but occasionally she was allowed to show real dramatic power. Along the way there were nine features with Dick Powell, two each with Barbara Stanwyck and Ginger Rogers, three with Humphrey Bogart, and assorted others with Clark Gable, Bing Crosby, John Wayne, William Powell, and Errol Flynn. She made seven movies with James Cagney, more than any other female costar. Warner Bros. paired her with Glenda Farrell, another snappy wisecracker, eight times. They were ideally matched, and it seemed Warner Bros. could not work her hard enough or fast enough. In the assembly-line sweatshop, she managed to be fresh and wise in every role given to her, no matter that she was suffering nervous exhaustion from playing another secretary, chorus girl, or gun moll for the umpteenth time. As an older character actress, her stock roles were madams, nannies, mystics, and matchmakers. She is best known to baby boomers as Lottie, the wise saloonkeeper in the late 1960s ABC-TV series *Here Come the Brides*, and as Vi, the harried waitress of the 1978 hit musical *Grease*, but quantity too often trumped quality in Blondell's career. The volume of her work presented a challenge for this writer. An accounting of so many movies and TV spots invites literary torpor. For the sake of narrative pacing, some Blondell work assignments that were quick and unremarkable are not mentioned in the text, while a complete list of her film and television credits can be found in the back of the book.

Joan was an object of desire for men and a symbol of trusting and loyal friendship for women. Though she had bad luck with romance in her private life, she always presented herself as in control and ready for fun. "Ann Sothern, who played types not unlike Blondell, would hold her nose up in the air when a man whistled after her as she walked by, though you could tell that she really liked it," remarked film historian John Kobal. "Joan, in a similar situation, would merely have smiled. 'Isn't that what men are like? God love 'em.'"

Her longevity cannot be attributed solely to good looks and a deeply appealing on-camera personality. Blondell was a professional down to her painted toenails. She knew her lines, hit her marks, and didn't complain. She was one of those rare movie stars who was equally liked by the cast, crew, and director. "She made everybody's job easy," said dolly grip Chico Anzures, who was briefly married to Joan's niece. "People don't realize the difficulty of remembering lines, staying in character, doing what the director wants, and moving so that you stay lit and in focus. Joan could do it all. She was up there with the best."

Joan took pride in her unassailable reputation, but she did not live for great parts in great movies. She was more focused on home and family. She loved animals and always had at least one pet in the house. She doted on her grandchildren incessantly. To her close friend, the acclaimed screenwriter Frances Marion, Joan was "impulsive, passionate, overgenerous; her life has been a kaleidoscopic shifting of incidents from comedy to drama. Rarely has she been able to stroll through peaceful meadows, though her sole purpose in living is to create an atmosphere of peace for those she loves. We who have known Joan since she was a young girl in her teens, and have seen her through some of the most grueling situations, never doubted that she would survive them and keep her sanity—not with her strength of character and strong fiber. We were always amused when people met her for the first time, saw her round and dimpled face, heard her rippling laughter, and said, 'What a jolly, carefree life she must have had!'" To another friend, columnist Jill Jackson, Joan was "the most generous person [she] ever knew. Giving, loving, highly dramatic, volatile, mad quickly and glad quickly." Bridget Hanley, her costar on *Here Come the Brides*, said, "I don't know how she had time to be friends to so many people."

Her husbands constitute one of the most intriguing marital trinities in Hollywood history, and she once said that the best of all three would make for perfection. George Barnes was the Academy Award–winning cinematographer of Alfred Hitchcock's *Rebecca*. Second husband Dick Powell was one of the most popular singers and actors of the 1930s and Joan's frequent costar. After their divorce, he went on to marry June Allyson and enjoy an immensely successful career as president of the groundbreaking Four Star Television production company. Joan's third husband was master showman Mike Todd. Before his famous marriage to Elizabeth Taylor and early death in a plane crash in 1958, he developed and marketed the Todd-AO film process that culminated in his Academy Award–winning smash, *Around the World in 80 Days*. A loving home life was Joan's elusive goal, and the failure of her marriages was her greatest sorrow.

Looking over Blondell's life, one is seized by the breadth of her accomplishments and the endurance of her charm. Arthur Bell of the *Village Voice* noted that her filmography is "an incredible history of the talking film, a sociological documentation of the tastes and trends of America during the mid-20th century. Joan personified the Depression. She was the *Kansas City Princess* who fought the war in *Cry "Havoc"* and was there when Gable came back and Garson got 'im. She wisecracked through the Jayne Mansfield '50s and dealt with Steve McQueen and Tuesday Weld in the '60s and entered the '70s with Elvis and James Garner and Suzanne Pleshette. Along the way there was vaudeville and radio and television and stock and Broadway." Put differently, her film career stretches the approximate time span from *The Jazz Singer* to *Star Wars*. Such deep entanglements with American entertainment reached beyond sound stages and into the most personal corners of her life. Her husbands all made indelible contributions to the movies, but almost everyone close to her was in show business. Her brother was a studio electrician; her sister, an actress. Her son became a noted producer-director, while her daughter and niece both became movie and television hairstylists. A grandson is a film editor; another is a musician. Among her in-laws there were two producers and a stunt man. Each may draw strength from the sister, mother, aunt, and grandmother who set the standard for professional integrity.

Joan did not see most of her ninety-two movies or countless television appearances. She was working too hard, and movie*going* was not a priority. But work gave her a purpose and control over her life that was forever missing at home. The sacrifices she made to family over three generations were made without self-pity or martyrdom. She worked out of need *and* desire, while her unending generosity was tempered by a sincere gratitude at being in show business. The costs were enormous, and when the women's movement hit its stride late in her life, Joan took notice. Her children and grandchildren were living in a different world, and perhaps she had been too pliant, too humble, and had taken too much responsibility for other people's happiness.

Joan never had an easy time of it and certainly made her share of mistakes. Her unfulfilled yearning for a permanent home is perhaps the most poignant consequence of her unstable childhood and failed marriages. But she would not be defeated by hard luck or the dark intentions of others. She fought husbands and ill health, raised two kids and a granddaughter, turned in performances that still offer much pleasure today, and won the affection of fans worldwide. Hers was a life dedicated to giving—time, money, and material gifts, most obviously. But she made an even greater impression in what she gave of her body, mind, heart, and spirit. And she is still giving, her presence brightening miles of film stock and videotape, while her memory brings tears to those who knew and loved her. Hers was a gaudy, spectacular, and troubled life, yet there is much to emulate and admire in how she lived it.

CHAPTER 1

The Next Town

Can I borrow your toothpaste? I left mine in Cleveland.
—Joan Blondell, *Goodbye Again*

When Joan Blondell published *Center Door Fancy* in 1972, it was labeled a novel, but everyone knew better. She maintained that virtually all events in the book were from her life. No one questioned her; the parallels were too transparent. The names were changed, but it was easy to figure out who was who. She was Nora Marten, vaudeville charmer turned movie star. David Nolan was George Barnes, cinematographer and first husband. Jim Wilson was Dick Powell, her singer-actor-producer husband number two. Jeff Flynn was Mike Todd, her volatile third and last husband, who offered eroticism alongside jealousy, public humiliation, and physical abuse. And Kern Brothers studio was Warner Bros., Joan's rewarding but oppressive employer for most of the 1930s.

The *roman à clef* included her vaudeville trouping childhood, her days as a fizzy comedienne of the talkies, and her doomed marriages. The stories she heard about her father's childhood were in there, too. Family oral history noted his French illegitimate birth, early life in an orphanage, and servitude to mean foster parents. He escaped, still a young man, via steamer bound for New York. Another story draws an obscure relationship between

10

Blondell and Richard the Lionhearted. Inexact U.S. census records have him born of French parents in Indiana in 1866 or 1869.

It appears fairly certain that Joan's father, Ed Blondell, traveled as a circus aerialist in his youth. On the worst day of his life, an accident of timing killed his trapeze partner, who was also his best friend. Out of fear, in tribute, or because of a haunting sense of responsibility, he never returned to the swing. His descendants avow that the story of the high flyer is true, and that is how Ed became a clown. In an era before unions, they painted a funny face on him and sent him out into the spotlight only minutes after his friend's heart stopped. Ed was in so much pain that the audience laughed at the strange expression on his face.

Joan's mother, Kathryn ("Katie") Cain, was born of pure Brooklyn Irish stock on 13 April, Easter Sunday, of 1884 (alternate records state 1890). She, too, lacked ongoing parental upbringing, as her seven older brothers took greater care than did her overextended parents. By the time she was a teenager, she had grown into a full-figured beauty with porcelain white skin and silky dark red hair.

Ed Blondell had since matured into adulthood, his broad face complemented by straight brown hair and a wide smile. He was making a modest living performing and producing vaudeville when he spotted Katie in the audience of a matinee. He introduced himself after the performance, then proceeded to court her in the Cain's parlor, always in full view of at least one brother. He was about two decades older than Katie, but there was a mutual attraction. Not surprisingly, he had a challenge in squiring a pretty young woman with so many protective older brothers. Katie was eventually convinced of his sincerity, as was her family. In 1898, thirty-something Ed married teenager Katie.

In 1887, the "Katzenjammer Kids" began as a newspaper comic strip by Rudolph Dirks. It told of two young twin brothers, Hans and Fritz, who were forever bedeviling hapless grown-ups. The kids were enormously popular, and in an early case of multiple media saturation, Ed mounted a stage version of their precocious antics in 1901. It played the Brooklyn

Music Hall under the advertised promise of "streams of laughter from start to finish. Comedy bubbling over with yours and other people's troubles." The show was a hit, and for the next few years it would sustain Ed and Katie on the vaudeville circuit.

From the Katzenjammer Kids emerged a new entertainment that brought Ed even more success. On 30 January 1905, he premiered a vaudeville skit called *The Lost Boy* at New York's Murray Hill Theatre. The title character was Reuben Plump, an oversized farm boy played by Ed who forever gets his hand caught in the sugar bowl. Plump was a slow fellow, and when his placid face registered the slow dawning of an idea, it made for excellent comedy. The routine, done in pantomime, was tinged with pathos and featured silly roles such as the ancient maid Gladys Passe, mummy King Ho Ho, and chief warrior Gadzooks. Early performances were met with sustained applause, and Ed Blondell and Company was soon touring on the Orpheum Circuit. Upon returning to New York in the fall, *The Lost Boy* played a week at the Hammerstein's Victoria Theatre on Forty-second Street and later at the Alhambra Theatre in Harlem on a bill with Harry Houdini.

Rarely did *The Lost Boy* accompany such a big headliner. More often it shared the spotlight with burlesque minstrels, xylophonists, trained dogs, sword swallowers, gymnasts, contortionists, fire eaters, yodelers, impersonationists, rope wranglers, or other specialty acts. If there was a major star on the bill, it might be cyclonic Eva Tanguay, ethereal Lillian Russell, or satiric Eddie Foy. For Ed and Katie, money was usually tight. Expenses such as costume repairs, transportation, food, and lodging were all the burden of the performers. With income a never-ending concern, the Blondells had mixed reactions to the news in early 1906 that Katie was expecting a child.

Ed continued to perform in *The Lost Boy*, as did Katie until her pregnancy was too obvious to hide. Just as Ed was preparing for a matinee performance, Rose Joan Blondell was born on Monday, 30 August 1906, in New York in a hotel room on Ninety-first Street off Central Park West. Her first cradle was a prop trunk and her first nursery was a backstage dressing room. The Blondell act was doing well when Joan was a newborn, and she spent her infancy touring with her parents through Europe. Her first birthday was spent in Paris. Show business legend has it she made her debut at fourteen months, toddling on stage during her parents' routine wearing nothing but a strip of flannel cloth around her waist.

Childhood was spent one week to the next in different cities. Joan's second birthday was celebrated in Paris, as was her first, but there were dozens of stops in-between. The young family was surviving on *The Lost Boy*, with New York most resembling a home base. They played a number of stages there, including the Novelty, Young's Pier, Colonial, and Keith and Proctor's Fifth Avenue Theatre. A son was born to the Blondells in Brooklyn in July 1909. He was named Edward Jr. and promptly acquired the nickname "Junie," which he kept for life.

Joan's third birthday, occurring when Junie was a month old, was spent backstage in Vancouver. She had grown into an adorable light-brown-haired, pigtailed child with a ready smile. She could be shy, but never when it came time to entertain. It was in Australia that she was formally integrated into *The Lost Boy*. She invigorated the act so much that an Englishman approached Ed to offer his services as international agent. At this time, Ed could afford to be discriminating. "This is a nice little contract," he said to a *Variety* reporter. "All they want me to do is to work for $200 less than my regular salary, and pay my fares over and back. Then they agree to give me four weeks, and if the first manager doesn't like me I can be canceled. All I have to pay the agent is 10 percent. I'll bet a hundred that there is a clause around here somewhere saying that there is an option on me for a longer time at that same $200 cut if I make good." There was indeed was such a clause, and Ed told the Englishman what he could do with his contract. *The Lost Boy* toured Europe nonetheless; Joan turned four on stage in London. Baby Rosebud, as Joan was called, later recounted some of her early adventures. She rode a Russian wolfhound in Paris and a huge turtle in Pago Pago. "In Australia, a man tried to get me behind the bushes with a bar of candy," she said. "Luckily, I was told to stay away from men with bars of candy."

At forty-four, Ed was at the top of his game. If anything, the act was a bigger success in Europe than in North America. One correspondent noted, "The Americanisms of Edward Blondell in *The Lost Boy* at the London Hippodrome are quite joyous, and this broadly comical visitor should have a triumphant tour in this country. To him ice is a 'hunk of water,' and he recommends a stuttering maid not to hold her words till they bust, but to scatter them around. He objects to a fork on the grounds that it leaks so badly when soup has to be dealt with and a tough steak which evades his knife is described as a nervous piece of meat. When asked if he is hungry this huge 'boy' admits that he fancies he could nibble away the edge of a bean, and he informs the stuttering girl that if she drinks like she talks she would be gargling all the time." The act was not favored everywhere. Ed scored a snide payback to a dead house in Dixon, Illinois: "Kind audience: You will pardon me but I am going to leave you flat," he announced in front of the curtain. "I came to Dixon to amuse, not to educate you. You will permit me to recommend an undertaker for this town."

The vaudeville life meant money in and money out. During flush seasons, the Blondells wore fine clothes and ate in good restaurants, despite their low status as traveling actors. From the beginning, the parents decided to keep the kids close by, even if servants could be afforded. As a result, Rosebud and Junie's childhood was spent in an endless succession of theaters, boardinghouses, hotel rooms, and trains. Daily rituals involved sweat-stained costumes, collars smeared with pancake, and the uncertain reactions of so many shadowy people behind blinding footlights. When Ed and Katie were on stage, fellow performers took turns at baby-sitting. The family usually went by rail, less often by bus. If an ocean was involved, they would go by steamer or cattle boat. Katie became adept at turning a hotel room into a cozy family retreat for the length of their stay. They would have their separate trunks with pots and pans, a Bunsen burner, table cloth, clothes, and whatever they needed to make a hotel room feel like home.

Vaudeville proved to be a fantastic, rigorous training ground for Joan. She learned the secrets of delivery, timing, and body language on the

road from her parents and their colleagues. Not that she was always a considered artist. She did impersonations that in retrospect she was certain
were terrible. But she was often surrounded by the best. In August 1912,
she and her family were en route to Australia with the robust comic Trixie
Friganza, pianist-composer Willie Paderewski, George M. Cohan acolyte Fred
Niblo (later a film director), Al Jolson, the Dolly Sisters, and the Singer's
Midgets. "Life on the boat was just one mad whirl," she said. "Costume parties,
marvelous entertainment by these world-famous performers. Yes, and
there was kid Joan herself right in the midst of the fray, begging to get
in the excitement and being petted and amused and entertained by the
stars themselves."

Formal education was strictly hit and miss. "I became educated with
no schooling," said Joan. "Once in a while I'd go to a school, but not often.
If the authorities were alert in some towns, they'd come backstage and say,
'Let's get to school.' I must have gone to anywhere from forty to fifty
schools in my life. For a week." She was never anywhere long enough to
grasp the principles of math, or make friends, or even find her way around
the playground. She did, however, learn how to read by virtue of playbills
and marquees.

In the early twentieth century, schools were incubators for disease.
In one of those rare moments that found Joan in a classroom, she contracted scarlet fever and diphtheria. The doctor nailed a quarantine sign on
the door, then told Ed and Katie to expect her death within days. During
Joan's illness, Katie walked the streets and met a stranger who "declared
the truth," as the Christian Scientists say. She told Katie to pray for truth
and understanding of God's ways, to be humble in seeking guidance, and
the healing would follow. Soon after that encounter, Joan's fever broke,
her painful red rashes cleared, and she recovered. Katie's Irish Catholicism
had offered little solace after the doctor had given up hope, but Christian
Science did. She was henceforth a dedicated convert. Convinced that
Christian Science brought about Joan's cure, Katie's belief in the efficacy of
her new religion was absolute and lasted the rest of her life.

By 1914, *The Lost Boy* was still politely attended, though the act was now called "old" in the trade papers. Vaudeville was beginning its long death march as "flickers" routinely accompanied live acts. The advent of the multi-reeled *Judith of Bethula* and *Tillie's Punctured Romance* heralded the coming dominance of feature films. But still Ed Blondell and Company toured. The family was in Australia during the outbreak of World War I.

Katie suffered a miscarriage in the middle of the night while on a Midwestern tour, landing her in a hospital for two weeks. The medical emergency did not disrupt the schedule. Joan went on in her mother's place, cannily playing an adult in skits she knew by heart. Vaudeville did not pay what it used to, and the family started to suffer. Flophouses and greasy spoons became the norm. Everyone, including a reluctant Junie and a recovering Katie, had to be in the show. Rehearsals were ongoing, and the eighteen-minute act was forever being polished to stay competitive and keep the offers coming, however low they paid. The family diet consisted of doughnuts and coffee during the day, meat and vegetables for dinner, and chop suey once a week in a Chinese restaurant. "When vaudeville was going downhill and things were really rough, my mother and father made a miraculous home life for us in cheap hotels and rooming houses," Joan said. "We learned the importance of our profession, [and] the importance of giving a good performance no matter how exhausted we were. We learned to cook on a Sterno stove and to sew; we learned compassion and we learned how to work."

Katie delivered a girl, Gloria, on 16 August 1915 in New York. By early 1916, the revamped family act was called *The Best Boy* and featured clever funny woman Gertrude Perry. Joan's portion of the act involved imitations, a gypsy dance, and a song or two. When she was learning the ropes, her father gave her advice that was as true as it was corny, and she remembered it forever: "Just go out there and love 'em; then they've got to love you back." When the Blondells played the greatest vaudeville house of them all, the Palace in New York, they were tucked away in the second act. When the show was again overhauled in 1917 and renamed *The Boy from*

Home, Katie was back on stage. The new routine went over well. "There is a lot of fun and just a soupçon of pathos in this bit of human nature, and Ed knows how to put both of them over," wrote the *Los Angeles Times*. Joan was happy to perform, avoid school, and dote on little Gloria. "I always thought of my sister as my own baby," she said. "I took her out in her little buggy, or walked along the street holding her hand, as she toddled beside me, people would stop and ask me whose baby it was. I always said she was my baby. I believed it."

A highlight of childhood came when father bought a Ford Model T. Everybody owned one, but it was a temperamental product. It would not start in the cold, and it rattled and overheated easily. It needed a running start to get up hills. It did forty-five miles per hour tops, but its greatest drawback was the crank start. If it kicked back, broken arms and wrists were the common result. The new car did not improve Junie's increasingly sullen disposition. Of all the Blondells, he was the most discontent with nomadic life.

When Joan realized how unique her young life was, she began to enjoy school. It became another kind of theater, and her classmates another kind of audience. They were enthralled at her stories of the gypsy life. This led to wild sagas that impressed even her teachers, though they were less gullible in believing them. One whopper involved a vomited lunch of ice cream and pickles. Joan explained that the cuisine was not to blame. She announced to her teacher, "I got a serious disease in the jungle when traveling with my father and every so often I have spells of throwing up." To satisfy the law, Ed received a special dispensation that allowed his children to attend various schools nationwide for short periods. Time and again, Joan would enter a classroom as a stranger among friends. To win their favor, she performed a few magic tricks she learned from her extended family backstage. After that came the stories of the Orpheum Circuit and life on the road. As soon as she had won their affection, she and her family would disappear to another town, another classroom, and another stage.

Between tours, the family stayed on Westminster Road in Flatbush. Much of Katie's family lived in Brooklyn, and Flatbush was a subway ride away from Manhattan theaters. Joan enrolled in middle school, but was getting too old to rely on charming recitations for passing grades. Katie insisted that she take piano lessons. "With me protesting every foot of the way, she loaded me on a trolley and escorted me to downtown Brooklyn, to the music studio of a man with a name something like Rumpelstilskin," said Joan. "For one solid hour, sitting at his piano, I suffered acutely. All the way home, I pleaded with my mother not to make me go back there again. She said firmly, 'You're going to learn how to play the piano. You're going to have a lesson every Saturday. The only thing that could prevent you from going back to Mr. Rumpelstilskin would be for him to drop dead.' The very next day, Mr. Rumpelstilskin did drop dead. And it gave my mother such a turn, after what she had said, she never mentioned piano lessons again."

Lack of stability nagged at Ed. When the Blondells were performing in San Diego, he attempted to settle his brood there and live on speculative real estate investments. He found a three-bedroom cottage in the suburbs on a dead-end street that suited everyone. There was a large, handsome pepper tree in the backyard for climbing. A grassy, undeveloped canyon nearby was ideal for thirteen-year-old Joan and ten-year-old Junie to explore. Joan found a "worry rock," a flat granite boulder on the edge of the canyon, where she told her secrets. During her time as a Girl Scout in San Diego, she felt an early rush of pride at winning a medal for life saving.

San Diego did not last long. The Blondells loaded the Model T and drove up the coast to the oceanside, canaled town of Venice, immediately south of Santa Monica, where they lived for eight months. It was here that Joan conducted herself as a more typical adolescent. She became a champion swimmer, was president of the drama club, and even played baseball on a boys' team. Ed rented dogs and cats for the intended benefit of his kids. He rented bicycles, too, and after a month or two, everything would be returned. Katie became a reader at the local Christian Science Church.

She and Ed devoted time every day to reading a quote by Shakespeare, Plato, or Aristotle to their children, a tradition that continued when Joan had children of her own.

In 1919, Joan met Johnny Kenney, president of the eighth grade. Johnny borrowed the family's car, drove Joan to a private spot three blocks away, and parked. They began kissing. She pushed him away when she worried that she might get pregnant. Her anxieties were relieved when Johnny gave her an introductory course in human reproduction. Joan's first menstruation took place during baseball practice, and she ran home frightened and confused. Katie merely looked down at her, smiled, and said, "My little woman." That was hardly comforting to Joan. It would be years before she developed ease and confidence in her sexuality. Large breasts added to her adolescent embarrassment as garbage men and truck drivers blatantly ogled her.

Ed opened a neighborhood tea room in Santa Monica called Fine De Lux Food (And Beaucoup of It), but no one stopped in for the first two days of business. Finally an elderly woman came through the front door, and the new Blondell restaurateurs turned solicitous. "We gave her vast tureens of soup, several steaks, gobs of potatoes, and a huge salad bowl," said Joan. "I think the poor little thing died of overeating." Fine De Lux Food suffered from the Blondells' priorities. They hung the "closed" sign if Joan was in a school play or Junie had a football game. The family reluctantly confessed they were ill-suited for a food business, and the stage act was resurrected. The resulting tour to Honolulu, Australia, and New Zealand was a dream. Joan remembered the white sand beaches of Hawaii and running through a rice field wearing only a bra and shredded-wheat skirt. In Australia she had a romance of sorts with the son of a hotel manager. The park-filled Christchurch on the South Island of New Zealand was a favorite stopover. "I have seen many lovely places," she said, "but never one as lovely as that quaint little town."

There were horrors in life on the road. While driving through the South, the Blondells saw something that looked like a meeting in a field under a large tree. As they approached, Katie could see that several black men were being strung up. She instinctively seized young Gloria and clutched her to her bosom saying, "It's a party. Look somewhere else." Joan was too far from her mother's protective embrace to miss seeing the lynchings. Whatever strength Joan gained by an early life in the theater, she never hardened to the violence in human nature. This was a young woman who avoided meat out of compassion for the animals she watched passing by from train windows. She never spoke of the lynchings.

Joan yearned to expand beyond vaudeville, and she found her chance back in New York in late 1923. She secured a small role in Gilbert Emery's *Tarnish* at the legitimate Belmont Theatre on West Forty-eighth Street. The drama starred silent film actors Tom Powers and Fania Marinoff and was directed by John Cromwell, later a respected film director. It made no great waves, but it did win Joan a scholarship offer from a talent scout at the John Murray Anderson Drama School, the launching pad for Lucille Ball and Bette Davis. "I couldn't take it," said Joan. "The family needed whatever I could earn and the scholarship was for tuition only. My ambition at the time was to make a buck so we could get the act together again and go again."

Before going back on the road, Joan was entangled in another production wholly different from vaudeville. She was an extra in director Max Reinhardt's spectacular Cathedral pantomime of *The Miracle* staged at the Century Theatre on Central Park West. There was movable scenery, forty-two windows, 470 costume designs, a choir, orchestra, fifty stage hands, forty electricians, and twenty-two assistant directors rehearsing the giant cast as it *clump-clumped* wooden shoes to effect the sound of teeming multitudes. The stage apron was thrust into the orchestra for more space, necessitating the removal of several hundred seats. The pageantry suffered from such characters as the Piper and a Blind Peasant, both of whom could not explain themselves as the production was without dialog. The six-hundred-person crowd remained *The Miracle*'s strong point, bursting through the lobby and down the widened aisles to the enlarged stage in mimicry of frenzied medieval devotion. "It produced an effect that was at times overwhelming, stupendous," announced the *New York Times*. Somewhere in that crowd was Joan and another show business newcomer, Bette Davis, both playing nuns and getting paid just enough for carfare. The production closed on 8 November 1924 when ticket sales could no longer cover the gargantuan weekly payroll of $40,000. Joan had left the production months earlier, celebrating her eighteenth birthday on stage in Albuquerque with her father in a vaudeville routine.

After closing in Grand Rapids, Ed decided again to quit show business for good. For reasons no one could remember, the Blondells moved to Denton, Texas, north of Dallas, where the sandy East Cross Timbers meet the black soil prairies to cut a swath down the middle of the county. The Blondells found a comfortable, small home on Oakland Avenue near the town center, then opened a dress shop. "It was a screwy thing to do, for there isn't a business brain in the family," said Gloria later.

Denton had a significant impact on the family. North Texas State Teacher's College (now the University of North Texas) was there, and Joan enrolled with the intention of becoming a teacher. She worked in the dress shop, but she flunked algebra and did not do much better at English and science. She gravitated toward theatrics yet again, appearing in a production of George Bernard Shaw's *Candida* produced by a local troupe. She enjoyed *Candida* and other forays into music or theater, including a minstrel show fund-raiser for the Kiwanis Club, but still she denied the greasepaint in her veins. Dress-shop saleswoman, teacher, even firefighter were higher on her wish list of professions. Twelve-year-old Gloria was showing a flair for drawing, and her work appeared on receipts, scraps of paper, and on mirrors in lipstick. Denton had the biggest impression on teenage Junie. He was smitten with a local girl named Eloise, and he soon announced his intention to marry her. He was itching to break free of the family and was looking for the right time. He never wanted to prance on stage, and he certainly did not want to roam the globe indefinitely.

Joan heard from a local girl that a search was underway for Miss Dallas in an upcoming bathing-beauty pageant. The winner of the contest would receive two thousand dollars and the chance to represent the city at the fall contest in Atlantic City. Joan grabbed an application and got to work. She bought a white bathing suit and dyed it regulation pink. She invented one tall tale after another, passing as native-born Rosebud Blondell. "It was a dirty trick to play on those Texas girls, the authentic Texans, I mean," she said. "But I had used a Southern dialect in our vaudeville act and I'm afraid my bootleg accent was even more real than the Texas brand! There was a judge on the committee from Kentucky, so I proceeded to 'indeedy' and 'suh' him to death. He later told me it was a relief, 'ma'am,' to hear a real Southern accent after all this Texas twang!"

Joan made the cut to the final five. "Girls, you are all too beautiful," said the presiding judge. "We've decided to pick the girl who has the most pleasing personality. Miss Blondell, step forward, honey." After the congratulations and shock abated, Joan telephoned Katie. "Mom—Ah'm Miss Dallas and you all has got to chaperone me to Atlantic City!" she cried.

"If we thought Dallas had been enthusiastic, it was a mild splurge compared to the one stage in Atlantic City," said Joan. "I tried to make it up to Texas, for posing as a native daughter, by being a peppy and popular representative of their state. On the hotel menu they featured a 'Miss Dallas Salad,' a 'Rosebudy Blondell Steak,' and a 'Texas Ice Cream Pie'!" She wore a cowgirl outfit, hollered "yip-pee," tossed ropes in the air, and shot toy guns. While there, she enjoyed sunbathing with the Misses Biloxi, Omaha, Seattle, and Minneapolis, her new-found and short-lived girlfriends.

Miss Dallas took her place among the contestants in her skin-tight pink one-piece bathing suit and high heels. Atlantic City's *Boardwalk Illustrated News* reported 5' 2½" tall Rosebud as "a pretty Texas lassie" who "made a deep impression on Pageant visitors for her continuous good nature." The Atlantic City Fall Pageant was judged by a point system: fifteen for "construction of the head," ten each for eyes, facial expressions, torso, legs, arms, hands, and "grace of bearing." An additional five points each was assigned to hair, nose, and mouth. When the numbers were tallied, Joan took second prize in the Southwest Division.

Though "Rosebud" did not bag the top prize, there was a party in her honor back in Dallas. When it was late and she grew tired, she accepted a ride home from an Oklahoma millionaire she believed to be "an awfully nice old guy." When they were in the car and on a dark street, he pushed himself on her for a kiss. She refused. "What are you playing me for, a sap?" he said. "I gave those girls [at the party] $200 for fixing this date with you. Now, little girl, don't pretend you weren't in on it." As she struggled to break free, he tore her dress and slapped her hard on the face. Joan was bleeding when he drove the car down a highway with steep embankments on each side. She jumped out and tumbled fourteen feet before landing in a gully. One ankle was broken, and one was fractured, but she hobbled to a gas station a mile away. She went home, a doctor came, and she was on crutches for three months. A Dallas lawyer took pity and told Joan she could send her assailant to a penitentiary, but the idea of court action and further confrontation terrified her. She declined the offer.

Texas ended badly. After the attack, the dress shop went under. The family was again on the road, with the palpably miserable Junie drafted to tote luggage and props. At some early age, Joan took up the family tradition of smoking to make her look more sophisticated, though she was too naive to be a Jazz Age flapper and too buxom to epitomize the current flat-chested ideal. She did, however, bob her hair. Joan learned many things in her early years. She learned how to work through bone-deep fatigue, to avoid involvement with people she would have to leave, to get by in small, deprived living quarters, and to endure the conflicting personalities of her family. She learned to flirt simply by batting her eyelashes and to endure simple, low-cost food, clothing, and accommodations. She learned how to practice child care for a sister who was younger by nine years. Most of all, she learned how to *troupe*. She would not, however, learn emotional self-sufficiency. That would be forced upon her much later and under particularly cruel circumstances.

Finally, the Blondells were back in New York in 1927, and Joan was again looking for something beyond vaudeville. She spent much of her two thousand dollar Miss Dallas winnings on clothes, housing for the family, and revising the act. With the remaining money, she bet that Jack "Manassa Mauler" Dempsey would win over Gene Tunney in their Philadelphia match-up. When Tunney won, Joan never gambled again and lost her stomach for prize fighting.

The Blondell's New York apartment was a one-room flat at Eighty-fourth Street and Lexington. Crowded into the tiny space were five cots, three stools, a gas stove, and an icebox. The toilet was down the hall. Ed managed to get vaudeville work, but it was low paying. Joan needed to bring in money for the family. She tried out for the Ziegfeld Follies chorus and proudly told the dance director that she was a beauty contest winner, Miss Dallas, to be exact. The noted choreographer and casting director Sammy Lee shot back that he didn't care if she was "Miss Manhattan Transfer!" Despite that inauspicious introduction, she was briefly with the Follies, then took a chorus job in the musical *Rosalie* with famed dancer Marilyn Miller. But Joan's ankles were still too weak for strenuous danc-ing since the attack in Texas, and she was soon unemployed again.

CHAPTER 2

Starlight

Her effectiveness in movies comes from her ability to be herself in front of a camera, to allow her personality to operate as freely as it does when she is taking a stranger into her home.
—Don Bachardy, *Stars in My Eyes*

When the Blondells arrived in New York for an indefinite stay, they were close to destitute. Twenty-year-old Joan and eleven-year-old Gloria took odd jobs, hating every one of them. Junie had a paper route. Father Ed did a solo routine as the live act before picture shows, but he never brought in more than ten dollars for a day's work. The reduced conditions of vaudeville necessitated his absence for weeks. Joan waitressed a bit, but didn't keep up with the practical skills she learned at the North Texas State Teachers College. Her tenure as purse salesgirl at one of New York's swankier department stores didn't last long either. She loathed the posturing formality of standing at attention waiting for customers to approach.

Joan secured a job in a circulating library at Broadway and Eighty-ninth for eight dollars a week. Her shift was typically 8 a.m. to 1 p.m., then again from 4 p.m. to 11 p.m., which was perfect for attending midday auditions. Her boss, kindly Esther Wright, recalled that Joan "was a good clerk on account of she would not let boys have dates with her unless they joined [Esther's] circulating library. One night there were seventeen boys lined up to join." Joan wrote their numbers on the wall near the telephone behind the circulation desk, which eventually looked like a directory of Manhattan's available young men.

Because of cramped accommodations and fevered emotions at home, Joan often slept in the back of the library on a small cot provided by Wright. One night at closing time, a police officer came in. He engaged her in friendly conversation and said he had noticed her ever since she started working for Wright. As Joan began the closing ritual for the store, he urged her down-stairs where packing boxes and business supplies were kept. The two were there alone, the light was faint, and the front door was already locked upstairs. His assault was fierce and sudden. He knocked her legs out from under her and she fell on the concrete floor. He went down with her, forcing a hand up her dress and tearing at her panties. From underneath him, Joan did everything she could to resist, first kicking and punching, then screaming for help. No one heard. When he was finished, he reassembled his uniform, warning Joan that he would kill her if she ever told anyone what happened.

It was nearly midnight and the street was empty. Joan wandered in bewilderment, her wobbly legs barely able to support her. Eventually, she reentered the library to spend the night on her cot in the back. Sleep was impossible; she was taut from the shock and a jabbing pain in her lower back. There were precious few resources for a rape victim in 1927, and Joan was ignorant of options, so she honored his demand of silence for decades. Only much later did she tell her grown daughter, and later still she went public in her thinly disguised memoirs, *Center Door Fancy*. But one detail is missing from the book: about the policeman using his big, blunt hands to bend her feet back until she writhed in agony. It would be months before Joan saw a doctor for ongoing lower back pains she suf-fered from falling on the rock hard floor, telling him that she slipped on icy pavement. X-rays revealed a fractured coccyx, and he recommended no heavy lifting, plenty of hot baths, and no motherhood.

When Joan returned to the theater, she was cast in a touring pro-duction of the courtroom drama *The Trial of Mary Dugan*, produced by the estimable cigar-chomping Al Woods. During the seven months she was on the road as a lisping chorus girl and understudy to the lead, she sent most of her paycheck to her family in New York. When the tour was over, she was back at the library, but she made sure never to be there alone. She secured a raise to eighteen dollars a week, the same salary she had made during the best of times at the dress shop in Denton. She earned no more than spare change in *My Girl Friday*, a tawdry production at the small but prestigious Provincetown Theatre in Greenwich Village.

Joan contended with her parents' worsening marriage. When Ed came back from one of his extended, wheezing vaudeville tours, he accused Katie of infidelity. After screaming and tears, and admissions by Katie that her life was a disappointment, Ed left again. One early morning soon after, Katie found a short note on the dining table. It was from Junie, announcing that he had run away to marry his Texas girlfriend. He added that he hoped father would show up again soon, but his departure was as much an effort to get away from his warring parents as it was to be with the girl he loved. The police recorded his disappearance as a teenage runaway and were not about to devote resources to finding him. Then Ed returned. Both he and Katie kept sparring, but they stayed together and kept the same address in hopes that their son would contact them. Everyone was relieved when Junie began writing letters, one announcing that he had married Eloise and another that he had landed a job in Denton dressing windows for the Woolworths Department Store.

While she was struggling to make a stage career, Joan and millions of others observed the singular phenomenon of Al Jolson opening his mouth to talk in *The Jazz Singer*. In 1928, she saw *Lights of New York*, the first all-talking movie, and took special notice. Movies with sound were quickly becoming commonplace. If movies were going to talk, then wouldn't they be needing theater actors with vocal training?

Joan could not pursue the promise of the movies, as survival took the Blondells in different directions. Ed was ill and in need of warmer climate, so he and Katie collected their meager cash and drove their Model T to Oakland, California, where Junie had moved with wife, Eloise, and their one-year-old daughter, Patricia. Gloria would stay with Joan, and both would send them whatever money they could. After an emotional parent-child parting, Joan was cast as Isabel Dawn's baby sister in a forgotten comedy at the Blunkal Players in South Brooklyn. Money was still tight. "The first day of rehearsing, my sister, Gloria, took the subway out to Brooklyn to have lunch with me—and me with only a nickel to get home on," recalled Joan. "So, I asked Isabel how I could get an advance on my salary and she gave me 50 cents, with which the Blondell sisters had a hearty lunch of tuna fish sandwiches and chocolate sodas at the corner drug store." With all the demands on Joan's time, she scarcely could look after Gloria, who, at twelve, was still young enough to need supervision. Joan went to the wealthiest person she knew and trusted, producer Al Woods, and borrowed one hundred dollars to pay for a car, driver, and expenses to send her baby sister safely across the country to reunite with her parents.

Everyone was now gone, and the moment was terrifying. A childhood in vaudeville brought discipline, excitement, and ever-changing surroundings, but not solitude. To compound her despair, Joan was closer to abject poverty than at any point in her life. Esther Wright had another hard-luck case using the cot in the back of the library. When friends failed her, Joan was very nearly on the street. "I've known what it is to wonder where I was going to sleep when night came," she said. "I've been at a stage of pocketbook flatness when half a sandwich, shared with another girl in the same predicament, was a banquet."

Joan was drinking black coffee and smoking a cigarette at the counter of a Broadway cafeteria when a young actor came in and sat on the adjacent stool. They began a conversation. He told her about an audition across the street for a new play called *Maggie the Magnificent* by the Pulitzer prize–winner George Kelly, who was all the rage after his recent stage hits *The Show-Off* and *Craig's Wife*. Joan was suddenly animated, gulped down the remaining coffee, tamped out her cigarette, and hurried across the street.

When she arrived at the audition, she found the place overflowing with hopefuls. "Every actor and actress alive wanted a part," she remembered. "There were so many waiting I was sure I'd never get to see Kelly. Finally I got into his outer office and found myself jammed up against a red-haired mug. He looked at me and said, 'Your eyes are so big they look like they're about to pop out of your head. What's there to be afraid of?' " His forthright, cocky manner was instantly appealing, but they did not introduce themselves.

When Joan finally got into Kelly's office, she found him to be polite and calming. "He sat me down and quietly began reading a few scenes from *Maggie*, sort of acting them out," she said. "I howled. It was so funny. The writing was so good. I guess he could see that I really dug it, felt it. I got the part. And he never asked me to read a line." Joan was cast in the supporting role of Etta, the brazen, gum-chewing wife of a bootlegger. James Cagney, the magnetic fellow who commented on Joan's popping eyes, was also cast.

Rehearsals started the next day. Kelly assembled the cast and said, "Now, boys and girls, we have hired you because we know you are experienced. I want the full benefit of all that experience. We think you know your business. Anything that occurs to you, please let me know—because I can't think of everything. So—if you would do me that favor of speaking up? All right now, let's go to work." The play was in rehearsal for four weeks, and Joan was overjoyed to be featured in the first quality drama of her life. Kelly proved to be a fantastic teacher, coaxing Joan to a level of performing she could only achieve with sensitive and encouraging guidance.

Maggie the Magnificent previewed in Boston and Atlantic City before opening in New York on 21 October 1929. Esther Wright was there, beaming. An assortment of Joan's uncles, aunts, and cousins were there, too, but the immediate family wasn't. Telegrams came from Ed, Katie, Junie, and Gloria in California. Joan was paralyzed with stage fright, but when the curtain went up she did her job as best she could, then accepted well wishes in her dressing room after the performance. The crowd dispersed, and Joan went back to her one-room apartment alone. She tried to call her parents and sister from the phone in the lobby of her residential hotel, but she couldn't get through long distance to California. Finally, she tried to sleep amidst the giddy thrill of the evening. At some unnamed hour of the morning, Joan awoke to incessant knocking on the door. It was Esther Wright, breathless under a load of latest edition newspapers. Each one had a review in it lauding this new discovery, Joan Blondell.

A more accurate title might have been *Maggie the Mediocre*; the play was not one of Kelly's best. Here was a story of mother-daughter friction that was neither innovative nor particularly interesting dramatically. But Blondell and Cagney made sparks, and they were routinely praised as the best part of an otherwise dull evening. Both of them made their work seem easy, but each was a coiled spring backstage. According to Joan, "Jimmy Cagney made such a big hit in that first show we did together, he had to have a bucket in the wings so he could throw up every night before he went onstage. He was so nervous it was unbelievable, yet look how cool he always looked." No doubt due in part to the Wall Street Crash of 1929, *Maggie the Magnificent* did not do well at the box office, lasting only thirty-two performances. Joan was hoping to "make good for [her] family, and maybe buy a new dress," but she was disappointed. "No one was going to the theater," she noted caustically. "Too busy jumping out windows."

Joan was in an agitated state herself, for reasons both personal and financial. In January of 1930, she was yoked to a miserable new play that closed during its out-of-town run in Pittsburgh. She was also caught in the heat of romantic yearning, and the object of her ardor was a fellow actor. "I believe it was the first time in my life I completely lost my sense of humor," she remembered. "I was just the girl who was crazy about him. I worshiped the ground he walked on, but he nearly wrecked my life through worry. His main ambition seemed to be to try and drink himself to death. I was the most miserable person in the world during the time I was in love with him. He was so darn good and sweet—but such a drunkard." In a moment of self-possession, she decided to sever contact with him and redirect her energies wholly to acting. It would not be the last time a man would cause her distraction.

William Keighley, an ambitious young producer-director who was preparing a play for Broadway, never forgot that dazzling couple he saw in *Maggie the Magnificent* on closing night. "Manna from heaven," he declared. "I was looking for an attractive yet tough young cookie and a strong, beautiful broad, and here were [Cagney] and Joanie on that stage, the living breathing counterparts of the two I needed for *Penny Arcade*." He contacted both of them, and they signed on in early February. Keighley was beginning a career in film while still producing on Broadway, and he simultaneously cast Blondell in the ten-minute short *Broadway's like That* with Ruth Etting and newcomer Humphrey Bogart. Under the aegis of Warner Bros.'s subsidiary, Vitaphone, Joan appeared in two more shorts, *The Devil's Parade* and *The Heart Breaker*, during the rehearsal period for *Penny Arcade* in the early weeks of 1930.

A light rain fell over Manhattan as *Penny Arcade* opened at the Fulton Theatre on West Forty-sixth Street on 24 March. A rough three-act drama of bootlegging and murder set in an amusement park, *Penny Arcade*'s seedy milieu was faithfully reproduced down to a hot-dog stand and the outline of a roller coaster against the cyclorama. But visual details did not compensate for dialogue that failed to reproduce the argot of the outdoor showman or cover up the transparent mystery surrounding the murder. *Penny Arcade* was strictly humdrum melodrama, but Cagney and Blondell in support took the attention away from leads Eric Dressler and Lenita Lane.

Al Jolson bought the film rights to *Penny Arcade* for $20,000, and he had a plan. He quickly sold it to the Warner Bros. film studio in California, but only under the agreement that Blondell and Cagney came attached with a three-week contract to film the play. Mighty Jack Warner hardly enjoyed being told who to cast in his movies, but he bought the property from Jolson with the rider that kept the two stage actors attached to the project. Blondell showed rare charm in her Vitaphone shorts, and Warner figured casting her in one movie was a minor risk. In a flash Joan was packing for Hollywood with the minimum promise of $250 a week for three weeks of moviemaking. The last Blondell in New York then trekked cross country by herself, stopping only for gas, food, or sleep. She made her way westward in a dented old Ford Model T bought for the occasion. When she arrived in Southern California, dirty and drawn, she checked into the new Roosevelt Hotel on Hollywood Boulevard and awaited day one on the set.

When Blondell and Cagney reported to work, they were met by Darryl F. Zanuck, the dynamic head of production at Warner Bros. "Well, we're stuck with you for one picture," he said. "Do you think you can play the roles?"

"No," answered Cagney and Blondell in sarcastic unison and without looking at each other. Both learned a lesson that day, as Zanuck took them literally and gave the top-billed roles to Grant Withers and Evalyn Knapp, while the two Broadway kids kept the smaller parts they had played on stage. Joan had the role of Myrtle, a tough-talking floozie, while the movie's name was changed meaninglessly to *Sinners' Holiday*. She was not photographed flatteringly with her naturally brown hair and splotchy makeup, but she showed an immediate ease with the camera.

Once production was underway, and Warner viewed the rough footage with Cagney and Blondell, all uncertainties about their futures disappeared. Recalled Blondell: "Cagney and I had done our scene the day before and we were [on the back lot] to do a little more. All the bosses came down: Warner, Zanuck, and all of them, with a contract, a long-term, five-year contract, and they signed us on that back lot in the broad daylight. So that's how that started, and from then on, it was one picture after another." By the terms of her original long-term contract, dated 23 June 1930, Joan was to be paid $250 per week, with the option of a first annual raise of $150 week, and $200 thereafter over four years, topping out at a gross income of $1,000 per week by 1934. Immediately she signed with William Morris Agency and shaved three years off her age, immaturing from twenty-three to twenty in an instant. Cagney, already showing his moxie as a shrewd negotiator, started at $400 per week. Happily for Joan, the new contract meant the Blondells could afford to be reunited. Ed Senior, Katie, Joan, and Gloria moved to a bungalow on a quiet street in outland North

Hollywood in the San Fernando Valley, where farm-bred white leghorn chickens still outnumbered humans fifty to one.

Soon the studio publicity machine was engaged, and reporters descended to scrutinize the two highly touted newcomers. Cagney withdrew from the glare, but Blondell kept them entertained. When one of them remarked on her beauty, she said, "Compliment my mother." When another remarked on her timing, she said, "Compliment my dad."

Warner Bros. was poised for Hollywood supremacy in 1929 with its takeover of the production and distribution company First National. The studio had room to sprawl in suburban Burbank, and profits peaked at a whooping $14 million. The Crash put a stop to empire building, and by the following year profits were cut in half. Warner Bros. quickly grew lean and became the studio most modeled on assembly-line principles of the Industrial Revolution. In the early 1930s, Warner Bros. movies were fast, cheap, urban, and tough. Many of their topics were contemporary, drawing on modern vernacular and headline news, usually to do with city corruption, violent crime, and bootlegging. Apart from their substantial value as entertainment, they are enduring nuggets of sociology and history. Warner Bros. depression movies had an on-the-street immediacy and the authenticity of Edward Hopper's paintings, Dorothea Lange's photographs, and John Steinbeck's novels. Its first generation of sound actors embodied gritty realism. Humphrey Bogart, Edward G. Robinson, James Cagney, and Paul Muni were not exactly upstanding family men in most of their early films at the studio. They were, simply, thrilling powerhouse actors. So, too, were the women, led in the early 1930s by the soon-to-be stars Bette Davis, Barbara Stanwyck, Ann Dvorak, and Glenda Farrell, in addition to Blondell. The directors took no less a visceral approach to their work. Men like Mervyn LeRoy, William A. Wellman, and Michael Curtiz were above all muscular filmmakers who believed in telling adult stories and pulling no punches. The pace at Warner Bros. meant that quality had to be sacrificed too often, but the talent was there to make amazing movies with the right combination of story and personnel. On backward reflection, it can be said that

Joan found herself in the company of an unusually capable and energetic group of filmmakers.

Joan's schedule was punishing from the start. Her second movie, *The Office Wife*, was made so fast it was finished and released before *Sinners' Holiday* premiered. Apart from her passing appearances in the three Vitaphone shorts, *The Office Wife*, not *Sinners' Holiday*, offered the movie world its first glimpse of Joan Blondell. Lovely Dorothy Mackaill was the star, playing a secretary who entered into complicated affairs with two men. Joan, her hair still a darker brown than it would later be, had a supporting part as Mackaill's sister. Joan was pretty and charming, and the camera loved her. She teased the audience in her opening scene as director Lloyd Bacon maneuvered the camera while Joan rolled out of bed, took off her lingerie, and drew a bath. A careful listen will reveal that she stumbled on not one but two of her lines, while the hurried pace of production ensured the camera kept rolling and the takes were used. Such gaffes made no tangible difference in the movie's financial success. Louella Parsons opined that *The Office Wife* "is what some of our slangy friends call a 'natural,' a story that will hold the interest of 'fifty million' wives and equally as many secretaries." Considering that it was based on a novel by Faith Baldwin, who made a fortune from topical yarns of women at work, Parsons was not taking great risk in her augury.

When *Sinners' Holiday* was released a month later, it was an unofficial audition for the Cagney-Blondell team, and they both came through spectacularly, especially Cagney. As the high-strung murderer, Cagney set the standard for his signature roles to come in *The Public Enemy* and *White Heat*. If Joan created a lesser stir than Cagney, there were no complaints. "We were getting paid, and times were tough, so we were happy and grateful!" she said. In the early days, Joan rebelled only when Jack Warner suggested she change her name to Inez Holmes. It was absurd, and she dared to tell him so. Why would anyone want to change a name as evocative of bright stardom as Blondell? It was so perfect, in fact, that it already sounded like an invention of studio marketing. Warner came to see the wisdom of her view, and eventually she would overcome her inherent shyness to again confront the boss.

Other Blondells were settling in Southern California. Gloria enrolled at Beverly Hills High School, earned excellent grades, and pursued her interest in the visual arts. Ed and Katie moved from Oakland to live with Joan. Ed took bit parts at Warner Bros. while Katie ruled the North Hollywood home, since Joan's one-movie-a-month work schedule hardly permitted her to shuck peas or trim the hedge. Katie still maintained her own life. She started going to Alcoholics Anonymous meetings because she found the seriocomic human parade of cases fascinating to behold. Where does humor come from if not from the worst tragedy, she reasoned. Word got out that Joan Blondell's mother was a drunk, so Joan had to ask her to stop going to the meetings. Joan meanwhile won fans at the studio, and none more ardent than James Cagney. He nicknamed her "Grandma" and declared her "a great taker of direction." His praise was unequivocal: "She could have done many better things than the roles they gave her. If she hadn't looked like a tootsie she'd have made a great Lady Macbeth." She was entranced by smart, tall, athletic Lewis Warner, son of studio boss Harry. But their brewing romance was destroyed just months after they met by Lewis's cruel death at twenty-two from pneumonia.

Joan was rushed into another supporting role in *Illicit*, a louche pot-boiler built around the emerging talents of fellow Warner's newcomer Barbara Stanwyck. Blondell played Stanwyck's friend "Duckie," a good-time girl too naughty to bother with undergarments. Blondell's character is drawn to be as wanton and exciting as Stanwyck's, but isn't given the screen time to prove it. *Illicit* is quite blue until the conventional finale, which has reformed playgirl Stanwyck becoming a dutifully adoring wife. Louella Parsons judged *Illicit* to be "as smart as next year's frock, as modern as television, and as sophisticated as a Parisian hotel clerk," while Joan's sharp performances inspired her to add that "Little Blondell has been scoring with unfailing regularity since her success in *The Office Wife*."

She was sporting an attractive new look in *Illicit*, as her lightened hair ideally complemented her bright, round face.

So far Joan's roles were limited to four types: sister, floozie, girlfriend, and gold digger. A pattern emerged, and Joan began to see what the business had planned for her. At Warner Bros., she was initially walked through minor roles in inconsequential movies, always managing to sparkle amidst mediocrity. *Other Men's Women*, a drama of rail men, featured Joan's first reunion with James Cagney. The set was made enjoyable by the presence of costars Regis Toomey and Mary Astor, who became good working friends to Joan. She played a diner waitress, and under the guidance of a quality director like tough-talking, hard-living William A. "Wild Bill" Wellman, she made a fine if brief impression. Her gift for one-liners decongested the movie of heavy drama:

> BLONDELL, *to two customers*. Anything else you guys want?
> CUSTOMER #1, *looking at her rear end*. Yeah, give me a big slice of you on toast—and some French fried potatoes on the side.
> BLONDELL. Listen, baby, I'm A. P. O.
> CUSTOMER #1, *to* CUSTOMER #2. What does she mean, A. P. O.?
> BLONDELL. Ain't Puttin' Out.

She thought nothing of the dialogue. She memorized what she was given and did what she was told. After spending her youth in flophouses and backwater theaters, she was only too eager to succeed in Hollywood. "God, the weather here," she said. "How can you beat that? Good weather, and a decent paycheck. If only they didn't overwork us."

On 14 January 1931, Warner Bros. announced production of *The Public Enemy*, a cautionary tale on the criminal underworld plaguing America's big cities. It was to be based on real mobsters who rocked Chicago in the gangland wars of the 1920s. Filmed in twenty-six days for $151,000, *The Public Enemy* distinguished itself as something above the routine crime dramas for which Warner Bros. was known. It endeavored to explore the root causes of law breaking, suggesting that young boys begin with petty crime, join gangs, then graduate to armed robbery, bootlegging, and murder until they are saved or come to a bad end. Prohibition, the constitutional amendment intended to curb vice, is seen here as contributing to a lethal new black market.

All of the film's merits as social drama are eclipsed by its greatest asset—James Cagney. He shot to the highest levels of stardom with *The Public Enemy*, but there are weaknesses in his breakthrough movie. Beryl Mercer overplays her role as his long-suffering mother, and Blondell as a gun moll is given too little to do. But mostly *The Public Enemy* is a startling series of potent images made possible by the collaboration of director William A. Wellman and Cagney. It remains a prototypical gangster drama, and certainly the most important film of Joan's career to date. Wellman promised Zanuck that he would direct "the toughest, the most violent, most realistic picture you ever did see." Wellman delivered. In keeping with *The Public Enemy*'s cynicism, Joan and Mae Clarke are a pair of night-club tarts we meet at a table shared by two men passed out drunk. Before the film is over, we get kidnapping, the senseless killing of a horse, machine-gun spray, sensational murders, and one unforgettable moment with Cagney, Clarke, and half a grapefruit.

In *Night Nurse*, a rookie nurse (Barbara Stanwyck) must fight a plot to murder two fatherless children. Sidekick Joan was insolent and gum-chewing this time, with a quip always at the ready. With *The Public Enemy*'s Wellman in charge, *Night Nurse* was coarse and uncompromising even by Hollywood pre-Code standards. Just as Wellman quickened heartbeats across America with the harsh sounds of bullets, screaming, and falling bodies in *The Public Enemy*, so, too, does he excite the screen in *Night Nurse* with screeching ambulances and inherently dramatic hospital props. As an amoral chauffeur, newcomer Clark Gable had an animal magnetism that caused Blondell and Stanwyck to swoon. "When he showed up the first day, Barbara and I had to sit down," said Joan. "There was something about him that was overpowering." In the history of Hollywood lingerie,

Night Nurse deserves honorable mention. Throughout the movie, Stanwyck and Blondell doffed their street clothes and medical uniforms so as to display silky private apparel. Joan's complicity paid off. The raise promised by her original contract came six weeks early, with her earnings now up to four hundred dollars a week as of May 1931.

In public, Joan adapted to growing fame. She observed with a smile, "When I first got into pictures, there would be something on the marquees saying 'Dallas' Own Joan Blondell,' or 'Battle Creek Michigan's Own Joan Blondell' or 'Chicago's Own Joan Blondell,' because someone would remember that I'd been to school there for a week. [So I became] America's own Joan Blondell." At home in North Hollywood, however, she and Gloria were treated like children living with their parents. Since Lewis Warner's death, there was no romance for Joan, only the growing affection of friends confined to the studio. As a talented and successful young actress, she was kept under glass. Her world was small, and her earnings were not hers. The Blondell's vaudeville ethos remained in place. Whatever was made was shared, sometimes excessively so. Even at four hundred dollars a week, Joan had to take an advance on her wages in July.

The reserved girl backstage at the vaudeville theater had not really gone away, and Joan was feeling a greater disconnection between her screen image and the real woman. She shunned public events such as premieres and large benefits. "The shyness only leaves me when I work," she once said. It left her in *The Reckless Hour*, released in August of 1931. Joan was called upon to wisecrack yet again, this time as the jealous glove-selling sister to haughty Dorothy Mackaill. Joan got whatever good reviews the movie earned. "Miss Blondell has a way about her that is fascinating because she can spout off the most obvious lines without making them the least bit obvious," noted the *Los Angeles Evening Express*. "It's her knack—and a good one." To *Variety*, Joan "nearly steals things."

In August of 1931, Joan signed a new long-term contract at Warner Bros. amidst much hope for the future. Jack Warner saw great promise in her, and it was his intention to focus on her potential for stardom. She was part of the wave of new blood that infused the movie industry as silent stars floundered under the microphone. Not coincidentally, many of the first generation of sound actresses who made it big in Hollywood came with New York stage credits. Joan belonged to a breathtaking sorority: Katharine Hepburn, Miriam Hopkins, Barbara Stanwyck, Kay Francis, Ruth Chatterton, Bette Davis, Claudette Colbert, Joan Crawford, Nancy Carroll, Irene Dunne, Ann Harding, and Sylvia Sidney all did stints on Broadway before movie contracts lured them westward. On consideration, Joan did not have to wait long for a major break; she was in Hollywood just over a year before *Blonde Crazy* came along. But already she was the veteran of eleven movies, and it must have seemed to her that she was bumping around that town forever.

Blonde Crazy was the happy reunion of Blondell, Cagney, and writers Kubec Glasmon and John Bright, all contributors to *The Public Enemy*. And just as *Blonde Crazy* was shooting, Joan received the good news, in September of 1931, that the Western Association of Motion Picture Advertisers (WAMPAS) had selected her as one of Hollywood's "Baby Stars," i.e., a real up and comer. The WAMPAS honor was well timed. Joan had appeared in two movies, *The Public Enemy* and *Night Nurse*, that would endure as classics of the Warner Bros. tradition, but *Blonde Crazy* was the first time she was given a movie worthy of her talent and a leading role.

Shot in the fall of 1931, *Blonde Crazy* was the fourth of the seven Cagney-Blondell matchups. Cagney once again gives us the hardened but sympathetic street mug, while Blondell juggles both worldliness and innocence in one adorable twenty-five-year-old package. Much of *Blonde Crazy* plays as a delightful, fast-paced comedy of lovable immorals out to fleece the rich. In an era that saw every imaginable grift, these two were just what audiences wanted. "The age of chivalry is past," Cagney announces to Blondell, his new partner in crime. "This is the age of chiselry." How Cagney, fellow con man Louis Calhern, and Blondell execute their various scams and counter-scams involving jewels, counterfeit money, and horse racing is wholly good-natured. As is noted in *Blonde Crazy*, "honest men are as scarce as feathers on a frog."

Blonde Crazy changes tone in the last half hour to become a more hard-boiled vengeance drama. The transition isn't satisfying, but the attraction of *Blonde Crazy* comes from the fantastic time Blondell and Cagney have working off each other. Joan exhibits a delightfully casual relationship with the camera in a bathtub scene where she gently chastises Jimmy for his voyeuristic interest, all the while giving the audience a sideways glance at her shapely and unfettered right breast. She makes it look easy, without pretense or self-consciousness. Considering her lack of experience with men, seduction, and romance, her acting here is remarkably instinctive.

As testimony to his great rapport with the screen, Cagney toys with Blondell's panties and bra without making an ass of himself, while Blondell lets it be known that she's no mere trifle. "Blondell's beauty as a 'broad' is that she can outsmart the man without unsexing him," wrote film scholar Molly Haskell. "Cagney's beauty as a male is that he can be made a fool of without becoming a fool." Indeed, the incongruously amusing sight of him in a bell-boy's uniform lets us in on the joke. Cagney's masculine power allows him to be subservient to no one, even when he is dressed in a uniform of capitalist oppression. Blondell's feminine power comes from her easygoing sexual self-confidence that never lapses into vampish excess. Together they create a barely contained erotic heat. And it may be said that *Blonde Crazy* has some of the wittiest indignant slaps in movie history. The shenanigans of the two mischievous stars are so endearing in *Blonde Crazy* that the tilt toward straight ahead drama feels like stealing candy from children.

Blonde Crazy was released in November of 1931 and was a sizable hit. Cagney received no raise after *The Public Enemy*, but held out and demanded one above his current $450 a week rate after *Blonde Crazy*. He was told no, so he walked, the first star to do so. He told Joan to follow him, but she couldn't. She did not have his early track record, she had no hit on the level of *The Public Enemy* to call her own, and she had a family to support. Neither was she inclined to be self-promoting or demanding of others. After much negotiating, Cagney came back for $1,000 a week. Joan stayed quiet, happy to earn her keep and add to the household account.

With *Blonde Crazy* such a success, Joan was beginning to understand her appeal. "I would get endless fan mail from girls saying 'That is exactly what I would have done, if I'd been in your shoes, you did exactly the right thing.' So I figured that was my popularity, relating to the girls," she said. "They just wanted more of the same thing. All you got were new clothes and new sets, but the stories were pretty much alike and I was the same type. But those early days of talkies were incredible, what with the sound-proof camera booth and everything. I think that's why they signed Cagney and me so fast, 'cause we just went through it like we were on a stage and they weren't used to that. We were showing something different, something fast and to the point."

Joan was next cast as a tainted chorus girl in *Union Depot*, a well-received ensemble effort set in a busy train station. Right on top of it came *The Roar of the Crowd*. There was concern that Joan would have to be replaced because *Union Depot* would not be finished on time. But Warner Bros. sped up its conveyor belt, and Joan was scheduled to begin one movie while the other was wrapping. In *The Roar of the Crowd*, she was to play Lee, Cagney's skittish girlfriend, while Ann Dvorak was to play Anne, the romantic interest to Eric Linden, a boyish actor playing Cagney's younger brother. When filming began, however, Blondell said, "I can't play a neurotic," and Dvorak said, "I can't play an ingénue." The two switched roles with the full blessing of director Howard Hawks.

Executives were watching costs on *The Roar of the Crowd*, renamed *The Crowd Roars*, since it required location scenes at Indy, Ventura, and Ascot Motor Speedway. The investment was worth it, for the racing footage of professional drivers is shockingly realistic. Hawks portrays the sport as gladiatorial, the dust, grease, and noise mingling with hysterical fans screaming as cars corkscrew through the air and burst into flames. Anne was a thankless role in a man's movie, and Linden did not offer the on-screen interest Cagney did, but Blondell generated some heat. Her emerging dramatic skill kept her character sympathetic even when she said, "You can take those hard-drinking, hard-riding men and put them in a truck and shove them over a cliff." Certainly we were meant to feel the pain of all women who get too close to daredevils, but the script asked her to be too embittered for a background ingénue.

At the end of 1931, just as James Cagney more than doubled his income, Warner Bros. cut salaries 20 to 30 percent to stave off Depression bankruptcy. With a $14 million debt, there was also talk of selling assets such as Warner's theaters. Joan became an ever more valuable commodity as she played variations on the same character in inexpensive quickies. She was hustled into *The Famous Ferguson Case* in early December, with a schedule that overlapped with the making of *The Crowd Roars*. *Ferguson* offered a stale critique of yellow journalism as Joan played a New York sob sister. The production's rushed schedule showed; director Lloyd Bacon let his actors over speak or stand idly by looking tentative. True to the studio's interests, it capitalized on current trends. *Ferguson* played off the rise of women in American journalism. More renowned fictional embodiments, Lois Lane and Brenda Starr, most notably, soon invaded the marketplace of popular culture.

It was now clear to Joan just how rough this Warner Bros. gig was going to be. The studio was a place of "hard, hard labor and gruesome hours," she said. "The studio did protect you because you were a moneymaker— but it was backbreaking and it was a good thing that you were young or you couldn't have stood it. The biggest treat was when you got time off to go to the bathroom." Contracted actors "were put on the payroll like bank clerks," according to film historian Charles Higham. They were "given strictly limited vacations—which could be canceled at a moment's notice— and put on suspension or even dismissed without recompense if they refused to play the roles to which they were assigned. The corps of producers and writers had strict instructions from Jack Warner to make sure that absolutely nobody was ever left idle for a moment. If no vehicle was fully prepared for a star, Jack Warner and Darryl F. Zanuck were to be seen pacing uneasily about, chewing hard on their expensive cigars."

Joan's daily grind reflects this pre-union corporate ethic. She awoke at 4, made grotesque faces in the mirror to warm up, slammed down coffee and toast, then drove her battered old Ford Model T to the lot. Traversing the empty streets as the morning light began to shine was the only time of an average day that Joan could be alone without immediate responsibilities to anyone. "We started work at 5 in the morning," she said, "makeup, all that junk, then *whammo on the nose!* Straight over to the set at 8, knowing all your lines. We'd work clean through the day until after sundown, then on Saturday and always right through Saturday night. They'd bring in sandwiches like straw for the horses and we'd finally make it into bed on Sunday morning as the sun hit the pillows." Menstrual cycles were charted, with two days allowed off each month for cramps. "They'd even plan us going to the ladies room," laughed Joan. If she was in command of tomorrow's shoot, she could enjoy a few pages of a novel, instead of a script, before falling asleep.

Warner Bros. movies of the early 1930s were usually shot in less than four weeks. Lloyd Bacon, who directed Joan eight times, actually used rehearsal footage in final prints. "Writers were pressed to crank out their stuff by the yard," wrote Cagney. With such a schedule expected of actors, directors, writers, and technicians, it is no surprise that much garbage was unspooled in movie houses across the country. But the industry remained solvent. Movies were *the* form of mass entertainment in an age when choices were few and two hours in the dark was a distraction from bread lines, bank runs, and foreclosures. There was enough talent, drive, and care to ensure that Joan and others of the Warner Bros. stable occasionally found themselves in movies of real distinction. Much has been said about how *many* movies Joan made during her years at Warner Bros., but less has been said about how *good* some of them remain to this day. In less than two years in the business, she had already made *The Public Enemy* and *Blonde Crazy.*

Joan was having trouble falling asleep one night. She was due the next morning on the set of a new studio, Goldwyn, where she was on loan for one movie. When she arrived just after sunrise, she was struck by the difference from her professional home at Warners. The sets were more plush, and the actors were treated to afternoon teas, soft music, private makeup artists, hairdressers, personal maids, and haute costumes. The Chanel gowns she wore glittered and clung seductively under hot lights, and her five-hundred-dollar-a-week paycheck was the result of a minor bidding war. Joan was platinum blonde here, with exacting attention paid to eye liner and dark lipstick. She looked gorgeous and, not surprisingly, she loved the indulgence.

She was making *The Greeks Had a Word for Them*, a comedy packaged by the industrious Samuel Goldwyn. She had come by it though indirect means, as a replacement for Carole Lombard, who dropped out after two weeks of illness. "Nobody believed she was sick," said cast member Ina Claire. "I think she knew it was a lousy movie and she just wanted out." Claire underrated *Greeks*, a breezy concoction about three mantraps adept at lightening the wallets of their blinded prey. The source material, Zoë Akins's Broadway play called *The Greeks Had a Word for It*, was considered too suggestive by the censors. "It" became "Them," as though audiences would not catch the innuendo anyway. Even with petty intrusions, *Greeks* was a step above the gruel Joan was usually fed at Warner Bros. The bracing dialogue and keen timing of the women offered worthwhile amusement. They spent the better part of the movie stealing each other's men, falling in and out of love, then kissing and making up over "drinkies."

The Greeks Had a Word for Them was hardly a landmark movie, but it was momentous in Joan's life. In the months that she had been in Hollywood, there was scarcely time to breathe, much less find romance. But behind the camera of *The Greeks Had a Word for Them* was slender and stylish George Barnes, a cinematographer who gave loving attention to Joan's photogenic beauty.

Joan flirted, and George made his moves, first pursuing her before she hurried off the lot and home to her parents. Idle conversation led to dinner. When they began dating, Joan suddenly found herself in the society of Hollywood elites. She was appropriately star struck. "I had been one of those kid fans of Ronald Colman," she said. "To me, Ronnie's home was the most homey I'd seen. The evenings were fabulous there. He and his friends were so distinguished, and he had divine humor. We'd all tell stories, and sometimes he'd get up and act them out while we'd all be sitting cross-legged on the floor and couch. Those were beautiful, wonderful evenings."

Barnes began as a still photographer and at thirty-seven had become one of the best cinematographers in the business. By the time he first worked with Joan, he had already earned four Academy Award nominations. His expertise was in soft-focus photography, which was particularly flattering to women. The look at Warner Bros. in the early 1930s was harsh realism. Under Barnes's thoughtful play of light and shadow at Goldwyn, Joan at last embodied the glamorous and radiant 1930s movie star. Here was a man who promised to take care of her, to spoil her even, at least for the length of the shoot. He was much more than a technician. His steady attention from behind a lens had an undeniable erotic charge.

What did Joan know of men sexually, except that some of them were rapists? Here was George Barnes giving her gifts and seducing her with mood music and liqueur by fireside on Saturday nights. On one of those nights, they made love for the first time.

CHAPTER 3

Hammer and Tongs

People like her never won awards. They just saved movies.
—John Kobal, *People Will Talk*

Thanks to George Barnes's connections, Joan was enjoying high-class company, but she remained unostentatious, disliking showy hats, jewelry, and makeup. She went to premieres only when ordered by the studio, as she was when *Union Depot* had a pull-out-the-stops opening at Warner's Hollywood Theater. It distinguished itself as a sharp, engaging drama that refused to go soft for an artificial happy ending. Joan invested the penniless chorus girl with a waiflike vulnerability that more closely approximated who she was than all those brassy, in-charge dames she usually played.

Joan, meanwhile, was grappling with her sexual attraction to George. "Here was a young woman who has been completely isolated, her life had been family and work," said Joan's daughter many years later. "She was not worldly. When she gets to George Barnes, she doesn't have a clear picture of what to look for in a man. She had her father, who adored her, but even her mother was jealous of that relationship. Like Ed and Katie, there's a major age difference between Joan and George. There you are, six days a week—your world is small. She was very pretty and very naive. He was kind and gentle."

George had a short neck and narrow shoulders, but he dressed well, was gentlemanly and good-looking. He also had a soft-spokenness that Joan and other women found appealing. In fact, George was a serial monogamist who was in his third marriage when he met Joan. It was all but over by 1932; he was in Hollywood and she was in New York. More seasoned friends, both male and female, told Joan that George was notorious for being a silver-tongued Romeo. Joan did not, or would not, listen to such warnings, instead telling movie magazines that she pursued him, not vice versa. And then there was the matter of his vocation. It is no surprise that she was seduced by a man who was charged with making her look every inch the alluring movie star. Actresses married cameramen with some regularity in Hollywood.

The Crowd Roars and *The Greeks Have a Name for Them* came out side by side in March of 1932 to strong reviews. *The Crowd Roars* was a box-office champion to boot. Meanwhile, Joan was back at Warner Bros. making *Miss Pinkerton*, in which she had the title role of a murder-solving nurse. The first day of shooting was grueling even by Warner standards. She was at the studio from dawn touching up her platinum dye, memorizing lines, reviewing blocking, and meeting with the cast and director Lloyd Bacon. She did not get to bed that night until well past midnight. On the second day of production, her character was called upon to fall asleep on a cot. Bacon shot four takes, and Joan performed her duties to perfection. In fact, it took three crewmen to roust her when the scene was complete.

Joan fulfilled her *Miss Pinkerton* obligations with an effortlessness that was becoming trademark, rising above clichéd material and the limited magnetism of her costar George Brent. By now, newspapers were running puff pieces about this new blonde charmer, explaining that she doesn't ever use cuss words or tell risqué stories. She has seen everything, but is utterly clean minded, frank, poised, and confident. Warner Bros. voiced concern about her image in light of a future with George Barnes, but she turned around and stated her dissatisfaction with the studio's diet of the same role in the same movie. "I'm so sick of that," said Joan for the first time publicly. "So sick of being the wisecracking, hail-fellow-well met, slap-me-on-the-back sort of baby!"

In early 1932 she made the trenchant *Three on a Match*, all about the divergent fortunes of school friends who meet ten years later. Vivian (Ann Dvorak) has married a wealthy lawyer, Ruth (Bette Davis) is a secretary, and Mary (Blondell) has taken to the stage after a stint in reform school. With its attention on violence, drugs, and kidnapping, *Three on a Match* was judged by the *New York Times* to be "tedious and distasteful," but it has become a minor pre-Code classic. It is a wonder of economic film making, as a fully realized story covering thirteen years is contained in sixty-three minutes. The plot hinges on Dvorak's character, who squanders loveless, conventional respectability and winds up ensnared in the underworld. The idiom-filled dialogue had forward momentum and gutter-inspired realism. With its uncompromising conclusion, *Three on a Match* became a primal scream against the injustices visited upon women.

Joan and George had meanwhile been dating only for a few months, but already she was clinging. "Whee—am I *jealous*!" she told a movie magazine. "When I see George even speaking to another girl, I go hot and cold all over. I suppose he feels the same way about me." Eventually, George met Ed and Katie, who were skeptical of his intentions. Gloria, now seventeen, didn't warm to him either. He was too smooth, she thought, and had been married too often.

In April of 1932, Joan made the quickie *Big City Blues*. She played Vida, a seasoned New York gold digger bemoaning the Depression. "Chorus girls used to get pearls and diamonds," she says wearily. "Now all they expect is a corned beef sandwich." With an older woman preying on a younger man, and a quotation from the sapphic novel *The Well of Loneliness, Big City Blues* was objectionable to many. At home, Joan patiently listened to the complaints of her increasingly cranky sixty-seven-year-old father, who voiced disapproval that his daughter was playing so many low women in movies like *Big City Blues*. He was similarly displeased when vivacious Gloria turned to acting. She was pretty, bubbly, and curvaceous like her big sister and caught the attention of industrialist turned movie producer Howard Hughes. No sexual favors were expected; Gloria did not even appear in front of a camera. She was just one of a whole bevy of unknowns Hughes kept at the ready since he launched Jean Harlow's career in *Hell's Angels*.

Joan completed twenty movies before she enjoyed her first real vacation. In the summer of 1932, she and George drove up to Gold Beach on the Pacific coast in southern Oregon for fishing and solitude. George needed to recuperate from a recent bout of pneumonia, but something else was slightly off about the getaway. An unknown source leaked that the two were married secretly in the wilds of Oregon. Upon their return, a dodgy Joan offered reporters nothing: "I didn't say I was married. I didn't say I wasn't. I'm not saying I am and I'm not saying I'm not."

They were not hitched on that trip. George was still married to wife number three, but the romance with Joan continued to blossom. Joan, the "naive sophisticate," as James Cagney so aptly called her, was told by George that he had not seen his wife in years, and he assured her that getting a divorce was mere paperwork. Those words offered some comfort to Joan when she was told by her doctor that she was pregnant. George was a perfect gentleman about it, kissing her gently and whispering "my poor baby" in her ear. He even escorted her to a discrete abortionist who made a lucrative if illegal business from movie stars. When Joan tearfully said she could not end her pregnancy, George took control. He assured her it was not really a child yet, abortions were safe, and she would be back on the job in a few days. Furthermore, she would not want to upset her parents and nothing and no one should come between them. Still Joan faced a wrenching dilemma. Alone one day on an afternoon break from the studio, she drove out to Malibu and walked into the Pacific, hoping the buffeting currents would induce a miscarriage. When that failed, she submitted to George's wishes and had the abortion. In the early 1930s, that meant cash only, back alley, no identification, and no recourse for malpractice.

Joan was appearing in a movie every month or two, as Warner Bros.' rotatory schedules ensured her being ever ready to shoot. All necessities of production—camera, lights, costumes, setting—were assigned personnel in advance. By the time a director received his orders, everything and everyone was already in place. It was not unusual for Joan and other contractees to make two movies simultaneously. Joan might shoot on one sound stage in the morning, then scurry to another in the afternoon, with the logistics worked out by the production department. "It's the same script, we just changed clothes," was the ongoing joke between Blondell and fellow studio actress Glenda Farrell. As for exhibition, Warner Bros. owned 525 theaters in 188 cities in America by late 1930, with admission costs at ten cents for children and thirty-five cents for adults. "You had to sell a lot of tickets at that price in order to make a profit," said William Schaefer, Jack Warner's longtime secretary. "The theaters were changing programs in the middle of the week and there were always double bills, so that meant four pictures would be used a week. They seldom ran longer than a week. So we had to make a lot of pictures during the year. In fact, we were making about seventy a year." Even with watertight planning, Warner Bros. announced a loss in 1932 of over $8 million. Joan and the other contractees were given weekly IOUs by the studio, which they cashed at the bank handling the Warner Bros.'s payroll, but only after noon on Fridays, when film rental income had been deposited. Despite the hand-to-mouth conditions, James Cagney demanded more pay. He was brought back for $1,750 a week, but Blondell's salary was unchanged at $500.

Joan finally had her chance at a solo turn with *Blondie Johnson*. This was her movie outright; she worked every day of its four week schedule. Conceived as a female *Little Caesar*, Blondie undergoes an extreme transformation at the hands of an indifferent society. As a Depression victim, she appears before a magistrate begging for assistance so that she may care for her sick mother. She gets no sympathy, then goes home to find her mother dead. She hardens quickly. "This city's going to pay me a living, a good living, and it's going to get back from me just as little as I have to give," she says with bitter certainty.

Blondie Johnson gently twisted movie storytelling and sexual stereotypes. This time Joan was not a gangster's female sidekick, she *was* the gangster. She became that way by the malfunctions of government, not because of a predisposition to be bad as was often the case in roles played by Cagney and Robinson. There is humor and authenticity in *Blondie Johnson*, and Joan enjoyed a personal success. She showed a new command on screen, occupying the space with full, confident strides and persuasively shifting from charity case to tough Mafiosa to vulnerable woman in love. It was a tidy hit at the box-office, grossing $325,000, more than twice its negative costs.

If conditions at Warner Bros. were sometimes brutal, Joan grew to love her steady cohorts. "Guys like Lloyd Bacon, John Adolfi, and Ray Enright were terrific directors, even though their budgets didn't let them do things they wanted to do," she said. "They were saddled with us, just as we actors were saddled with them, [but] the all-important compulsion was to finish on schedule and under budget. . . . We helped each other at Warners. We were always on time and there were no 'star complexes' or 'temperament.' " They virtually lived together. "We seldom said hello or goodbye; it was just sort of a continuation," she said. Audiences going to a Warner Bros. movie in 1932 knew they would be in the pleasurable company of stars and character actors who were almost constantly on America's screens. The big names are familiar still, but for almost eight years Joan lived in the company of a wide variety of actor types suited to whatever product Warner Bros. served. There was snoopy, spinsterish Ruth Donnelly, buffoonish Hugh "woo-woo" Herbert, gullible roly-poly Guy Kibbee, fast-talking opportunist Glenda Farrell, pompous Alan Mowbray, dynamic and resolute Regis Toomey, tall and craggy Grant Withers, dapper Warren William, youthful and slight Eric Linden, sadder-but-wiser Ann Dvorak, blue-collar type Allen Jenkins, and fey fussbudget Edward Everett Horton. Farrell said, "Warners never made you feel you were just a member of the cast. They might star you in one movie and give you a bit part in the next. . . . You were still well paid and didn't get a star complex. We were a very close group."

George Barnes pulled strings at Fox, where he was currently working, and got Joan the starring role in the sudsy, off-color *Broadway Bad*, a movie he was assigned to photograph late in 1932. At the same time, his wife finally agreed to a divorce. On her way out, she caustically wished his new love all the luck in the world. On 3 January 1933, Joan and George left town and drove east, with Joan's parents and Gloria trailing them in another car. It was a long day's drive, and the night was inky black when they reached Phoenix and checked into a hotel. The next morning, Ed took George aside to give him a tattered old envelope containing a single piece of paper. It stated, in essence, that Joan broke her maidenhead at the age of eight in an accident on the edge of a costume trunk. Ed Blondell, oblivious to his daughter's rape and current sexual habits, certified that she was a virgin.

To elude her fans, Joan wore a red wig and tortoise-shell glasses. She and George registered as "Rose Blondell" and "Scott Barnes" and were married in Phoenix at First Presbyterian Church in a secret wedding. Present were witnesses Allen Vincent and Elizabeth Wilson, a movie magazine writer given an exclusive provided she kept quiet before the ceremony. When the Barnes returned to Southern California without a honeymoon, they settled on Lookout Mountain, a meandering collection of residential streets in the Santa Monica Mountains above Hollywood. Their new seven-room, two-story, white stucco home came with a steep, shingled roof, cobblestone drive, and a view across greater Los Angeles to Catalina. Joan was drunk on the joys of domesticity. Her culinary experiments ran to barbecue sauce, salad dressing, dried beef à la king, homemade ice cream, and shortcakes. "It's great what love can do," she enthused. "I—who couldn't boil water. Why, I've learned to cook and I love it. I—who had just as soon live in a hotel as a house. Why, I go around touching every little vase and picture in our house. I think marriage is grand—and maybe if I hadn't smiled at George and kept smiling at him until he noticed me, I wouldn't be married to him now. I'm glad I didn't wait for him to propose. I'm glad I did the chasing. It's swell!" As a dedicated reader, she filled the shelves in the den with books, with particular devotion to titles by Hemingway and Shaw and the idiomatic poetry of John V. A. Weaver. For a time, she declared her favorite book to be *If I Were King*, Justin Huntley McCarthy's 1901 historical novel of monarchical France.

The house was never solely occupied by the two of them. Gloria found an apartment with friends, but Katie and Ed lived with Joan and George. Two less opinionated members of the household were Thing, a dachshund, and Abadaba, a Boston bull terrier. Joan accepted the arrangement. "I could be happy in a little store or some business somewhere else if Hollywood wouldn't let us make a go of our marriage," she said. "This town hasn't got into my blood. I like it—it has been good to me—but I'm my father's child, and if the callboard for happiness ever indicated any other place, well, a Blondell has never yet been afraid of 'the big hike.'"

For now everything was focused on her new husband and making the marriage work, which was no small challenge considering the scant time the newlyweds could spend together. Joan was so swept away by marriage that she asked Jack Warner to allow a name change to Joan Barnes, but he said no. It was his turn to remind her that she refused the name Inez Holmes more than two years earlier. The attempted gesture underscores Joan's great but transient happiness. She remembered looking out of the picture window of her new living room soon after marriage and seeing George "winding up the road below in his lovely car. He was coming to me. My first and youngest feeling of joy was that moment."

Joan was so ecstatic in marriage that she attempted to be a housewife and live off George's income exclusively. She was due back at the studio to shoot *High Life*, but she proved her sincerity for "the big hike" by refusing the work, returning the script to the studio via her agent at William Morris, and opting for a layoff period. The studio sent the script right back and told her to, in essence, report to work or face the consequences of breach of contract. The flare-up proved to be almost pointless, as delays on the commencement of *High Life* allowed Joan to revivify and return to the studio willingly.

Joan was often seen about town on George's arm. Louella Parsons reported spotting them dining at the Beverly-Wilshire one night and dancing to the music of Gus Arnheim at the Cocoanut Grove the next. They spent a weekend in Palm Springs with friends. So much home cooking was making Joan too curvy, so she began a regimen of reduced calories and increased exercise. She bicycled on the steep hills around Lookout Mountain, skipped rope, and tried to live primarily on salads and vegetables. She thought it would be easy, since she avoided meat in her youth. She was also taking a harsher assessment of her screen presence, appalled that her eyes popped open, her shoulders pulled back, and her breasts jutted forward whenever she acted with emphasis.

Joan was part of the Warner Bros. entourage in attendance at the first inaugural speech of President Franklin D. Roosevelt, proving that her temporary insubordination did not endanger her place at the studio. Though Jack Warner was a diehard Republican, he believed the appearance of his top stars at Roosevelt's swearing in would come back to benefit the Depression-racked studio. The dire circumstances were laid bare two days later, when Warner Bros. announced that all studio employees were to take a 50 percent pay cut for eight weeks. The Academy of Motion Picture Arts and Sciences attempted to intervene and force Warner's hand, but that failed. Meanwhile, the studio kept its doors open with the enormous smash *42nd Street*. Musicals were thought to be dead by 1932, but along came Broadway choreographer Busby Berkeley to recharge the genre by staging the most original and exciting production numbers ever seen. The plot of *42nd Street* was perfect for a musical—all about the backstage machinations in putting on a musical within a musical. Joan was considered for the role of "Anytime Annie" Lowell but was too busy with other assignments, so it went instead to Ginger Rogers. Joan was, however, firmly cast for a key role in *High Life*, the movie she originally blanched at that had not yet gone into production. It was to be a splashy musical, and the studio's follow-up to *42nd Street*. No one argued with success, so the plot of *High Life* concerned—what else?—putting on a show.

High Life transformed itself into *Gold Diggers of 1933* during its filming on Sound Stage Seven as *42nd Street* tunesmiths Harry Warren and Al Dubin penned a slew of new songs, including "We're in the Money," "Pettin' in the Park," and "The Shadow Waltz." Berkeley was one of the few artists at Warner Bros. to be given a virtual blank check after *42nd Street*. The swirling, intoxicating kaleidoscope that he achieved with his all-female choruses in *Gold Diggers of 1933* confirmed the studio's judgment. Rogers and chorus open with "We're in the Money," festooned with giant coins fulfilling the sartorial duties of bikinis, boas, and hats. It is a lavish ode to American optimism, punctured by the arrival of the sheriff and his posse to close the show for lack of funds. In *Gold Diggers of 1933*, the Depression is literally waiting just outside the stage door.

The movie's last production, "Remember My Forgotten Man," stood apart. Gone are the rows of alabaster lovelies singing lilting melodies of love. Instead, there are 150 male extras as soldiers or hobos. It may seem that the downbeat "Remember My Forgotten Man" came out of nowhere to put a damper on all the fun that preceded it, but *Gold Diggers of 1933* has frequent references to the harsh realities of the time. The number was simply the culmination of an anger and anxiety that had been treated more lightly in the movie's earlier reels.

Joan was not the most musical of stars. Her dancing was passable, but she was wanting vocally. Her singing voice was, in fact, everything her speaking voice was not—flat, limited in range, and uninteresting. Berkeley was not deterred. "It was a spectacle type of number and a good one to use in those dark days of the Depression when many people had forgotten about the guys who had gone to war for our country," he said. "I did something extraordinary in that number, too, when I had Joan Blondell sing the song because Joan Blondell can't sing. But I knew she could act it. I knew she could 'talk it' and put over the drama for me."

Joan is galvanizing in "Remember My Forgotten Man." In her few moments with the song she is sultry, vulnerable, bitter, and yearning. She is then followed by the magnificent Etta Moten, who provides the song a vocal melody. Later still, the soldiers, then bums, make for a powerful musicalization of politics and history. "Remember My Forgotten Man" is perhaps the most socially urgent song ever conceived for an American musical film.

Though it is specific to the Depression and the treatment of World War I veterans in a nation wanting for food and work, "Remember My

Forgotten Man" has never gone out of date. What is government's responsibility to the dispossessed? What are the effects of war and neglect on women? Joan's character speaks to an ambivalence of the moment when she looks at a hard-luck veteran and says, "I don't know if he deserves a bit of sympathy." As someone reduced to streetwalking, the question could be asked of her as well. In six minutes and forty-five seconds, Berkeley treats us to prostitution, homelessness, veterans marching in the rain, bread lines, and desolate womanhood. The final image is a three-layered design of choreographic genius. In the back is a human canvas of marching soldiers in silhouette on multileveled semicircular pathways. In the middle is Joan, her arms outstretched in V formation for the final tableau. Surrounding her is a mass of hungry men, the former vets. They reach out to her in communion, each a victim of society's betrayal.

Jack Warner did not originally conceive of "Forgotten Man" as the finale of *Gold Diggers of 1933*, but it was so powerful it could not be inserted anywhere else. Joan was modest about the whole experience and hesitant to admit that she was at the center of an emblematic image of the Depression. *Gold Diggers of 1933* cost $433,000 to make and earned a $2 million profit. Those figures placed it alongside *42nd Street* as the biggest moneymaker of the year for Warner Bros. and among the top five of the year overall. It had everything a hit could ask for: comedy, romance, music, a smattering of low-pressure drama, social commentary, and Berkeley's awesome visual designs. Everybody, from Joan to silly Guy Kibbee and opportunistic Aline MacMahon and newcomer Dick Powell, as Ruby Keeler's singing boyfriend, filled their roles perfectly. Public and critical response to *Gold Diggers of 1933* was instantly positive. "Smash girl-and-music special has everything and should mop up everywhere," with "fat parts for all the featured players," announced *Film Daily*.

After *Gold Diggers of 1933*, the studio sent Joan on a personal appearance tour to Washington and Philadelphia. She and George combined professional obligations with a visit to New York to see friends and relatives, catch some theater, and drop in on Joan's former librarian boss, Esther

Wright. Though she was paid to market her latest movie, Joan wanted only to move on. " 'The Forgotten Man' number in *Gold Diggers of 1933* mortified me," she said. "I remember there was a bread line and someone fell down, but that's it. I remember I had a pregnancy test made when that was filming." With great dread, Joan learned she was indeed expecting, and again she was escorted by George to an abortionist. Joan, unprepared and unaware, didn't ask George about children during their courtship. Only after they were married did he make it clear he did not want any. He couched his feelings in adoration of her and a desire to prolong their honeymoon with a kind of endless romantic stupor. But he also rejected conventional forms of birth control, which were then condoms and diaphragms. Joan was trapped. For a time, she wanted nothing more than to please George, so the grim ritual of abortion repeated itself.

Back in California, Joan and George were both assigned to *Goodbye Again*, an undemanding comedy in which she loves Warren William, but he pursues Genevieve Tobin. Reviews were flattering and business was brisk, but more attention was paid to *Footlight Parade*, another backstage musical with production numbers by Busby Berkeley. *Footlight Parade* was made with the most practical of intentions: to capitalize on the box-office magic of *42nd Street* and *Gold Diggers of 1933*. But it was no slavish imitator to success. *Footlight Parade* offered a whimsical plot on the rise of talkies and the fall of live prologues. George was brought on to supervise the photography and James Cagney to star as a dynamo producer. As expected, Cagney enlivened the proceedings considerably. His dancing was a major revelation for anyone who missed his nimble feet in vaudeville.

Footlight Parade emerged as fast paced, knowing, and arguably the best of the Warner Bros. Depression musicals. Joan delivered one of her most endearingly comic performances. Though she had no musical responsibilities, her role in *Footlight Parade* was larger and more sympathetic than in *Gold Diggers of 1933*. She is the sweet and witty secretary who patiently waits for Cagney to come to his senses and realize that it is her, not Claire Dodd, that he loves. She has a delicious ongoing duel with Dodd, who plays Vivian

Rich, a hustler prone to phony French. Amidst funny insults, Joan calls her "Miss B-Rich," but the moment goes by so fast it could easily be missed. When Miss B-Rich makes designs on Cagney, Blondell throws her in the street at 3 a.m. and utters her most famous line: "Outside, Countess. As long as they've got sidewalks, you've got a job!" To add to the fun, Warner Bros. dependables Hugh Herbert, Ruth Donnelly, and Guy Kibbee were given character showcases. Fresh-faced cherubs Dick Powell and Ruby Keeler formed the other romantic couple, a foregone conclusion after their rapturous serenades in *42nd Street* and *Gold Diggers of 1933*.

Footlight Parade had it all. The *Los Angeles Post Record* stated, "You will see the most extravagant, eye-paralyzing chorus scenes in *Footlight Parade* that have ever graced a movie screen." The declaration may still be true. More than thirty minutes at the finish of *Footlight Parade* are devoted to three stupendous productions: "Honeymoon Hotel" for Powell and Keeler; "By a Waterfall," featuring one hundred bathing beauties in a colossal aquacade; and "Shanghai Lil," in which Keeler mimics someone's idea of a Chinese prostitute ("I miss you very much a long time") while Cagney not so quietly outclasses her with his precision dancing.

"Those musicals were tough," Joan said years later. "Much tougher than a straight movie. And the hours were awful because we didn't have unions then. We worked anytime they wanted to work. You could come in to work at 6:00 a.m. and work till midnight and then be back at 6:00 the next morning. And you might have breakfast at 6:30 and then not break for lunch till 3:00 in the afternoon. You'd be ready to fall over. Then you'd work all day Saturday, and they made it a point to work all night Saturday night. . . . I don't think it was like that at all the studios, I think they specialized in it at Warners. They had something hot going for them: the musicals and the gangster things. And they had a bunch of us who were *hot*, and they were going to wring it dry. And they did."

Footlight Parade was not as huge a money earner as *Gold Diggers of 1933*. It cost $703,000 and had more than a $1 million profit. That was still a spectacular return in 1933 and enough to convince Jack Warner not to tinker with success. In a pique of non-creativity, he saddled Joan with cheap *Gold Digger* rip-offs, but without the music, Busby Berkeley, zippy dialogue, or a trace of flair. In *Havana Widows*, Blondell and Glenda Farrell are a pair of high steppers who set sail for Cuba in search of their own Daddy Warbucks, only to find Guy Kibbee waiting as bait. Audiences were not impressed, and the *New York Times* declared it "a helter-skelter lark that sounds as if it were written by the studio mechanics."

The Barnes got out of town immediately after *Havana Widows* to vacation at the carnivalesque Tent City in Coronado near San Diego. Joan was suffering under the private strain of the abortions and the public strain of a career that was too productive for her own good. The booths, Ferris wheels, sailing, and swimming of Tent City were distracting and restorative, provided Joan could go undetected. Dreading a new movie assignment, she sent a Western Union cable to Jack Warner making her position clear. Her complaints were not exclusively financial; she would have gladly kept her current rate of pay if it meant fewer films per year. Joan was simply exhausted beyond endurance as reflected in a cable sent to the studio: "Please be advised that I have no desire to render my services in a picture to be produced by your studio on September 11, 1933 or any other time till the above mentioned studio does right by our Nell Stop Truthfully Im so sick and tired I dont care if I ever work again. Joan Blondell." The studio once again issued a threatening "you are under contract" instructive, followed by suspension of pay. She pleaded to Warner to "please replace [her]" as she was "trying to get much needed rest."

Just as she attempted to evade *Gold Diggers of 1933* but made it anyway, Joan's efforts to be replaced on the new *Convention City* proved fruitless. She had left William Morris and was now represented by Frank and Dunlap, the very agency that represented James Cagney as he sought higher paychecks. As she wandered among the amusements of Tent City, Joan's representative George Frank met with Warner Bros. lawyer Roy Obringer to forge a deal. Frank did right by her, just as he had for Cagney. She came back from a six-week suspension with a $250 per week raise, making her gross earnings $1,250 weekly. Good fortune was mixed with rest to vastly improve Joan's state of being. In the fall of 1933, she found herself complimented by the mariners of the Seamen's Church Institute of New York, who enjoyed a regular diet of the latest Hollywood products in their advanced, up-to-date auditorium. They declared Joan Blondell one of their five favorite actresses.

Convention City, it turns out, was a treat. Joan was happy to be reunited with affable Dick Powell in a nonmusical setting, and happier still by the delightful premise. Amiable old Guy Kibbee is a salesman attending the annual Honeywell Rubber Company convention in Atlantic City with his wife, the reliably prim Ruth Donnelly. He can't resist a romp with Joan, and so throws caution, and his toupee, to the wind. Early audiences were in stitches, unaware that the script underwent much sanitizing due to the objections of the Production Code Administration (PCA). The administration felt that *Convention City* "seemed to indicate a pretty rowdy picture, dealing very largely with drunkenness, blackmail, and lechery, and without any particularly sympathetic characters or elements." The producer, Henry Blanke, avowed that *Convention City* started an active effort to blue-pencil Hollywood: "Me. I was the one. Single-handedly I brought on the whole Code. Yeah. Ask [Code enforcer] Joe Breen. He'll tell you. Ask him about *Convention City*." When Jack Warner watched the rushes, he fired off a memo to director Archie Mayo with the caution, "We must put brassieres on Joan Blondell and make her cover up her breasts because, otherwise, we are going to have these pictures stopped in a lot of places. I believe in showing their forms but, for Lord's sake, don't let those bulbs stick out." There was also the naughty language to consider. "We were forever doing things among ourselves with double meanings," said Joan. "Finally, they would have people in the front office just watch for what we'd say off-color."

Convention City proved to be a pebble in Jack Warner's shoe. It was released to strong objections over the low morals of its characters. After it left theaters, there was continued interest in screenings by exhibitors and convention organizers. Due to the controversy, Warner simply wanted it to go away forever. To ease his anxiety and placate the Production Code high-muck-a-mucks at the same time, he had all prints and negatives incinerated.

Like the Hanging Gardens of Babylon, today we can only imagine the experience of seeing *Convention City*.

In late November, soon after she had started a movie called *I've Got Your Number*, Joan woke up in the middle of the night ghost white and bleeding heavily. Her doctor made an emergency house call and diagnosed peritonitis, requiring immediate surgery and hospitalization. Joan's uterine wall had been punctured as a result of the suction and scraping during one of her abortions, causing infection and hemorrhaging. The doctor said in stern tones that it must not happen again, that abortion was no substitute for birth control. George once again took charge of the waiting reporters, telling them that his wife was suffering from appendicitis.

Soon enough Joan was back on the set of *I've Got Your Number*, a comedy featuring her as a switchboard operator, the perfect occupation for an ace wisecracker. Pat O'Brien played a telephone repair man, and the actor became a cherished, platonic confidant among the studio players. So, too, did Glenda Farrell, who played a small part in *I've Got Your Number* as a bogus medium. Joan told her ghastly domestic tale to both of them. "We were all brothers and sisters," said Joan. "Pat O'Brien and I told each other everything, one experience and one joke after another. We'd work together and help each other. There was a camaraderie and professional way of working." Joan also found a kindred spirit in Barbara Stanwyck, whose actor husband, Frank Fay, was behaving similarly to George. Both were increasingly drunk and uncommunicative.

Joan had further medical problems stemming from the abortions, and newspapers simply reported *another* case of appendicitis. Her pay was suspended "until such incapacity has been removed and you are again able to resume your duties," according to a letter from Jack Warner to Joan. But this particular suspension came with an addendum: Joan was needed for one more key scene in *I've Got Your Number*, and she was bedridden. "Therefore, it is hereby agreed that we may photograph such scene or scenes in your home tomorrow, December 20, 1933, and for which we shall, of course, place you back on our payroll for such day's work," noted Warner. After that, the suspension "shall again be in full force and effect and continue thereafter until you are able to report back to our studio." The camera and sound crew, and their equipment, caravanned up the hairpin turns of Lookout Mountain to get their scene with Joan, who offered moviegoers a peek into her real bedroom. One by one the Warner personnel filed in to film her under the covers, with her large picture window covered by curtains. Eight actors, including O'Brien and corporeal Eugene Pallette, were in the shot with her.

I've Got Your Number was finally completed in early 1934, despite the infection, hospitalization, surgery, and bed rest of its leading lady. Still, other misfortunes plagued Joan, including a house fire on Lookout Mountain. It did not cause extensive property damage, but it did kill the Barnes' Siamese cat. Then Warner Bros. shoved Joan into *Smarty*, an odious programmer shot in eighteen days. *Smarty* came out just prior to the PCA's crackdown on sins of the flesh, so it could still mention "diced carrots" as veiled code for "impotence." More tawdry was the comedy and romance made from homespun violence—*Hit Me Again* was the project's working title.

The cumulative effect of exhaustion, depression, fire, abortions, and soul-freezing movies like *Smarty* put Joan over the edge. She had developed a habit of fluttering her eyelashes on screen, but it was out of necessity, not affectation. When she could not finish a sentence without effort, she called her doctor and said, "I'm stuttering and I can't stop blinking my eyes. I can't work another day." Her doctor believed overwork was driving her to the edge of a nervous breakdown and prescribed sedatives and rest. Joan took his advice, went straight home, washed down two pills, fell into bed, and slept for forty-eight hours.

After recovering, Joan drove to Death Valley alone for a few days of introspection. She knew that her marriage to George, not even a year old, was already in trouble. Joan had totaled seven abortions, each only equally horrible. The charade of "everything's fine" was excruciating, particularly with her parents in the same house. Amidst the arid majesty of sand dunes and salt flats, she admitted to herself a lifelong desire for motherhood.

Before leaving Death Valley, she vowed to stand up to George, and, her health willing, she would go full term with the next pregnancy.

When she was back at work, she told acquaintances her time off "was just a case of nerves." In February she revealed to George that she was pregnant. Once again George whispered "my poor baby," and once again he planned a visit to the "doctor" who worked down a darkened alley. When confronted, Joan looked at George, then looked down. Placing both hands on her abdomen, she said, "Not this one." George did not believe her resolve at first, but he came to. He confronted her regularly over the following weeks, hoping she would agree to end the pregnancy. Each time she refused.

After Joan completed *He Was Her Man* with James Cagney, she was chosen as the WAMPAS "baby star" who, in the opinion of the membership, has made the most progress since the 1931–32 season. The event in her honor was held at the Elks Club in Hollywood with a dinner dance, where she was given a silver achievement trophy. She justified the award with more work during her pregnancy. In the gag-heavy *Kansas City Princess*, Joan and Glenda Farrell played a pair of manicurists intent on separating men from their largesse. George was the cameraman on this one, and his presence on the set exposed their marital pathology. By a combination of coercion and insecurity, Joan refused to take off her wedding ring, even though her character was unmarried. A crew member's application of adhesive tape, greasepaint, and powder took care of the dilemma. Many considered it a gesture of devotion. Those who knew Joan well considered that she may have been afraid of her naked finger, afraid that once the ring came off, she would never put it back on.

Joan's middle was thickening, but the studio kept her busy. "I made six pictures while [pregnant]," she said. "They'd get me behind desks and behind barrels and throw tables in front of me to hide my growing tummy. And I never had more than two weeks before starting a picture." In the summer of 1934, domestic tranquility was reported from the Barnes home. They had hired two African American servants from New Orleans named Chalmett and Clarence, who called their mistress "Miss Joan." Also added to the brood was a Pekinese that was a gift from George to Joan.

Joan did everything she could to make life on Lookout Mountain joyous. In August, friend and costume designer Orry-Kelly gave her an unusual baby shower. Gender roles were reversed to the delight of all, as the guests were men bearing shirts, dresses, booties, and bibs. Joan was also engaged in a movie of more promise than her last two dogs, *Smarty* and *Kansas City Princess*. *Dames* was the unofficial *Gold Diggers of 1934*, complete with Busby Berkeley and much of the same cast. Its amusing plot managed to poke fun at the new efforts at moral uplift in popular entertainment. The subject could not have been more timely, as *Dames* was produced on the eve of the PCA's crackdown of Hollywood smut.

The Code, a wordy treatise on what is proper and improper for American film content, was drawn up in 1930 by the Motion Picture Producers and Distributors of America (MPPDA), also known as the Hays Office. It declared, "No plot shall present evil alluringly," and "The fact that the nude or semi-nude body may be beautiful does not make its use in the films moral." But the Code did not have fangs until July of 1934, when the Catholic Church's Legion of Decency led a campaign to clean up Hollywood. A previous effort had already touched Joan's career with the panic over *Convention City*. Now hordes of citizens demanded cleaner movies and were organizing boycotts. Facing the potential ruination of the industry, studio executives saw no alternative but to play along.

Dames was carefully inspected by the Hays Office. Little was reportedly offensive, but what was there was puerile. In another Berkeley fever dream, he envisioned Joan in a cat-and-mouse production number, with her as a feline inviting a rodent to "come up and see my pussy sometime." The Hays Office made sure that number never got past conception. There were further objections to Joan's character forcing herself into a man's train compartment, too, but *Dames* otherwise won the Code's seal of approval.

The plot is pure dross, but there is much to recommend *Dames*, not the least of which is ZaSu Pitts doing one of her flibbertigibbet routines. But the real amusement of *Dames* lies in its lampooning of prudish hypocrites, those closet tipplers and goons who tell other people how to live their lives. The movie's fictitious Ounce Foundation for the Elevation of American Morals coincides neatly with the PCA and managed to make fun of the overlords of motion-picture censorship. Miraculously, Will Hays, Joseph Breen, and other Code executives either ignored or did not notice this laugh at their expense.

Joan had a fun role in *Dames* as a cutie-pie blackmailer. She offered a textbook lesson in comic delivery with her mark, the flummoxed old Guy Kibbee. She also had a memorable number called "The Girl at the Ironing Board," in which her laundry comes to life with the help of very thin wires maneuvered by dozens of off-camera crewmen. She is endearing, as expected, but the sight of her falling in love with pajamas, flannels, and night shirts is nothing short of loony. With no personal allowances made for her pregnancy, Joan was again feeling stressed. But she amusedly noted the contortions used to keep her expanding midriff out of sight, including high-angle shots, carefully placed furniture, and unfashionable billowy dresses.

The studio could not deny Joan's pregnancy any longer, so by the fall of 1934 she was granted maternity leave. She gleefully readied Lookout Mountain for the baby. Due to the kidnapping and murder of Charles Lindbergh's child in 1932, Joan developed a catalog of fears that preyed on her mind—entrapment, abduction, molestation, and blackmail. She and George accordingly equipped the nursery with the latest in kidnap-proofing protective features on the door and windows, a burglar alarm, and a watchman to be always on duty once the baby was brought home from the hospital. Believing three names carry dignity, Joan and George settled on Georgia Joan Barnes or Norman Scott Barnes. The boy name was inspired by friend Norman Foster, Claudette Colbert's actor-director husband. Whatever discord sounded between the Barnes, it was hidden from the public. When they dined out with the Fosters just three weeks before the baby was due, one newspaper noted that "never was there a happier pair of prospective parents."

George was privately despairing at the thought of his life transformed. For him there was no joy in impending fatherhood, but he tried to overcome his trepidation. He gamely presented Joan with a fancy bassinet, with a card that read, "To my baby, from your baby, for our baby!" He also gave her a charm bracelet with trinkets meaningful to them both—two small hearts, an engagement ring, a house, and a stork with open wings.

"We're all ready for the stranger," said George behind a false smile. "The nursery has been ready for weeks."

"I think it will be any minute," said Joan. "I'm praying for quintuplets, but I'll probably only get one."

Joan waited as does any expectant mother, though her unusual profession of movie star meant that she had to endure some negative reviews of the just-released *Kansas City Princess* on the eve of her first contractions. Both came on the first of November. The obstetrician was summoned to Cedars of Lebanon Hospital in Hollywood, while George escorted Joan into his car for the trip down the hill. Recent showers necessitated a slow drive on slippery pavement, but the real nightmare began at the hospital. Joan's labor was complicated by her rape and consequent fractured coccyx. Not only that, but the baby was breach, with the cord wrapped around its neck. Labor lasted over twenty hours, and for much of that time there was the fear of a stillbirth. Joan finally delivered a bawling Norman Scott Barnes on 2 November to a cheering obstetrics staff. The cord was cut, and Norman was washed, dried, and swaddled. Joan did not hold him right away. She was already unconscious, and remained so for the next twenty-four hours.

Mother and son stayed in the hospital for eighteen days, but they were allowed only fleeting time together. When at last they were given leave to go home, Joan was weeping. "You see, this is the first time I've had the feeling he is really mine," she told reporters as she was wheeled from her room. "Before he's just been brought in a couple of minutes at feeding time and then whisked right out. But now I'm going home and they've given him to me for keeps and am I happy!"

With that proclamation, Joan and Norman were met at the patient exit door by George and Katie. George avoided contact with his infant son, by busying himself with discharge paperwork and Joan's suitcases. Katie, in contrast, was a radiant grandmother, holding the child at every opportunity. The four were soon loaded into George's car and off to Lookout Mountain, where the "cutest little fellow" was installed in his kidnap-proof nursery. Never before was Joan less invested in being a movie star than when Norman was born. And never was she more invested in her marriage to George. Here was an eight-pound reason to stay together. Yet in the coming months, the veneer of happy couplehood would be difficult, then impossible, to maintain.

CHAPTER 4

Nearer to Heaven

In woman dressed and adorned, nature is present but under restraint, by human will remodeled nearer to man's desire.
—Simone de Beauvoir, *The Second Sex*

Christmas 1934 was quiet on Lookout Mountain. Relatives came loaded with gifts, Joan cooked, Norman slept, and George brooded. Preoccupation with the holiday allowed Joan to postpone contemplating why George seemed distant from her and their son. They were happiest when out of town. For New Year's Eve, they tent camped in the desert. Later in January, Joan went searching for a nanny and found a want ad listing for Gesina Lanke, a woman who once cared for Joan, Junie, and Gloria. She was rehired, but Joan had to confront the growing problem at home. Norman's birth was a Pyrrhic victory, and the cost was marriage to George Barnes.

It began with increased drinking, which led to long intervals of silence. Often George would sit in the living-room easy chair with a cocktail and cigarette and stare blankly down on the lights of Hollywood. Joan tried various methods to communicate: she told jokes, got angry, finally pleaded with him to say something, *anything*, but nothing worked. Slowly George's tortured psychology revealed itself. His need to possess her was so great that he rejected the child who took her away from him. He showed little affection for Norman, and any attempts Joan made to discuss their child's immediate or distant future were shunned. George stayed at home as much as possible, turning down the social gatherings with friends that he and Joan once enjoyed. The new George lacked the need for simple human contact, and Joan had to confess to herself that she was falling out of love.

Joan's first movie after Norman's birth was *The Traveling Saleslady*, inconveniently photographed by George. Since the marriage, he shot Joan from the neck up whenever possible. Her sexy curves were no longer for others to see, causing friction with directors and charges of possessiveness at home. Of course, Joan was depressed at the deterioration of her marriage, but it does not show on screen. *The Traveling Saleslady* was a daffy concept movie with a lambent Joan showing her stodgy father how to run his toothpaste business. She teams up with his rival and a wacky inventor/ex-bootlegger to patent "Cocktail Toothpaste" that comes in flavors like gin, whiskey, and scotch. Joan recalled the social service provided by such movies: "That was when people wanted to get relief from all the pain of living. And, oh boy, they got it going into those pictures. Nine times of out of ten it was some darling frothy comedy and you looked as pretty as possible in it."

There were disputes about Joan's salary. She came back from her six-month non-remunerated maternity leave holding steady at $1,250, but agent George Frank sought to negotiate a deal at $2,000 a week. "I do not know what they have in mind, but it looks like another one of those things," wrote studio lawyer Roy Obringer to production chief Hal Wallis. "Blondell is daily asking, through Frank, what the company intends to do." Joan held out for more money, refusing wardrobe fittings for the upcoming *Broadway Gondolier* until an amount was set. A compromise was found at $1,600, which the studio was quick to explain did not constitute a raise. The additional $350 was a bonus and could be revoked at any time.

Broadway Gondolier was not a happy set for Joan, but it turned out to be a respectable comedy with music. The setting was supposed to be Venice on a warm evening, but it was shot in California during an unusual cold snap. Dick Powell wore long red flannel underwear, but Joan had to shiver in her décolleté gown. It offered her more tart-tongued repartee, with Powell in fine voice warbling bits and pieces from *Rigoletto* and current pop tunes, but Joan's despair was detected by at least one critic. She "utters comedy lines but looks sad in the process," wrote the *Hollywood Citizen News*. Actually, Joan appears to be trying a new kind of humor based on playing it straight rather than delivering the expressive face and voice that was her stock in trade. *Broadway Gondolier* was also the first pairing of her and Powell as a romantic couple. They played their scenes together with a convincing tenderness of feelings as captured through the lens of George Barnes. They clicked, and *Broadway Gondolier* earned sizable profits.

Whenever schedules allowed, Joan and George did what made them happiest as a couple—they went weekend camping in the Mojave Desert. The following Monday, Joan required extra time in makeup to disguise her sunburns, while life at home grew more discomforting. Work was a temporary salve, at least when George and she were assigned different movies. Though Joan was now Warner Bros.'s top musical comedienne, Jack Warner never let her get too self-assured, thus denying her the circumstances that made James Cagney so expensive. "You made one good movie, followed by two or three stinkers," she said. "That enabled Jack Warner to keep you humble." Nor should Cagney's walkout be evidence that insubordination was easy. His unparalleled success on screen made him the studio exception, while lawyers were ready to enforce compliance for everyone else. Warner saved money on writers, rarely buying expensive books or plays for adaptation. The scripts for most of the studio's topical dramas were based on remakes or on stories taken from newspaper headlines, while the musicals differed only by character names and a few chord progressions.

Joan fought against her own exploitation, but only so far. "I never saw rushes or dailies," she said. "Who'd have the time? I'd stagger away from the lot and go home and collapse. I did every film they put me in. Sure, I'd have preferred meatier roles, but I wasn't a fighter. Bette Davis fought and it paid off. But that wasn't too important for me. I was never a career girl." She was forever committed to other people's causes. She gave annually to the Hollywood Junior League and Tailwaggers, a local charity for stray dogs. She joined dozens of other stars as striking Screen Actors Guild members seeking to improve conditions of extras. She attended the opening of a beauty salon run by the esteemed Westmore family, which included ace makeup artist Perc. She cheered as Gloria opened in Los Angeles in the hit play *Three Men on a Horse*. She even spearheaded a campaign for Bette Davis as a write-in candidate for the Best Actress Academy Award for *Of Human Bondage*.

Joan did, on occasion, look out for her own well-being. In August of 1935, as her marriage was disintegrating, she wrote a revealing screed to Hal Wallis:

I've been thinking! Thinking about my work at the studio and how I can best attack it for the good of all concerned.

I'm getting stale! And it has occurred to me that since it seems impossible to get away from doing the same role and practically the same picture over and over again, that perhaps a complete change of the general atmosphere might help. A change of director, for instance.

I haven't a thing in the world against Ray Enright, personally! It is simply that we have done the same thing together so often, and know each other's tricks, such as they are, so well, that there is nothing more to be gained for the good of a picture by a continued association. . . . Maybe a new director might give me a new slant. . . .

Another thing that I would like to call your attention to, is the fact that you told me that I would not do more than two pictures a year with Farrell, and then not one on top of the other. I hope that this will be the case, as it will upset me considerably if it isn't, and hardly work towards the change that I am trying to bring about for better performances and a more pleasant attitude of mind. Naturally, I take it for granted that the studio would like to feel that people under their employ were happy in their work. . . . I am not! And that is why I hope that you will give this let-ter full consideration.

Imagine yourself eating the same meal over and over again, accom-panied by the same people and the same small talk calling for the same small answers from yourself. After about the sixth meal you would become pretty weary and your answers would cease to have any life to them what-so-ever. That is pretty much the position that I am in. . . .

I hope that you will not take this letter as just another momentary outburst of temperament, but will try to do what you can about it. . . . With kindest regards, I am, sincerely, Joan Blondell.

Joan was granted a private meeting with Wallis after he read her letter, but the results were not promising. Defeated, she wrote to him five days later: "My body belongs to Warner Bros. for a few more years. I am more or less reconciled to the fact that there is nothing that can be done about it but do their bidding, this notice, I say, should relieve you from that ever present annoyance of me being the 'bane of your existence.'"

Joan came to an equally sobering conclusion about her marriage. Efforts to live with George again failed, leaving her to file for divorce. She cited drunk driving, public humiliation, and mental cruelty. In court, a dis-traught Joan spoke so softly that the judge had to ask her to raise her voice. For ten minutes, she listed George's conjugal infractions and unpaid bills. He ignored her and their guests in their home, reading books and newspa-pers instead of socializing, and refusing to converse. She declared no com-munity property and asked only for custody of nine-month-old Norman. The divorce was final on 4 September when she appeared before a Los Angeles Superior Court judge.

Joan took her place alongside other newly coined Hollywood divorcées of the mid-1930s. Joan's closest shoulder to cry on in the divorce war was friend Barbara Stanwyck, but Claudette Colbert and Joan Crawford were in like circumstances. For Joan, secrets were told only after the marriage was over. In talking to George's uncle, Joan learned what her husband had refused to divulge. George's childhood was ruled by a demanding, harsh, invalid mother and a Milquetoast father. He had spinal meningitis as a child, but as the only child he was expected to massage his mother's aching body, brush her hair, run her errands, feed her, and empty her bedpan. His forced servitude gave him a cynical view of marriage, children, and parents. As an adult, he would not discuss it. Joan did not know and therefore could not offer more direct sympathy until their marriage was over. George's next move scuttled that effort. Before the divorce was settled, he announced his engagement to twenty-one-year-old dancer Betty Wood. Her resemblance to Blondell was undeniable.

Joan was downhearted after the breakup, but Gloria, Katie, and Ed soothed her regrets and melancholy. Lookout Mountain went on the market while Joan and Gloria set about packing. Joan moved to a smaller white-brick Colonial-style home in Toluca Lake, a rental owned by actress Helen Twelvetrees, just minutes from the Warner studio. It was perfect; Joan wanted to be close enough to run back and forth to see the baby during her work day. Gloria, now a contract player at RKO, took the spare bedroom, while Katie and Ed found their own apartment. Joan was happy when brother Junie announced that he, Eloise, and their two children were moving to Los Angeles from Oakland, where Junie had a dead-end job at a five-and-ten-cent store. Happiness was nipped when the marriage unraveled in Southern California. Eloise and the children soon left California and returned home to Texas. Junie stayed and, thanks to Joan's negotiating, found work as a studio electrician. Junie was not tall, just five feet eight inches, but his thick, muscular build was ideal for wrangling heavy cables and lights.

Norman was Joan's chief joy. He was a burbling, chubby, and energetic child, sitting up and crawling ahead of schedule. Joan loved being a mother too much to worry about its interference in her career. "This business of a baby spoiling the fan's interest in a female star is all bunk," she announced. "Audiences today are more intelligent than they used to be. They like to see an actress give a good performance more than anything else. And a baby helps a female become a better actress. My baby is help-ing me. He takes me out of myself. Makes me understand many more emotions than I have ever felt before."

No one remembered exactly when Joan met Dick Powell, or when she stopped seeing him as a fellow contract player at Warner Bros. and started seeing him as a potential suitor. By the time they made *Broadway Gondolier*, they had already appeared in four movies together. They were first spotted dating in late September of 1935, less than one month after Joan's divorce. Joan began to see why he was one of the most well-liked men in town. He was personable and upbeat and a great asset to any party. He had a rendition of "When Irish Eyes Are Smiling," sung slightly off-key, that James Cagney said was "one of the funniest things [he'd] ever heard."

Dick Powell was born on 14 November 1904 in Mountain View, Arkansas. In 1914, his parents moved the family to Little Rock, where he grew up with two brothers. As a young man he discovered a talent for music. "I started out with two assets," he once said, "a voice that didn't drive audiences into the streets and a determination to make money. I've always worked like a dog." He mastered the piccolo, sax, trumpet, and banjo, then joined a number of bands and toured in vaudeville. His dark, wavy hair, dimples, twinkling eyes, high cheek bones, and prolonged upper lip provided him with boyish appeal. He loved the spotlight, but his ambitions were stalled by an ill-advised marriage to a Little Rock native. They stayed together only two years, in part due to Dick's constant touring. On contract at Warner Bros. since 1932, his movie popularity had come as quickly and completely as Joan's. He saved and invested wisely. When he had enough money, he bought a house for his parents in North Hollywood. The only scandal that accompanied him so far was his short affair with actress Marion Davies.

Just as the Blondell-Powell romance began to simmer, Joan cranked out a team effort with Glenda Farrell called *Miss Pacific Fleet*. After her forthright letters to Hal Wallis, Joan believed this latest show-girl part was

an insult to her attempts at securing variety if not quality in her assignments. She felt trapped and had run out of ideas for getting positive results
from the executives. She decided to protest by leaving the set promptly at
5 every afternoon. She reasoned that her unhappiness could be expressed
and she could get home to Norman at an early hour. Jack Warner was
irate. "From this day on I personally want to handle any disgruntled actor,
writer, or director," he informed Wallis. "By this I mean any extreme cases
like Blondell and those who threaten they will not work any more and
quit at five. This is a lot of bunk and I want to handle this." He and Joan
had it out in a heated telephone call, which ended with his punitive withholding of her $300 bonus. Blondell retained a high-priced downtown
lawyer and through him claimed the $300 was part of her guaranteed
salary. She then used the withholding of that money as a point in canceling her contract with Warner Bros. under the studio's breach of terms.
Warner blinked this time, fearing he'd lose a lawsuit, public sympathy, and
a profitable star. After several weeks on suspension without pay, Joan's
$1,600 weekly take was reinstated.

Miss Pacific Fleet was pawed over by several screenwriters, but it was
wholly dependent on the charms of Blondell and Farrell. They remain a
curious pair in movie history. Unlike Laurel and Hardy, the comedy of
Blondell and Farrell was based on similarity, not difference. Perhaps that is
why they are rarely acknowledged as a team, despite their eight movies
together. In so many ways they are alike: short, blonde, flirty, with pen-
ciled eyebrows, flawless diction, and a gift for elevating routine dialogue
into real entertainment. Affectionately nicknamed "the gimme girls" at the
studio when costarring together, both brought an experienced but not
jaded demeanor to their work. Even their attitudes toward acting were
similar. Both worked hard and rarely complained, Joan's recent tussle with
Warner and Wallis notwithstanding. Their prime differences were pedigree
(Farrell was born in the wilds of Oklahoma), temper (Farrell exploded
more often than Blondell), and on-screen effect (Farrell did not excel at
sweetness and romance as did Blondell).

They became great friends. Glenda was divorced from a World War I hero, so she and Joan could offer each other a guiding hand with men. Joan became a frequent guest at Glenda's Spanish-style home in the San Fernando Valley. "No one would be able to enjoy a case of the blues with Glenda around," said Joan. "She would start to console you and before you realized it, you're laughing." Glenda's son Tommy Richards well remembered the great comradeship. "Joan and my mother were 'bosom buddies,'" he said. "When they were at Warners together, during their lunch hours, they would go out shopping, and the director would say, 'Where are the girls?' They'd have to go chasing them."

As an exorcism of her first marriage, Joan became more attentive to her appearance. Orry-Kelly designed a dress for her private use, but it was too small. Joan was back a month later, thirteen pounds lighter and with four inches less around the hips. The gown fit perfectly. Sympathy and admiration in Hollywood were hers. "Although Joan has been hard hit, she doesn't mope or whine," reported *Modern Screen*. "She doesn't believe in dramatics, or in being morbid. And she hates the sight of a long, suffering appearance. Nor does she try to laugh it all off, for it is a serious thing to her."

Joan's new figure was shown to good advantage in her next feature, *Colleen*, in which Ruby Keeler wins Dick Powell. This was their last romantic teaming on screen and, not coincidentally, Joan and fellow supporting player Jack Oakie ran off with the picture. Joan was radiant as Minnie, an adenoidal chocolate-dipping swindler. The highlight of her performance, and the movie, was a comic duet with Oakie called "A Boulevardier from the Bronx," in which the two drolly explain the rituals of the nouveau riche. As a musical comedy of the *42nd Street* and *Gold Diggers of 1933* kind, *Colleen* does not measure up. But in itself, it has ample charm. Blondell is a funny dish and a welcome alternative to Keeler's girlish, dull sincerity.

Joan was assigned the leading female role in the hard drama *Bullets or Ballots*, but the script had a difficult time with the Production Code. "It looks very much to us, in its present form, to be quite definitely the kind of story which the Association, at its meeting last September, agreed not to make," wrote Code administrator Joseph Breen to Jack Warner. Its bracing premise had good cop Edward G. Robinson pretending to be thrown off the force so he could infiltrate the syndicate and blow it wide open. The script was finally accepted by the PCA in February of 1936 after months of tinkering, and William Keighley, the man who ably guided Joan early on in *Penny Arcade*, was assigned to direct.

Like so many other funny people, Joan wanted excel in drama. When *Bullets or Ballots* came along, a familiar anxiety returned. She began nail biting in her anticipation to make good. She need not have worried; she gave a wise performance as a shady Harlem nightclub owner and more than held her own next to Robinson and costar Humphrey Bogart. Although the movie is dominated by men, Blondell grows persuasively more bitter as she believes Robinson is using her as a cat's-paw to the mob. She softens just as persuasively when she learns the truth. But for all its merit, *Bullets or Ballots* cannot decide what side to play. Syndicate crime is the cause of so much social cancer, but Joan's small-time numbers business is tolerated in the spirit of American entrepreneurship. Fortunately, the mixed message does not overwhelm the pleasure of watching a crackling good crime picture.

In a show of improved self-confidence, Joan began to comport herself more like a movie star and less like an overworked career woman and mother. She hired friend Maurice Leo to oversee her fan mail. For a time she favored botanicals, appearing publicly in flowered silk dresses and flower-bedecked hats, and with flowers in her evening coiffures. Compliments on her beauty increased threefold. Her rebound was further aided by a calming acceptance of George Barnes's troubled character and the increasing attention of Dick Powell. George was fading from memory; they never worked together again. She purged her home of any pictures of him, and he never once contacted her to see Norman. "Now that I dress carefully and do everything a girl should do to make the most of herself and her opportunities, people show decidedly more interest in me," she said. As a result of her efforts, "Joan Blondell" had become a brand name, associated on screen with gentle impertinence and bubbly good cheer. Such expectations guaranteed that she would eventually bristle at the role she was forever expected to play.

Romance with Powell was getting serious, and it was time to meet the parents. Dick's mother found Joan to be "a lovely girl and a perfectly beautiful one." Joan's parents similarly voiced their approval of Powell. Even Gloria, currently touring in *It's a Wise Child* on stage, thought Dick Powell was good enough for her big sister. Compared to George Barnes, he seemed lightweight and easy.

Warner Bros. decided to unite the pair in two more movies. The first, *Stage Struck*, was cursed with Joan's sprained ankle and Dick's throat problems. But Joan once again proved amusing as a temperamental actress of marginal talent who finances her way to fame in musical comedies after shooting her husband. (Echoes of Beulah Annan and Peggy Hopkins Joyce were likely to be intentional.) No one was much impressed by *Stage Struck*, but something unmistakably big was happening in both Joan's and Dick's careers. As a romantic couple for the tabloids, they became greater than the sum of their parts. Press coverage on Joan focused on the trivial—her diet, hobbies, likes and dislikes—suggesting fan preoccupation and voguishness. It was important to millions that Joan owned a pair of wire-haired dachshunds she called "the Thundering Herd" and that Norman was a fearless explorer of the backyard when he was not at the selective preschool attached to the Education Department at UCLA. It was in print that Joan hated pickled beets, planes, spiders, and answering phones, and that she liked motorboating, cider, pajamas, soda pop, swimming, tennis, hiking, hamburger, and chop suey. When Orry-Kelly declared Joan's mouth the most beautiful in Hollywood, that was news. Significant, too, was the fact that Dick Powell visited her in her dressing room to go over lines. Fan mail for Blondell and Powell increased, and Warner Bros. began treating both of them like toprung stars. She had her own hairdresser and a voice coach on request. She was moved into a suite on the Warner lot with a large living room, fireplace, two bedrooms, kitchen, and a separate makeup room furnished with fine antiques.

Rumors of matrimony began circulating just as Joan embarked on a movie without her betrothed. *Three Men on a Horse* was an earthy, roughneck comedy based on a hit Broadway play that once starred Gloria. Now Joan played the gladsome but dim Brooklyn-born "Film Fun" cover girl named Mabel. *Three Men on a Horse* featured a great deal of yelling, with rat-a-tat dialogue on the very edge of incomprehensibility. In *Gold Diggers of 1937*, she played a chorus girl, while Dick was a dull life insurance salesman. Finally, their newfound mutual attraction translated warmly on screen. As the last *Gold Diggers* musical, there were hummable tunes sprinkled throughout, including "With Plenty of Money and You," "Speaking of the Weather," and the lavish showstopper "All's Fair in Love and War." But the formula was gasping from over familiarity, and this would be the last time Blondell and Glenda Farrell shared the screen. From now on, Farrell would be consigned to the *Torchy Blane* B-picture murder mystery series.

Joan and Dick frantically completed *Gold Diggers of 1937* in time to stage their showy wedding. On 11 September 1936, they filed a marriage application amid hundreds of gawking civic employees at the Los Angeles County Marriage License Bureau. On 17 September, they announced that they would be married in two days on the yacht *Santa Paula* at San Pedro shortly before it was to sail from Los Angeles to New York. (Less attention was paid to the wedding of George Barnes to Betty Wood in Fresno that same week.)

On 19 September, the San Pedro docks were jammed with fans hoping to catch a glimpse. When they did, they found a couple exceedingly handsome in their finery. Joan wore a gown of dusty pink marquisette and a large pink picture hat and carried a bouquet of orchids and baby's breath. Dick was in a dark business suit, white shirt, and blue-stripped four-in-hand tie. They calmly entered the flower-ladened honeymoon cabin of the *Santa Paula* to take their vows. Between loving gazes, Joan and Dick paused to wave and smile at the cheering fans lining the nearby docks. Joan's hairdresser-confidant, Ruth Pursley, was maid of honor, and Dick's good friend, actor Regis Toomey, was best man. Present also was Junie with Constance Ray, a flaming redhead he married on the rebound from his first divorce. For reasons never divulged, Dick's parents were not there. The onboard reception for fifty guests was attended by Busby Berkeley, James Cagney, Glenda Farrell, Orry-Kelly, Mervyn LeRoy, and, as a business courtesy, Hal Wallis. Joan gushed, "I'm deliriously happy," as she lifted her glass of champagne. "This is the greatest event of my life," said Dick.

The voyage from California to New York through the Panama Canal took two weeks. A stopover in Havana included a costume ball at the home of Luis J. "Daiquiri" Bacardi, wherein Joan was a Tahitian maid and Dick was a beachcomber. It was a perfectly temperate night, with Dick singing in the open air between well-wishing speeches to the newlyweds. When the *Santa Paula* arrived in New York harbor on 6 October 1936, Warner Bros. arranged to have a flotilla of eight tugs come out to greet her. Five airplanes performed acrobatic loops, while one biplane pulled a fifty-foot banner that read "Welcome, Joan and Dick." Regis Toomey and Gloria were waiting at the dock, along with a phalanx of press agents and reporters. Garlands of flowers were dropped on the decks of the liner from the planes. Dozens of river craft began a chorus of whistles and honks, creating a happy din that could be heard up the canyons of Manhattan.

The Powells had planned to stay at the Ritz Tower, but Joan changed her mind during the honeymoon. Upon arrival, the Powells and their small entourage were taken instead to the Waldorf-Astoria. Joan, Dick, Regis, and Gloria were ushered into a private room where they breakfasted on bacon and eggs, while reporters and hundreds of misguided fans waited at the Ritz. The Powells' twenty-fifth-floor suite was piled with flowers and gift boxes when they arrived. One card labeled for "Mrs. William Powell" must have been from a casual acquaintance.

When Joan looked out the window of their suite, she saw a horde of people looking up at her. She had hoped to drag Dick to all the places in New York she knew as a kid, but mostly they had to dodge the public. Dick was a friendly guy, freely giving autographs to fans, but the stress of a fishbowl honeymoon sent him to bed with an ardor-suppressing cold. Actor George Brent had given Joan a copy of the sensational new 1,037-page novel *Gone with the Wind* as a joke present for her honeymoon, but she finished it before returning to California.

Joan and Dick left New York by train on 17 October, stopping at the tony South Shore Country Club in Chicago to visit Dick's relatives. They did not linger, for both were needed at the studio to prepare for *The Singing Marine* (Dick) and *The King and the Chorus Girl* (Joan). Some fans had difficulty separating reality from the movies. "People took all that love stuff so literally with Dick Powell and Ruby Keeler, who were always playing opposite each other, that several times the fans were actually *furious* that I took him away from Ruby," said Joan. "When we got married, they thought she should marry him. It didn't bother them one bit that she was married to [Al] Jolson. It was just that I had no right to do that."

Dick had orchestrated the refurbishing of an English-style house on North Maple Drive in Beverly Hills to coincide with the honeymoon. He was shrewd with property and was one of the founding investment developers of a huge complex at Beverly Boulevard and Fairfax Avenue that included an ice hockey arena, bowling alley, stores, and restaurants. Dick was also an attentive stepfather to Norman and won Joan's further affection when he knocked the wheels off of a trailer home in the backyard, set the body on blocks, and filled it with Norman's toys. Joan was thrilled that Dick wanted more kids as Joan had "no intention of letting [her] one child grow up without brothers or sisters." Joan was enjoying domesticity like never before, in part because Dick, unlike George, was a fully participating spouse. Marriage this time came with an equitable division of labor. She loved home decorating and leaned toward Early American on North Maple Drive as she had on Lookout Mountain. Her new den looked like a West Coast Sardi's, with signed eight-by-ten glossies of movie stars lining the walls.

Production of Joan's first movie after the honeymoon, *The King and the Chorus Girl*, was suspended on 11 December 1936 for Edward VIII's abdication speech. "I'll never forget the day that the Duke of Windsor made that speech on the radio about giving up his throne for the woman he loved," Joan remembered. "Time stopped on the set for this moment that seemed the most romantic thing possible, in or out of the movies!" Joan and Dick reading "The Gold Diggers" on *Lux Radio Theatre* as a holiday treat to their fans was only slightly less so.

Meanwhile, the martinet of censorship, Will Hays, issued directives to ban any movies that resembled the unfolding drama in England. By amazing coincidence, *The King and the Chorus Girl* suggested a story very much like Edward's, but it was in production before the abdication. The idea had been scripted by Norman Krasna and Groucho Marx, then sold to director-producer Mervyn LeRoy. He finagled a huge $2 million budget from Warner Bros., then further broke the rules by casting Belgian actor Fernand Gravey to play an effete, brandy swilling ex-monarch. Reviews for Joan as a Follies Bergère cancan dancer were exceptionally positive. She "is at her best," wrote the *Los Angeles Evening Herald Express*. "In fact, I think this portrayal is the finest she has ever put on the screen. She has the subdued finesse of a Lubitsch heroine." She plays someone untutored to the ways of royal protocol, yet is never vulgar or made the object of mockery. Gone is the expected brassiness of her other heroines. Here she is more subtle, playing an undercurrent of dramatic star-crossed love. "Dorothy in *The King and the Chorus Girl* . . . turned out to be my favorite role," said Joan a decade later. "This was because Dorothy was a sympathetic part, a girl with some intelligence and character—the kind of person chorus girls often are. It was one of those lucky breaks that sometimes come along when you are under contract, have made a dozen poor pictures, and are wondering if the public will forgive you and forget them."

Joan's income in 1936 was $84,799, a paltry sum considering her output and profitability. That same year Claudette Colbert made $350,000 in comparison. This is due in part to the studios—Colbert was at Paramount, a movie factory far more flush than Warner Bros. But the disparity must in part be attributed to Joan's lack of fighting spirit in financial matters and her continued undervaluation at the studio. "What was foremost in my life, in every phase of it, has been my home . . . and whoever is in my home, be it a husband, or children, or whatever," she later said. "The instant they said 'Cut' I was whammo out of that studio and into the car, *zuuuup* out of the gate and *home*. Half the time I'd forget to put on my shoes, I wouldn't even stop for that. In order to be a top star and remain a top star and to get all the fantastic roles that you yearned for, you've got to fight for it and you've got to devote your twenty-four hours to just that; you've got to think of yourself as a star, operate as a star, do all the press that is necessary. . . . [W]hat meant most to me was getting home, and that's the truth."

Still, the glamour makeover continued into 1937. Joan was seen posing in black crepe, black net, and black princess gown with a brief bolero for *Modern Screen*. She began offering advice on color, fabric, hair, hosiery, and accessories. In February, she and Dick left their prints in wet cement at Grauman's Chinese Theatre, sealing their stardom. When she caught the flu that winter, she wrote the beginnings of a screenplay for her husband, all about a naïve country boy in the big city. But she recovered quickly, and the script was never finished. For the sake of domestic harmony, it was for the best. Dick may have been mature in the ways of business and money, but he was stymied by his screen image. "I'm 32 and I'm still playing boy scouts," he moaned.

Just as Dick was feeling like a perennial juvenile, Joan found a winner in *Back in Circulation*, a solid comedy-drama about the workings of a scandal sheet. Playing a hot-tempered ace reporter, she had another chance to work with good pal and topnotch Hollywood party giver Pat O'Brien. *Back in Circulation*'s concern for mud slinging, press feeding frenzies, and bloodthirsty media competition is still timely. Joan played a tough-as-nails reporter, ruthless in her quest for a scoop. And it is *her* movie. Like in *Blondie Johnson*, she's in nearly every scene. A script titled *The Perfect Specimen* had meanwhile passed through the fingers of Marion Davies, Carole Lombard, Rosalind Russell, Miriam Hopkins, and Olivia de Havilland before Blondell saw it. It suffered from a credibility gap, as audiences were asked to believe that rich old May Robson could encage her virile grandson Errol Flynn within the family compound. Since Flynn lacked the *je ne sais quoi* for comedy, the burden of turning this wobbly premise into entertainment fell on the players surrounding him, including Warner Bros. stalwarts Edward Everett Horton and Hugh Herbert. The result was as pleasing as could be expected.

After *The Perfect Specimen*, Joan was cast in United Artists' *Stand-In* as part of a studio talent swap. The deal proved most fruitful for Joan. *Stand-In* genially satirized the movies in a tale of mercenary bankers who swoop in to cannibalize the carcass of the once mighty Colossal Studios. What *Stand-In* lacked in laugh-out-loud slapstick or goofy characters it made up for in breakneck speed, snappy dialogue, and ample knowledge of moviemaking culture. More important, *Stand-In's* happy disposition belied a hard political message altogether rare in an industry dedicated to entertainment.

Joan, playing a former child star named Lester Plum, is the stand-in who explains her function to Atterbury Dodd, played by a bespectacled Leslie Howard. The star must never be "fatigued or mussed and above all she must never be so vulgar as to perspire. Hence, her stand-in does her sweating for her." She then guides him through the subtle arts of movie producing, as well as the rumba and jiujitsu. Inevitably, love blooms for Miss Plum, who stands by while Dodd accepts the gauche advances of Thelma Cheri, a less than talented star played with amusing egomania by Maria Shelton. Various movie business types pass by the story, including a phony accented director, venal board members, and a stage mother with a demon child in tow. We are even treated to a boozy producer played with vim by Humphrey Bogart.

Stand-In's respect for the little people of Hollywood is reflected in its anti-capitalist, leftist ideology as rendered by original story writer Clarence Budington Kelland, the man who was also behind the 1936 populist classic *Mr. Deeds Goes to Town*. Dodd is a pawn for the bankers, but he must stop treating labor as "cogs" or "units" if he is to win Miss Plum. In a vivid allegory to revolution, a horde of nameless studio electricians, prop men, costumers, extras, and carpenters hoist the evil banker-saboteur over the studio walls. And it is the stand-in, not the star, who ultimately gets the man. At the final fade, however, Lester Plum is still a nameless face in the machinery.

The creators of *Stand-In*, director Tay Garnett, screenwriters Graham Baker and Gene Towne, and producer Walter Wanger, were not known for their leftist sympathies. If anything, Wanger tilted in the opposite direction. Perhaps they saw *Stand-In* primarily as a comedy of inside jokes. It is as much a romantic comedy as it is an agitprop treatise. As an exposé of the "real" Hollywood, *Stand-In* was significantly lighter in tone than the earlier *What Price Hollywood?* or *A Star Is Born*. Its primary delight to audiences came in taboo-shattering disclosures of trade secrets. Then there was the witty dialogue sprinkled with asides such as "In Hollywood, when you turn the other cheek, they kick it." Joan was singled out as downright brilliant, and *Stand-In* may be the first lighthearted movie of her career that fully capitalized on her unforced sexual allure as well as her considerable intelligence and flawlessly timed delivery of clever lines. As a bonus, she performed a savage travesty of Shirley Temple singing "On the Good Ship Lollipop." Joan enjoyed the working environment of *Stand-In* immensely, though she did not warm to Bogart, who had worked with her before in *Three on a Match* and *Bullets or Ballots*. "He wasn't a man one ever felt close to—nobody did," she said, "but I liked him."

Soon after *Stand-In* wrapped, Joan was hospitalized for neuritis and exhaustion. She climbed aboard a boat for Avalon, Catalina, to recover, but Warner Bros. was on her tail. She had been assigned to the hillbilly wrestling comedy *Swing Your Lady* with Bogart and was needed for costume fittings and production meetings. She read the script, thought it was the dregs, and refused to jeopardize her health by accepting. In added insult, her role was not the lead and the director was Ray Enright, the very man Joan had gently complained about to Hal Wallis. This was to be their eighth withering collaboration. The success of *The King and the Chorus Girl*, *The Perfect Specimen*, and the positive heat surrounding the unreleased *Stand-In* brought Joan career momentum, and she felt that *Swing Your Lady* would be a regression to lousy parts in even lousier movies. *Now* was the time to break into the quality productions enjoyed by fellow light comediennes Carole Lombard and Constance Bennett. She cabled the studio from

Avalon stating she "had no intention of reporting to the *Swing Your Lady* set," then impudently added that she "would rather do *Gone with the Wind*."

When Joan was back in Los Angeles, she was given a private meeting with Wallis to discuss her situation. They were cordial enough, but Joan did not waver in her refusal to do *Swing Your Lady*. Wallis then met with Joan's new agent, the powerful Charles K. Feldman, who threatened to take his client away from Warner Bros. and sign her to a studio that would give her the vehicles she deserved. Feldman suggested three movies a year with privileges outside the studio, but Wallis vetoed the idea. He reminded Feldman that Blondell did not have the right of story selection in her contract. Feldman acknowledged this, but added that *Swing Your Lady* did not deserve to be made. Wallis disagreed. Still Feldman struggled to get Blondell a better deal at a studio that he felt owed her some gratitude. This time Joan prevailed. *Swing Your Lady* featured Penny Singleton in the role earmarked for Joan, who went on four-week suspension. As expected, the finished product was a howler. Just as *Swing Your Lady* was hissed off Warner's screens nationwide, *Stand-In* was previewed to cheers.

For the Powell's first anniversary, Dick purchased violinist Jascha Heifetz's sixty-two-foot yacht. The plush Danish import was lined with mahogany and teakwood and had already crossed the Atlantic twice. The Powells named her *Galatea*. In return, Joan presented Dick with a sports roadster with a custom-built motor. Joan showed some business sense when she agreed to a variety of product endorsements, including Lux soap, Pepsodent toothpaste, Doublemint gum, Chesterfield cigarettes, Coca-Cola, and Cashmere Bouquet Beau Cakes. Warner Bros. always took a share of her earnings, as her every outside appearance required the studio's approval.

On 11 December 1937, Warner Bros. announced that Joan was put on loan to Columbia. She was to appear with Melvyn Douglas in *There's Always a Woman*, but script problems caused a delay, and Warner Bros. balked at releasing her. With no production start date, a peeved Joan and Dick left Norman with Katie and took the train east for a working holiday. The mob was only slightly less jammed than it was on their honeymoon.

In New York for Christmas, Joan mentioned that she would be leaving Warner Bros. to freelance. Her announcement was premature, but the point was made that she was damn near the limit of her endurance.

For Joan and Dick, January 1938 was all about children. When Joan learned that she was pregnant, there was no talk of abortion, and on 15 January, Dick appeared in court to argue for adoption of Norman. Not surprisingly, George Barnes agreed without hesitation. The family of three, with one on the way, was now fully consecrated. As for the ever lachrymose Joan, all she could say between tears was, "This is something we have fervently wanted. It makes us both more gloriously happy than ever before."

There's Always a Woman finally began shooting with Melvyn Douglas and Joan at Columbia in late January of 1938 after the details of Joan's upcoming maternity leave from Warner Bros. were settled. Future congresswoman Helen Gahagan Douglas watched her husband, Melvyn, and Joan do multiple takes of a lingering kiss. When it was over, she said to her husband, "Sometimes I wish you worked in a bank." *There's Always a Woman* proved to be a zany, agreeable, and well-written comedy-satire of murder mysteries in *The Thin Man* mold. Joan was afforded one genuinely funny scene. During an interrogation, the police crack under pressure, while Joan remains chipper under a bright lamp, blithely filing her nails and dabbing on makeup. Her energy is on a different setting here, unbound by the stale conventions of her Warner Bros. roles. Audiences felt her reinvigoration. In April, while *There's Always a Woman* was playing in theaters, a poll of moviegoers declared Joan "Public Gold Digger #1" in the tradition of Mary Pickford's moniker as "America's Sweetheart," Theda Bara's "The Vamp," and Clara Bow's "The 'It' Girl."

There were tensions at home. Dick felt trapped at Warner Bros., both by his contract and by the man-boy image the studio insisted for him. When he refused to appear in a routine Busby Berkeley musical, Jack Warner put him on twelve-week suspension. He was a wonderful father to Norman, including him in everything from fishing to gadget making around the house, but he could be vain, cheap, and prone to fulminations about the decline of civilization. And perhaps his feelings for studio type-casting ironically commented on his approach to sex. It usually happened on Friday nights and was signaled by Dick making eye contact with Joan, then hitching his eyebrows twice. A thorough preparatory cleansing fol-lowed—mouthwash, shower, hair combed, nails clipped—before pajama-clad foreplay. A like procedure followed their duty-filled romantic moment.

Joan's work schedule during her second full-term pregnancy was not as arduous as it was during her first. She did two easy radio gigs, but was otherwise suspended on unpaid maternity leave as of 5 March 1938. Apart from a tumble from her limousine onto the curb at the Academy Awards, she suffered few physical stresses this time.

After a ten-hour labor, eight-pound Ellen Powell was born at Cedars of Lebanon Hospital at 4:30 p.m. on 30 June. Mother and father were elated, and relieved that this delivery came without complications. Norman was an adoring big brother, tenderly stroking the tiny crown of Ellen's head and calling her "my baby."

The taskmaster was not moved. Jack Warner gave Joan just three weeks of uninterrupted motherhood before announcing plans to shoot her next movie.

CHAPTER 5

Freelancing

I was raised in the house of mirrors in the land of moving illusion.
—Ellen Powell, 1994

On 31 August 1938, Joan reported back to the studio for her first day of work with director James Flood and costar Pat O'Brien. She was now taking in $2,500 a week, the highest salary she would ever have at Warner Bros. It had been a whopping seven months since she made her last movie, *There's Always a Woman*, and Joan was suffering from a mother's separation anxiety. On the first day of shooting, she called home between scenes.

"How's the baby?" she asked Katie, now known by the family as "Nana." She smiled at the answer, hung up, then lifted the receiver to place a call to Dick on Stage 12.

"Ellen is fine," she reported. After a moment's pause, she said, "I'm fine, too."

"And O'Brien is fine," said the actor.

"Flood is fine," said the director.

"I'm not," said an electrician adjusting the hot lights overhead. "I've got a toothache."

The return movie was *Off the Record*, a seventy-minute trifle with O'Brien and Blondell as romantic sparring partners. This was a veritable replay of the superior *Back in Circulation*, complete with like plot angles, a newsroom, and Pat O'Brien. (Both had the same working title of *Unfit to Print*.) *Off the Record* was not as bad as *Swing Your Lady*, but it was an undistinguished programmer and a decided letdown after *Stand-In* and *There's Always a Woman*. Joan knew this during production and exercised her dismay again by leaving the set every afternoon promptly at 5.

Joan's insubordination caused another uproar with Jack Warner and Hal Wallis. She claimed fatigue, but the executives were convulsing over the bad precedent and the lost production time. Lawyer Ralph Lewis told the studio that a physical examination was in order "because, after all, under your modern contract you have a clause covering the suspected incapacity of an artist going into a picture. . . . [I]f developments after commencing the picture should indicate [that Blondell is not fit to work], causing the artist to be partially incapacitated, or making it dangerous for the artist to render services then, if the artist is unable to render full services certain penalties shall be attached."

Certain penalties were, indeed, attached. On 8 October, at the completion of *Off the Record*, Joan was back on unpaid leave. Her salary recommenced on 19 November with the onset of *The Kid from Kokomo*, a roughhouse comedy in which she played a bubble dancer. Joan told the press that she wanted to make *May Flavin* instead to remind the brass that she was an actress of significant range. That idea fell on deaf ears. The indignity that was *Off the Record* became a veritable slap in the face with *The Kid from Kokomo*. If Jack Warner wanted to make her happy again, he had a peculiar way of showing it. *The Kid from Kokomo* was so bad, in fact, that Warner more likely wished to bully Joan off the lot by giving her a skid row assignment. Predictably, *Kokomo* stunk up theaters for a few days, barely met its costs, then crept away to rightful obscurity.

Recent indignities boosted Joan's resolve to leave Warner Bros. permanently. Younger actresses such as Jane Wyman and Ann Sheridan were getting increased attention. She was thirty-two, and if she hoped to enjoy a few years of quality roles as a leading lady, she would have to leave *now*. It helped her tremendously to have Dick's unwavering support for her cause. He experienced typecasting career endangerment as much as she did, so he was more than sympathetic. On 11 December 1938, the inevitable happened: The *New York Times* reported that Joan and Dick had promulgated their departure from Warner Bros. a full year after the original such announcement was made. Dick's summation of his studio tenure sounds like it could also have been said of Joan's: "Warners coined money with those musicals and I was never paid what I knew I was worth to them. But it wasn't just money. They always handed me the same stupid story. I never had anything sensible to say." Not only was Dick unhappy with his assignments at Warner Bros., he was unhappy with his profession. "He hated to sing," said Joan. "He didn't like acting either. He wanted to be a producer. He was a businessman." In leaving Warner Bros., Dick said, "I have found sanity. I know that this is the sure track. I love Joan and the children and they love me. We have time for one another and we have a real home at last. . . . I have been in a fog. I nearly made a mess of my life. But, thank God, I woke up to what I was doing!"

There was little recognition and not much appreciation for Joan's indentured years at Warner Bros. No big gala on a sound stage was ever given to either for their efforts. "I suppose I was a fool not to have fought [for better roles]," Joan said. "Because I was under contract they only gave me scraps or the parts they couldn't get Carole Lombard for." But she was not all self-pity. She had an amazing run, and she knew it: "I was part of the '30s, the Depression years. People needed to laugh, to be released from despair. They needed to forget fear even for a few hours. They needed to sway, to hum—I contributed to that. Isn't that terrific?"

Many years later, Joan had explicit opinions on her place at the studio. "All the others on the lot would tell me to walk," she said. "They absolutely did. Cagney was a big fighter with me, he'd say 'Would you just beat it? Get out of there, just walk out, that's all you have to do. Then you'll get what you want and decent money.' " She implied that acting was not much more than a job to her. "None of the pictures stand out," she said. "I can tell you where I lived at the time, who I was in love with, but I can't tell you about a picture.

It was more that we were all carried up knowing that we were all in a hit *cycle*, everything that we did was in demand. What we were doing was being eaten up by the screen. So we did it and let it fly." She assessed her output in a moment of cynicism: "There was a pattern. I was the fizz on the soda; I just showed my big boobs and tiny waist and acted glib and flirty. Once you do something like that, it's hard for the studio to let you out of that trap."

Joan left the studio without misgivings. "I've had more than enough of this," she said during her twilight at Warner Bros. "I shall never again get into that sort of a mess. I am going to sign up for a picture or two a year with Columbia and in this way leave myself free to do what I like with the rest of my time." Her last Warner Bros. paycheck, with bonuses, was dated 7 January 1939 and came to $2,916.67. With that, Joan packed up the 10-cent makeup basket she bought just before coming to Hollywood and left the studio gates a free woman.

The Powells had nothing to fear as far as post–Warner Bros. employment was concerned. In early January, Dick signed a contract at MGM. Before going to work for Columbia, Joan was announced as the female lead in *East Side of Heaven* at Universal, a comedy with music featuring Bing Crosby as a warbling cabbie. He and Joan play an engaged couple whose lives are derailed when a scene-stealing baby is placed in their care. Crosby produced *East Side of Heaven* himself, carefully overseeing the production while crooning "Sing a Song of Sunbeams" and "My Melancholy Baby."

If Joan dreamed of an immediate rise in the stature of her movies, she was soon disappointed. Here she looks abandoned by director David Butler and Crosby, with little to do but smile, look pretty, and act the part of an efficient telephone operator. Nor did she warm to Crosby off camera, finding him distant and cold. With bad weather and Joan's throat infection, *East Side of Heaven* finished behind schedule on 6 March. But it received good reviews and drew big crowds. Its profits were so high, in fact, that they were credited for keeping an ailing Universal from going under.

It was during the production of *East Side of Heaven* that Jimmy Starr of the *Los Angeles Evening Herald Express* reported that Joan turned down the role of the madam Belle Watling in the hugely anticipated film version of *Gone with the Wind*. Acting very much like unsupervised talent, Joan felt the role was too controlled by the Hays office, her choicest lines losing their bite. That is what she said, but perhaps she was not ready to accept a part so far down the cast roster. Whatever the machinations, lesser-known Ona Munson took on Belle and brought with her a self-possession reminiscent of a typical Joan Blondell performance. Joan meanwhile took the Columbia deal she alluded to on her way out of Warner Bros. She traded a prestige film for leading lady status, playing a coy waitress in the light *Good Girls Go to Paris* with Melvyn Douglas.

Joan wanted nothing more than stability without overwork, and to keep an address for more than a year or two. Dick had other plans, and this brought considerable friction to the marriage. There were arguments about where to move, whether to buy or lease, add a wing here, knock down a wall there. He saw a home as an investment and broke Joan's heart when he sold their property on Maple Drive without her consent and after she had personalized it. In March, the Powells moved to a 1920s Tudor-style house on Selma Avenue near Fairfax, previously owned by actress Fay Wray and her husband, writer John Monk Saunders. It was one block from Schwab's drugstore and next door to screenwriter Frances Marion's huge estate known in Hollywood as "the Enchanted Hill."

The house was set among eucalyptus trees, with a broad front lawn framed by low hedges. Joan did not grieve Maple Drive long and got busy applying her eclectic taste. The living-room ceiling was traversed by rough-hewn timbers which Joan contrasted with an assortment of modern and Victorian furniture. Sheffield sterling silver was put on display in the dining room. For entertainment, there were ping pong and pool tables, a tennis court, and a barbecue pit. Dick had a tool bench in the garage, where he could practice his hobby of auto mechanics. Fan magazines evoked a picture of domestic utopia. Though he abhorred singing professionally, Dick practiced his scales and whistled around the house, the yard, and in the shower.

That summer, Joan and Dick talked about doing a "Burlesque" on the "rustic circuit" as a break in movie work, but the idea was abandoned for something less taxing. They decided instead to get out of town separately. Leaving the children in Katie's care, Joan took a train to New York between productions of her two contracted movies at Columbia to visit Gloria. Dick, meanwhile, took the *Galatea* on a fishing trip. Perhaps the Powells had a row, for Joan offered her recipe for coping to a *Screenland* reporter: Say to yourself, "Skip it. You'll live, darling — you'll live."

Back home and returned to work, Joan was given a huge cake on the set of *The Amazing Mr. Williams* for her thirty-third birthday on 30 August 1939, with fellow actress Lucille Ball, among others, stopping by to wish well. *The Amazing Mr. Williams* was another madcap pairing of Joan and Melvyn Douglas in pursuit of a murderer. Much of the humor derived from Kenny (Douglas) spending time in drag and showing more interest in solving crimes than romancing curvaceous, willing girlfriend Maxine (Blondell). When the movie finished on 27 October, Joan and Dick left immediately for another trip to New York—together this time. They were by all appearances happy, committed to their children, and delighting in a shared sense of humor. With him in a purple dressing gown and her in lounging pajamas, and coffee percolating on the mahogany side table, they fielded softball questions from high-ranking *New York Times* film reporter Bosley Crowther.

Dick did no film work in 1939, and he preceded the drought with a string of failures, but there were no financial worries in the Powell home. Dick had recently completed *Naughty but Nice* and singing royalties kept him awash in money. His ventures into real estate were exceedingly rewarding, as property values rose exponentially during the great twentieth-century migration into Southern California. Joan appreciated that Dick's boyish charm belied a clever businessman. As for movies, he was frankly demoralized by seven years of playing the All American crooner. Contract-playing in Hollywood held little appeal to him.

In contrast, work fed Joan. She could have reduced her output at this point in her marriage, but instead she sought to hold onto her popularity.

Though she spoke of arduous conditions and claimed acting was just a job, it was a lifeline for her spirit. She was far more inured to performing than she was to being a wife and mother. Professionally, acting was her entire world. Personally, when caring for her children, it meant nothing. The public and the private only fitfully reconciled.

Joan had a brief stint at MGM, and given the prestige of that studio, she might have expected elevated assignments. Her first, *Two Girls on Broadway*, was a remake of the studio's 1929 landmark musical *The Broadway Melody*. Once again Joan had thankless chores. Newcomer Lana Turner was billed over the seasoned professional. To make appearances worse, the script called for Blondell to lose fiancé George Murphy to younger sister Turner. It looked official—Blondell had now entered the danger zone for actresses of a certain age. To end any doubt, the tag line for the movie shouted, "The Girl They're All Talking About . . . lovely Lana, America's Blonde Bonfire, in her hottest, most daring role."

Joan wearily assessed her career. "After having cracked the same jokes in different gowns for nine years, I find them just a little stale. The startling performance I had hoped to give some day seems to matter less now and I content myself with being adequate. I would love to go back to the stage, but mountains of scripts won't help me. It is one alone and a good one that I need." Yearning for variety, she turned to radio. *The Gulf Screen Guild Theatre* featured her with Eddie Cantor in a self-satire of a man coping with five daughters. She had meatier fare with *The Campbell Playhouse* on CBS, where she performed *Only Angels Have Wings* with Orson Welles and Regis Toomey. She was roasted by Edgar Bergen and his sassy dummy sidekick Charlie McCarthy on *The Chase and Sanborn Hour:*

> BLONDELL. I'm a daancer. Maybe you caught my act at the Country Club. I have talent. . . . I'll go far.
> CHARLIE. I hope you do, and the farther the better.
> BLONDELL. Ain't cha got an opening for me?
> CHARLIE. Yes, we have. First door to the left. I saw your act, sister.

BLONDELL. Didn't you like it? Maybe you caught me at a disadvantage.

CHARLIE. I did. It certainly was a disadvantage. . . . The curtain was up.

BLONDELL. Well, I admit the opening was a little slow—but didn't you think the <u>endin'</u> was awfully good?

CHARLIE. Well, it was a relief.

BLONDELL. Anyhow, d<u>aa</u>ncing really ain't my spe<u>ci</u>ality.

CHARLIE. That's evident.

BLONDELL. I'm really a Shakespearean actress. "To be or not to be. . . . [W]hat a question!"

CHARLIE. What an actress! Get out of here.

Joan was learning that being the wife of Dick Powell came with fiduciary benefits. On 7 January 1940, they negotiated a generous husband-wife contract at Paramount. This was to be Powell's first movie since *Naughty but Nice*, filmed in December of 1938 as his swan song to Warner Bros. The prophetically titled *I Want a Divorce* at Paramount came with ten weeks of work, with 37.5 percent of gross receipts in excess of 1.7 times the production cost, split between the Powells along with a $25,000 advance to be paid to each at $2,500 per week. With the Powells in firm control, and Joan billed over Dick, the perceived career slippage of *Two Girls on Broadway* was kept at bay. In *I Want a Divorce*, Gloria Dickson as Joan's sister gets unhitched, then proceeds to drink and party her way through lonesome despondency. Meanwhile, attorney Powell goes into divorce law, only to find his marriage to Blondell suffering as a result. The ache of a broken home is effectively rendered, while the hold-on-to-what-you've-got message was easier dramatized for the movie than realized by the Powells off camera.

In yet another run at variety, Joan went back to the stage in the Sheldon Davis farce *Goodbye to Love* with British actor Patric Knowles in June of 1940. To exercise his business skills, Dick produced with Al Woods, who had employed an unknown Joan in *The Trial of Mary Dugan* back in 1927. Cast in a supporting role, and allowed to shine in the second act, was Gloria Blondell. Woods was one of the leading stage producers of the day, so where was the risk? Certainly it was not in Joan's throwback character, a chorus girl and gold digger very much in the style of women she played ad nauseam at Warner Bros. *Goodbye to Love* opened at the Lobero Theatre in Santa Barbara as a jumble of comedy setups. Audiences were polite to the actors but dismissive of the material. After the poorly received opening, Joan suffered some kind of breakdown on the train north. When she arrived in San Francisco, an ambulance was waiting at the station. She was sent to a hospital for "nervous and physical exhaustion," and the planned 10 June opening was postponed one week. When it finally did open, reviews were horrible and business was spotty at the downtown Geary Theatre. It closed on 7 July at the El Capitan Theatre in Los Angeles after a piddling one-week run there, never to be seen anywhere else.

Joan's emotional derailment during *Goodbye to Love* was never explained. Was she mortified by audience reaction? Had Dick said or done something cruel? What of her career? By the early 1940s, Warner Bros. cohorts Ginger Rogers, Barbara Stanwyck, and Bette Davis were at professional acmes. Davis, in fact, was thriving at what the actors called "San Quentin," routinely playing the studio's most coveted female roles. Joan, in comparison to all three, was floundering, her pivotal post–Warner Bros. moment wasted on unremarkable appearances. Whatever Joan suffered, *Goodbye to Love* did no damage to sister Gloria's expanding social opportunities. Living bicoastally, she frequented the Russian Tea Room in New York, then the Cocoanut Grove in Hollywood as one of Howard Hughes's girls. Matters were complicated when she fell in love with Albert R. ("Cubby") Broccoli, a sailor and bodyguard assigned to her. Hughes fired him, then Broccoli and Gloria chartered a plane to Las Vegas, where they eloped.

That same summer, the League of American Mothers declared Joan "The Most Glamorous Mother in Hollywood." She was confused by the honor, seeing "glamour" and "mother" as mutually exclusive. "The greatest penalty of screen success is a familiar face," she said by way of seeking privacy. Then *I Want a Divorce* was released to blistering reviews. Bosley Crowther, who had been so polite in a recent feature article on the Powells, turned acidic: "Miss Joan Blondell of Hollywood once solemnly informed this department that she would like very much to break away from the frivolous type of films she had been playing for several years and really get her teeth into something nice and dramatic. Well she has had her wish. . . . And now, with the kindest intentions, we would like to suggest that she consider a reconciliation and return to her old bed and board. . . . Now, we don't say Miss Blondell is not a dramatic actress; we simply say she isn't in *I Want a Divorce*." Joan would not come back to Paramount for twenty-five years.

As for life at home, all appeared well. Evening backgammon was a favorite pastime, and the private screening room ran films for the neighborhood kids. Joan's brother Junie was happy in 1940 after his brief second marriage was annulled. He was thriving in his new trade as studio electrician. He met Nebraska-born stenographer Gretchen Dussell while ballroom dancing, and they were married early in the year. Joan and Gloria liked their new sister-in-law immensely. She was a tiny person, well-spoken, and a wonderful cook. Best of all was her loyal service to family. If anyone needed to relocate, and the Blondells did so with startling frequency, she was always there with boxes, old newspapers, and packing tape.

Joan received an unusual offer to star in the reformatting of *I Want a Divorce* as a radio serial. She hesitated, but air-waves veteran Dick urged her to say yes. Once committed, she was consumed with the job, cranking out a program each week. "These 22 weeks on the air have been stimulating," she said, "for I have had to stand on my own feet again. You forget all about real acting in pictures. You have to concentrate for one minute and then you have perhaps a couple of hours rest. You have no worries about timing or anything else, for the directors, the camera men do it all for you. But on the radio you have got to be alert; you have to prepare as well as execute whatever evolutions the script calls for." Joan had more variety of roles in those five and a half months on radio than she had in ten years on screen. "One week I have to be a rascal and the following one a little martyr," she said. "But the important thing is that I am always getting myself into trouble. The drama develops during the first fifteen minutes. Then the wedding march prepares for another fifteen minutes in which everything is cleaned up, and just before the commercial I am on the right path again. One week I married a man who had a grown-up son who hated the sight of me. In the midst of this situation a flood swept the town and we all had to swim out of the house. I had to breathe so heavily into the microphone, to give the impression of drowning, that I had hardly any strength left when the show came to an end. But my mother, who listens in regularly, remarked that I would develop into a tragedian some day."

Thanks to Dick's skill with savings and real estate, the Powells invested in vacation property. In honor of their love of the sea, they signed a ninety-nine-year lease on an old Irvine Ranch house in Newport Beach. It was not large, just three bedrooms, but it was open and airy, and it included a private dock. The outside was painted in gunmetal blue-gray and adorned with yellow flower pots filled with geraniums. Balboa Bay was their front yard, and they had their own pier for mooring a dingy, canoe, Chris-Craft, and the *Galatea*. The Powells were there every weekend they could get away, with Joan driving on her own after working on Saturdays. They would picnic on the sandy, deserted Shark Island, walk along the empty lots called the African Trails, collect shells, and be silly. Away from Hollywood, Joan could be with the children in a role approximating traditional American motherhood. She spent time at Newport Beach cleaning house, planting flowers, or preparing fresh abalone or crab.

The Powells dined at the Balboa Bay Club for Sunday brunch and special occasions. The restaurant was done in old wood and overlooked the water, with staff customarily in sailors' hats and jackets. On one Sunday outing to the club, Joan's order arrived on new china. Upon inspecting her entree, she picked up her napkin and started *whack whacking* on her plate. The sailor-garbed waiters rushed over. "What is going on? What's wrong, Miss Blondell? Miss Blondell, what's wrong?" they asked in an overlapping chorus. Pointing down to her plate, she said, "Look, look, it's a spider!" It was, in fact, the yacht club insignia. The episode quickly entered the playbook of family jokes.

In between Newport weekends, Joan appeared in *Topper Returns*, the third outing in the series of comic tales revolving around convivial spooks. Otherworldly characters were in vogue in 1940s American films: Claude Rains in *Here Comes Mr. Jordan*, Rex Harrison in *The Ghost and Mrs. Muir*, Spencer Tracy in *A Guy Named Joe*, Charles Laughton in *The Canterville Ghost*, and Henry Travers in *It's a Wonderful Life*. The *Topper* series had lost a bit of its sparkle by the time Joan arrived. *Topper Returns* featured special effects and sight gags instead of the witty repartee that so distinguished the original. As Joan is the only ghost on hand, she is denied the benefit of good chemistry with a fellow spirit. All by herself she removes any trace of morbidity in the tale. She makes being a ghost look fun, and she holds her own against the memory of Constance Bennett as the female star of the first two *Topper* movies.

Her next effort, *Model Wife*, was the last movie she made with Dick. They play employees of a hoity-toity salon run by an imperious biddy who prohibits her staff from being married. But Joan and Dick secretly are— and to each other. All's tidy until the boss's son woos Joan and enrages Dick. Gloria had a small role in *Model Wife*, while agent Charles K. Feldman fashioned a deal unusually advantageous for movie stars in 1941. He bought the rights to film the story at Universal with producer-director Leigh Jason, Powell, Blondell, and the screenwriters hired for a percentage of the gross. With negative costs at a mere $180,000, this movie was a cash cow for the Powells. They were so emboldened by the success of *Model Wife* that they ventured into *Miss Pinkerton*, a radio program with Joan as a detective and Dick as a police sergeant. It had only a parenthetic relationship to Joan's 1932 movie heroine of the same name, while a combination of boredom, money, and contracts caused the Powells to abandon the project soon after its first broadcast.

Then came the modest but endearing *Three Girls about Town*, a gift from Columbia to rank beside *Stand-In* from United Artists. In this Joan is the eldest of a trio of sisters Hope, Faith (Binnie Barnes), and Charity (Janet Blair). Due to unforeseen events, they need to dispose of a corpse that keeps resurfacing. The movie is filled with madcap setups and a heady array of types such as the exasperated policemen, drunken convention-eers, smarmy journalists, moralizing biddies, Milquetoast desk clerks, sassy dames, dour morticians, and tippling Irish charwomen. No one did been-around-the-block-but-not-yet-jaded better than Joan. As a hotel hostess, she upbraids a newspaper editor at the speed of light. Pacing while holding a phone, she begins with a steady, low growl, almost monotone, speaking as audibly fast as possible: "You may be a great big editor with a finger on the pulse of the public and a knife in its back BUT," she slows a bit, "if you don't stop defaming our character I'm going down to your office to per-form some plastic surgery with my bare hands!" Ringing with nimble dia-logue and flabbergasted personnel, *Three Girls about Town* is altogether delightful and one of the best comedies Joan ever did. Perhaps it would be better remembered if it had a more distinctive title. Joan once joked that she had made *Three on a Match*, *Three Men on a Horse*, and *Three Girls on Broadway*. (There was no *Three Girls on Broadway*. Joan likely confused *Two Girls on Broadway*, *Three Girls about Town*, and *Three Broadway Girls*, an alter-nate title for *The Greek Had a Word for Them*.) She said that left one last option: *Three Girls on a Man*.

Later in 1941 Joan did *Lady for a Night*, her third movie in a row with able director Leigh Jason. She was paid thirty-five thousand dollars and received top billing for this "women's picture," supported by no less than John Wayne. Lavishly costumed for its 1880s setting, *Lady for a Night* was comparatively opulent coming from the small Republic Studio, and Joan was initially eager to do it. "The story is wonderful," she said. "For the first time in years, I'm not thumbing through the pages of the script to see what days I'm off." Joan's character is impetuous, proud, and sympathetically wicked by virtue of unalloyed social ambition. Here is one of the few movies that fea-tures her as the star, and she responds with high energy and a credible south-ern accent. Her costars, however, do not offer much in return. Wayne sleepwalks, while Hattie Noel as a loyal, fun-loving black maid is reduced to a stereotype. *Lady for a Night* touched on a bit of everything—comedy, social satire, family drama, courtroom suspense, romance, Gothic horror, and music—but did not fully succeed at any. It did, however, give Joan one residual honor. A B-17F airplane was named *Memphis Belle* after the crew saw the movie, though the pilot avowed the name was more as tribute to his Tennessee fiancée than to Joan.

On one particularly clear blue December day in Newport, the Powells set out for a picnic across the bay in the Chris-Craft. Dick captained the boat, as was his routine, while Joan and the kids watched gulls soar and swoop. Dick noticed another Chris-Craft with two men in it who were waving for them to slow down. Dick steered the decelerating boat near the other. Both boatmen looked terribly anxious, one telling the Powell family that a Japanese air raid was on its way to the West Coast. When the Powells returned home and turned on the radio, the details of the Japanese attack on Pearl Harbor were being announced.

Everything changed in that moment. As was her custom when frightened, Joan opened the Bible. She chose to read the Twenty-third Psalm loud enough for everyone in the house to hear: "The Lord is my shepherd, I shall not want; he makes me lie down in green pastures. He leads me beside still waters; he restores my soul." She then shuttered the windows while Dick secured the boats. Norman rounded up Boy, the family dog. Three-year-old Ellen clutched her blanket and watched attentively at the action surrounding her. She knew something was wrong and became quiet and wide-eyed. With the place closed and locked, they all piled into the Cadillac. "Now, Dick, don't drive too fast," said Joan. "Joan, I'm in command here," he said while fumbling with his keys. "Be quiet!" They sped home.

As soon as it was clear the West Coast was in no immediate threat of Japanese invasion, Joan and Dick left the kids with Katie and took a combination business-pleasure trip to New York. Hotshot impresario Mike Todd was in early development for a Broadway show called *Beat the Band*, and he believed Dick was the right leading man. After auditioning and discussing the project with Todd, both men lost interest, leaving *Beat the Band* to eventually be produced by George Abbott as a vehicle for Jack Whiting.

This trip was a pivot of sorts for the Powells. A boredom had settled into their five-year marriage. No longer were they on the town arm in arm. Now they were stepping out separately, offering excuses of family duties or the flu to account for the oft-absent spouse. Dick went alone to see *Best Foot Forward* at the Ethel Barrymore Theatre and was taken with sprightly young cast member June Allyson, who sang the praises of the barrelhouse, blues, and boogie-woogie in the "Three B's" showstopper. Dick went backstage to meet her, and she was agape that a star of his rank would single her out. Joan began going solo to the exclusive Cub Room of the Stork Club, that see-and-be-seen nightclub on East Fifty-third frequented by the café society of Broadway, Hollywood, and Washington. There was no rationing at the Stork Club, and patrons could almost forget that the United States had newly joined World War II.

Mike Todd frequented the Stork Club as well. The man was singularly charismatic. He could walk into a room and suck up all the available oxygen with his bear-trap mouth, ubiquitous cigar, and rattling voice. *Beat the Band* was an incidental moment in an outsized life, except that it offered him an introduction to Dick Powell's wife. Mike Todd was used to getting what he wanted. And right now he wanted Joan.

CHAPTER 6

The Interrupted Family

How small after all the cup of human enjoyment is, how soon overflowed with tears.
—Kakuzo Okakura, *The Book of Tea*

Nineteen forty-two brought on blackout shades, civil air patrols, war bonds, victory gardens, and gas shortages. Tens of thousands of women began riveting, welding, and assembling in defense industries. With husbands gone, children were left without parental supervision. Juvenile delinquency staged a comeback and reform school enrollment increased accordingly. Neither Norman nor Ellen was in need of such intervention, but their parents were preoccupied elsewhere.

James Cagney loaned his New England farm as barracks for servicemen. James Stewart joined the air force, and Robert Montgomery commanded a PT boat in the Pacific. Dick's secretary Harold Kinny joined the Coast Guard. Joan's brother-in-law, Albert Broccoli, joined the navy. Dick volunteered at the United States Organizations (USO), as did mother Katie and sister Gloria. He sang innumerable patriotic songs in sailor suits at fund-raisers and enlistment drives and on film. He made wooden guns for the kids and taught them how to fire at enemies, with the Selma Avenue tennis court used for military drills of Norman's Cub Scout troop.

Joan felt the call of duty, but her war efforts earned her wages where Dick's did not. She went on the road for six months in 1942, visiting many of the seven thousand camps in the United States with a six-a-day USO vaudeville troupe. In a fifteen-minute routine, she told jokes and did a striptease. But just as she started to undress, and the soldiers registered interest, her zipper got stuck. No amount of tugging, by her or an eager volunteer from the audience, made a difference. With an exasperated shrug, she'd say, "Sorry fellas, but what can I do?" and exit.

She spent an additional three months visiting the American bases in the freezing North Atlantic. She mingled with the boys, danced, shared meals, and swapped jokes. She patiently danced with soldiers, one at a time, in brief shifts. Because the men had been so long deprived of feminine company, the brass was concerned about possible groping or assault. They had machine guns posted around Joan to keep the servicemen under control, though there were no reports of unwanted advances.

Despite her ready smile, Joan's war tours were grueling. Men she had breakfast with could be dead by lunch. She had some terrifying bad weather in small planes, sealing her lifelong phobia of air travel. She ate badly on tour, inciting tooth and gum problems. "Being a truck horse, I was built to take whatever came along," she said. "There is no time for being tired, or for complaints. You keep going, because you can't let the boys down. You laugh when you want to cry, and act happy and gay when you're so sad inside it hurts."

In April, Joan sold war bonds on a whistle-stop Victory Caravan tour of twelve American cities with fellow show-business headliners. Their collective presence in itself was enough to stupefy the train station gawkers, but they offered a generous three-hour mélange of songs, dances, comedy, and dramatic readings wherever they went. Between stops, stars such as Cary Grant and Bing Crosby relaxed or slept in their own compartments, lounged in the dining room or observation car, drank, played poker, did crossword puzzles, or chatted. At each stop they checked into a hotel for rest in advance of a parade that would display them to the throngs. The surreal, intoxicating two weeks ended on 29 April 1942, when Joan and her colleagues were feted by Eleanor Roosevelt at a reception on the White House lawn.

After being dispatched again to Newfoundland in the North Atlantic, and then to Hollywood's USO Clubhouse for an appearance with Marlene Dietrich, Joan traveled to Camp Polk, Louisiana, for a four-day stint. The U.S. Army Commanding Major General reported to the Brigadier General of the War Department the following statistics of Joan's visit:

number of men who saw Joan Blondell	30,000
number of theater appearances	6
number of men before whom she performed	7,000
dances she attended	3
number of men with whom she danced	150
number of united (officers) with whom she messed	8
number of men with whom she messed	1,200
number of autographs given	500

In summary, he wrote, "Miss Blondell is deserving of high praise for her tireless and unselfish way in which she accomplished the ambitious schedule which we had laid out for her." Joan so endeared herself that she was made honorary staff sergeant and had two tanks and a bulldozer named after her. At the Colored Service Club, she was asked if Cab Calloway would make a good movie actor. "Well, he's hep to the jive, rides the groove, and ain't a square from Delaware," she said as a smile traveled across her face. "With his sweet and smooth style, he should be able to dent the public." At the Air Corps Flying School at Lake Charles, Louisiana, she dressed in a fur cape over a dark blue crepe dress to assist in the induction of twenty-one teenage boys. She demonstrated her superior marksmanship by firing a Thompson submachine gun, a .45-caliber revolver, and a .30-caliber machine gun. She gave greetings over the public address system, rode a tank, witnessed a demolitions exhibition, performed skits, stood for photos, visited the army hospital, lunched with nurses, and judged a jitterbug contest. In a field house packed with cheering soldiers, she was elected unanimously as "the favorite date of a Yank in a tank."

She enjoyed telling the story of one poor soldier stationed in "some godforsaken place up in Canada":

After the show we were all huddled around a stove in a Quonset hut, and I noticed a tall, thin boy staring at me, and I could tell he was just too shy and nervous to approach me. He was standing by the door, shivering. So before he froze to death, I went over to him and said hello. He was from the South, and he said he had a terrible problem and could I help him. He was engaged to this marvelous girl, but all the guys in his platoon were saying that with him being away and her being in show business, she was probably seeing other fellas. "Now, Miss Blondell," he said, "you're in show business. Just 'cause I'm away doesn't mean she isn't gonna wait for me, does it?" I told him to pay no attention to his friends and said that it was just an old-fashioned notion that people in show business were fast. He was terribly relieved and practically in tears thanking me. When we were ready to go and I was walking out to the plane, he ran up and said, "Miss Blondell, you've made me so happy. I just want you to see a picture of my girl." He handed me an eight-by-ten glossy. There she was in black lace underwear with her things bursting out of her brassiere, and she had a black boa that she was holding between her legs, trailing behind her. Her name, Trixie Dixon, was etched in white in the corner, and her manager's name and phone number was printed at the bottom. At the other corner, in ink, was the inscription:

Honey—I really love you No Shit
Trixie

Joan returned to her family in time for Christmas. "If I don't get [a furlough] pretty soon, I won't have a husband to go home to," she said only half jokingly. Her war work continued stateside, with letter writing and phone calls to hundreds of servicemen's families. Norman and Ellen were meanwhile forming early memories. Not surprisingly, they recall more of their father and grandmother during this time than their mother. Katie, a flinty but loving matron by the 1940s, was living in the in-law accommodations over the garage. She and Ed were arguing too often to live together peaceably, so he found an apartment in Hollywood. Gloria was a devoted aunt, particularly to Ellen, enrolling her in art classes.

There were others supporting the Powell home. Maurice Leo, a slender man with a balletic turnout and campy sense of humor, worked for Dick as his secretary. There was a Japanese gardener who disappeared when the war started. Chalmet and Clarence, the African American couple Joan hired as domestics during her marriage to George Barnes, still served as cook and butler, but Katie ran the house. She was kind when anyone was hurt or sad and always had a comforting prayer. Due to her embrace of Christian Science and rejection of her Irish Catholic heritage, Ellen and Norman were raised with the former. But neither the children nor Joan were as devoted to the church as was Katie. She had a rich spiritual life, combining Christian Science with the occult. Ouija boards and séances were not uncommon on Selma.

For all of her preoccupations with the supernatural, Katie was prone to ignoble behavior. When several green, spiked flower holders were missing, she told Norman she believed Chalmet had taken them. Norman told Chalmet of Katie's suspicions. When confronted, she denied everything, then came to Norman and asked why he said that, attributing his response to devil possession. The episode shook Norman's confidence in his grandmother and gave him his first unsavory taste of the lies grown-ups tell.

Life for the children was regimented. Katie made sure Norman and Ellen said their prayers, went to Sunday school, and respected their elders. Dinner was ready exactly at six o'clock, served properly on silver at the formal dining table. Katie instructed the children on etiquette, while Joan was not usually able to have dinner with the kids. There were ongoing kidnapping fears, undiminished since Norman's birth. Dick hired a security guard who reported to work every night at six and went home every morning at six. He carried a .45, but he used it only once to kill a rat in the basement.

Though Katie was the dominant female caregiver to Ellen and Norman during the war, it was Joan who gave Ellen *the talk*. As the two sat in Joan's dressing room, she briefly looked out the window with a thoughtful glance, then turned to address her daughter. "It's time I told you about the birds and bees, and more about your body and the differences between boys and girls," she began. "When you grow older, to a stage called puberty, maybe in your early teens, you will unexpectedly bleed in your underwear. Your body is preparing itself to have children. . . . My period, that's what it's called, began when I slid into home playing baseball with boys. I was a great pitcher. When I got up, I felt something different in my drawers and went home to look. I was terrified when I told my mother. She just looked at me and smiled, 'my little woman.' Women have to go through this, Ellen."

"It's not fair if boys don't have a period," she said.

"Boys can't have babies, but don't worry, something much worse happens to them." She paused before explaining herself. "They get erections."

Whenever they were in town at the same time, Joan and Dick entertained. After two or three cocktails, Katie was a favorite among the partygoers of Hollywood for her riotous laugher and tales of growing up with seven older brothers. Composer and friend Hoagy Carmichael, whose songs "The Old Music Master" and "I Get along without You Very Well" were recorded by Dick, was particularly fond of Katie. He performed a quick piano ditty called "Down in Nana's Canyon," noting that the Blondell matriarch's impressive cleavage was a convenient storage place for a number of gewgaws.

Joan crocheted a brightly colored rug for the living room and bought early American furniture. A light-carpeted sitting room had a fireplace, desk, and the effects of Dick's avocations, including a relief of his boat, a ship in a bottle, riding crop, and pith helmet. He had a musket, sword, and pistol collection that hung on various walls in the public rooms near Joan's Victorian figurines. The master bedroom was void of any symbols of aggressive masculinity. It was all early American, nineteenth-century cameos, cut glass, and porcelain. The dining room was paneled in dark wood with thick ceiling beams and matching floral drapes and wallpaper. Since Dick's tastes leaned toward modern and Joan's toward antiques, the effect was mixed. Joan laughed at the scheme, calling their home "early English on the outside and Kansas City on the inside."

Norman was enrolled in a private school, where he became a quiet, well-behaved boy. Though she revered her father, Ellen was always more defiant, learning to detest the consequences of her parents' fame at an early age. She went to the respectable public Gardner Street School, but the appearance of her mother caused embarrassment. "She would get so much attention, and that's tough on a kid," she said. "My mom would try so hard to be so inconspicuous, and try to participate in school matters like the PTA or the paper drives during the war, but it didn't work. She was always 'Joan Blondell,' not 'Ellen's mom.'" Joan coveted her children's education, insisting that they have the continuity of learning that she lacked. Every night that she was at home, without fail, she would read to them, or have them read to her. When she was away, she made sure Dick, Katie, or Gloria took over book duties.

Dick usually kept a sunny disposition. He tinkered around the house, helping the kids build model planes or play musical instruments. Ellen showed no interest in dolls, gravitating instead to shooting caps and climbing trees or daydreaming about horses and sailing ships. This caused some conflict with Joan, who tried styling Ellen's hair and dressing her in pinafores. At Christmas, there was always a tiny nativity scene on the piano, and every year Joan would thoroughly review the characters with the kids. Dick had installed an advanced music system and alternatively played '78s of classical music or the up-to-date Bing Crosby and Sammy Kaye.

When Joan came home after work, she often fell into bed without taking off her makeup. It was not uncommon for days to pass in which schedules necessitated no more than brief exchanges between her and Dick. Only rarely did the family gather around the radio to hear the news or to enjoy the kids' favorites programs such as *Amos 'n Andy*. "We'd all sit there as a family," said Ellen with faint incredulity.

The unraveling of the Powells marriage began in early 1943, when Joan ventured to New York at Dick's urging. Mike Todd's pursuit of Joan had been delayed by the onset of the war, but when she wound down her work in the North Atlantic, he made his next move.

Born Avron Hirsch Goldbogen in 1907 to Polish immigrants in Minneapolis, Todd was part P. T. Barnum, part Houdini, and part huckster. He was one of nine children born to a poor rabbi, but somehow his powers of fund-raising and risk-taking were astounding. He once bet a man that he could raise one hundred thousand dollars in one night. He won the bet. Abel Green of *Variety* noted, "He may parlay himself into the poorhouse or Fort Knox, but in either case he will sup on caviar and champagne."

When he came to show business producing, he had transformed into the Gentilesque Mike Todd. His early Broadway efforts, such as *The Man from Cairo* in 1938, did not do well. *The Hot Mikado*, performed at the 1939 New York World's Fair and featuring an erupting volcano and waterfall on stage, did much better and foreshadowed Todd's penchant for spectacle. He spent the war traveling through Europe selling bonds and producing variety acts for the soldiers in army camps. Ever the showman, he envisioned a baseball game in the Nuremberg Stadium and a showboat on the Rhine, but they did not come to pass. The best he could do was an assemblage of circus performers and an evening of opera recitals.

Such modest producing would soon be out of character. In 1943, Todd was red hot with two hits on Broadway, *Star and Garter* with Gypsy Rose Lee and *Something for the Boys* with Ethel Merman. Since he had spun gold for two other brassy dames, Blondell reasoned that his interest would serve her well. In March, Todd agreed to produce Lee's play *The Naked Genius*, the autobiographical story of a stripper who pens a murder mystery. But fury was unleashed when Lee assumed that Todd would produce the play for her, not Joan Blondell. Todd's coddling, pricey gifts, and promises of future roles quelled her temporarily. Despite all appearances, she was not carrying on an affair with the married Todd, and neither, for the moment, was Blondell.

Todd put together *The Naked Genius* as a sort of theatrical seduction for Joan, who he found to be inalienably desirable. She, in turn, iced her already stagnating film career, and threatened the well-being of her children and home life, to take on Broadway. Of course, the gossip mill started churning out stories about Joan and Mike. Dick was accepting of the arrangement at first, respecting Joan's career opportunity and privately wondering if circumstances would allow him to exit his marriage.

Joan was barely reading the first-script draft when she received a phone call in New York announcing that her seventy-seven-year-old father was dying. Ed had been admitted to a Compton sanitarium, gravely ill with testicular cancer. For years, he seemed to his children to be living in the past, happy only in the company of cronies at the Friars and Lambs Club. Norman, too young to appreciate his link to bygone days, found him cranky and intimidating. His marriage to Katie, marred by long-standing accusations of infidelities, was estranged at the end. He never adjusted to show business after vaudeville died and kept his old props in a trunk just in case of a revival. But to Joan he was her jocular, talented father who gave her the strength and mental agility needed to succeed in a ravaging profession. She beat her way back across the country as fast as possible, overcoming her fear of flying to save time. She did not get back soon enough; Ed died on 27 March before Joan's plane touched down. At his morning service at Forest Lawn in Glendale two days later, his family paid tribute in the company of a few surviving vaudeville buddies.

Show business does not allow protracted grieving, and within a few days Joan was negotiating work. *The Naked Genius* was stalled, so Joan followed an offer from director Richard Thorpe at MGM. He thought she would be perfect as the burlesque dancer turned war nurse in *Cry "Havoc,"* a World War II drama with an all-star female cast to include Margaret

Sullavan and Ann Sothern. The action centers in the bomb shelters and makeshift hospitals of Bataan before the American surrender, with the human interest derived from diverse women plunged into mortal peril. Joan's witty on-screen summary of a dance routine, all flouncy and teasing, commented backward to her war service and forward to her theatrics with Mike Todd.

Joan stayed home through the early summer, with *The Naked Genius* rehearsals at long last commencing in August in New York. Philip Ober was cast as a press agent, but he was disgusted with the proceedings and walked out. The redoubtable director George S. Kaufman was rightfully worried about *The Naked Genius*'s viability and sat in the front row forcing a grin to stave off despair. Lee was there to fiddle with the script, but she, too, eventually bailed.

With Norman, Ellen, and thirteen-year-old Mike Todd Jr. in the audience, *The Naked Genius* opened in Boston on 13 September and was promptly disemboweled. Kaufman could not keep up with his own scribbling notes and rewrites. Todd, meanwhile, grew less coy in his interest in Joan. He made double entendres and ogled her breasts incessantly. She was not amused and certainly did not yet see Todd as a romantic partner. His impudence actually became a source of marital solidarity during the early weeks of *The Naked Genius*. Joan was forever calling home to tell her husband that Todd was an A-one jerk.

Before the Boston run was finished, shrewd Todd sent gifts to the critics with thanks for their "constructive criticism." Then he, Kaufman, and Lee rewrote the show, sexing it up considerably. Joan's frumpy bathrobe gave way to sheer negligee. The disarmed critics started commenting on Todd's unusual grace. With Joan's sex appeal reawakened on stage, box office was strong. "There were daily dialogue changes and complicated revisions of Joan's stage business, which added no motivation or logic to her role," noted Mike Todd Jr. "She could barely get through a performance. There was no improvement in the play, but business continued to be good throughout the Boston run."

Similar financial rewards came with the Baltimore and Pittsburgh engagements. Todd kept tinkering, determined to see it to a New York opening. Having put up his own sixty thousand dollars for the production, he always gave the impression he had more money than he could spend. He was a master at self-promotion and publicity and did not appear the slightest bit nervous at huge financial risks. In rescuing *The Naked Genius*, he put seven dogs, a rooster, and a Rhesus monkey named Herman on stage alongside the swelling human cast of forty-three. Then he lowered expectations by running ads that proclaimed, "Guaranteed not to win the Pulitzer Prize, it ain't Shakespeare But It's Laffs," alongside a barely dressed cartoon woman at a typewriter.

Still, Todd was trying to gild a sow. Kaufman stopped directing altogether, and he and Lee urged Todd to close out of town. Blondell, who had to take the nightly pounding in front of an audience, grew despondent. Todd fought on, and "Joan forgot about trying to make any sense out of what she was doing onstage and let her warmth and personality come through, which did help—somewhat," said Mike Todd Jr.

By the time *The Naked Genius* was on the docket for a 21 October opening at Broadway's Plymouth Theatre, everyone but Todd was looking to escape. Lee and Kaufman wanted their names off the credits, with Kaufman conspicuous by his absence on opening night. As expected, reviews were awful. "There are sad and dreary tidings from Broadway this morning," groaned the *New York Times* critic. "For last night Mr. Todd, against the advice of friend and foe, brought in *The Naked Genius* to mock the world and to prove, alas, that Gypsy Rose Lee is a choice item only in person and not in manuscript." Remarks about Joan were assiduously tepid. She "is okay for figure, manner, and accent, and she seems to be having fun—all of which is proper," reported the *Times*.

Todd was not a drinking man, but he got drunk on opening night. He took Lee to "21," where he tried to atone with a Cartier gold compact. He then said that his wife, Bertha, would grant him a divorce, and he intended to marry Joan Blondell. Lee quietly rose from their table and left, the compact still there. The next day, Todd had a huge Bouguereau nude delivered to Lee's house with a note that read, "You won't leave this on the table at '21.' Love, Mike." In summarizing his character, Joan said simply that he "wanted to own the world."

The Naked Genius played to full houses and pulled in $20,000 each week. That did little to ease Joan's anxieties over what she saw as a personal embarrassment replayed publicly every time the curtain went up. "Oh, did I want to get out of that one," she said. "It was all kind of an emotional thing. The play was silly and gay and lavish—but I wanted to get home" Todd was downcast at having failed Blondell artistically. Ethel Merman and Gypsy Rose Lee were mere professional investments, but Joan was a prospective wife if he could sideline their respective spouses. To straddle her with a witless, dull play was unforgivable. While holding court at his Park Avenue penthouse, he promised brighter projects in her future, then buried her in jewels and fur.

Todd pondered a sentence in the morning paper about the stratospheric ticket prices of *The Naked Genius*: "To pay $3.30 instead of the screen's highest $1.10, and be insulted besides, does not create the ultimate in good will." He polled two audiences and found that about half of the crowd was unhappy with their investment of time and money on *The Naked Genius*. Todd then ran an ad stating he wanted a long career on Broadway and was not in the business of disappointing audiences. On 16 November 1943, while chomping on one of his beloved Havana perfecto cigars, Todd stunned Broadway by announcing that *The Naked Genius* would close in less than a week. "In show business you can't please everyone, but I believe pleasing less than half is not a good percentage," he announced. "Therefore, in my eagerness to keep faith with the public, I am closing the show despite the fact that it is earning a very substantial profit. I believe the money I might be losing as a result is not as important as the loss of goodwill of the people who might not like *The Naked Genius*. In this game you're as good as your last show." The decision paid off richly. Kaufman, Lee, and Blondell all heaved a loud sigh of relief, and columnists one-upped each other in praise of Todd's good sportsmanship. Todd didn't mention the sweetheart deal made behind the scenes. He had convinced Twentieth Century-Fox to invest $150,000 in a film version of *The Naked Genius*, with an additional $200,000 guaranteed if the play lasted for at least thirty-five performances on Broadway. Todd closed the show after performance thirty-six, ensuring his maximum take for the film rights at $350,000.

When the whole fetid enterprise was over, Mike apologized to Joan. "I'll make it up to you, sweetheart."

"I hope the picture turns out better," she said. "But I doubt if the Hays Office will approve the title."

"So they'll change it to *The Half-Naked Genius*," quipped Mike.

It was filmed as *Doll Face* with Vivian Blaine. It was not as bad as its stage predecessor, but its sole distinction was a performance of the Perry Como hit "Hubba Hubba Hubba."

Todd's pursuit of Blondell was no secret at this point, and his long marriage to beautiful and jealous Bertha Freshman was on the ropes. He saw his wife once or twice a week at most, and a previous affair had soured the relationship before Joan entered the picture. Joan and Dick, meanwhile, could hardly have been more distant emotionally or geographically. While Joan was away, Dick broke the long-term lease on their Newport house with the justification that it was too close to the Pacific and therefore vulnerable to a Japanese invasion. Joan was brokenhearted, nonetheless, and felt betrayed. There was a change in the tenor of phone calls home. Joan and Dick kept conversation topics to the children and rarely spoke of each other. He was out more often when she called—at the studio, doing errands, or meeting with friends. Katie was blunt and said she believed he was seeing another woman. Todd, meanwhile, continued his aggressive campaign, promising Joan not just love, but excitement, something that barely existed in either of her first two marriages.

Joan had commitments in New York that extended beyond the run of *The Naked Genius*. She appeared at the tenth annual Night of Stars variety show to benefit the United Jewish Appeal at Madison Square Garden for the reconstruction of Palestine as well as the Friars Frolic at the Winter

Garden Theatre. It was December, the first snow had fallen, and she was desperate to get home to her children. Traveling through North America's midlands on the Super Chief, she felt a profound uncertainty about her marriage and about what Todd now meant to her career and life. Todd, by phone and telegram, continued to declare his love.

It seems likely that Joan and Mike, as of late 1943, had not yet been adulterous. Joan declared her fidelity in marriage, and there is no reason to doubt her. The immediate problem, however, was *appearances*. It looked suspicious to anyone taking notice: Impresario sinks his own money in a stage vehicle for a beautiful star who is then lavished with gifts and promises of love everlasting. In the coming weeks, the chatter would get louder and the denials more unsustainable.

As expected, relations with Dick were barely cordial at home. The Powells were nearing the crucible of their marriage, and both knew it. Certainly, Joan looked guilty of carrying on a torchy affair during those long months back East, leaving Dick feeling justified in pursuing his own extramarital agenda. According to next-door neighbor Frances Marion, Joan was informed by thirdhand sources of "a certain young lady, dressed like a prim and proper school girl though she had long since emerged from her school days, who came for dinner and left just before the milkman arrived." She was June Allyson, the Bronx-born hoofer who bewitched Dick on stage in *Best Foot Forward*. Now she was in Hollywood to do the film version and get a toehold on Powell's affections.

Despite the imminent ruin of her marriage, Joan reacquainted herself to housework, her children's schedules, and life among friends and family in California. She and Dick gave each other the superficial accord of barely tolerated roommates. Home life was further strained by "Mike Todd this" and "Mike Todd that" in various phone calls and letters. Even before Joan left New York, he had offered her the Ethel Merman role in *Something for the Boys* on tour. He called daily urging her to return to New York to negotiate *Boys* and begin rehearsals. Dick offered no resistance to another separation, but he considered the potential heavy consequences to his marriage if she should go. Joan stalled for time to get through another Christmas at home for the sake of the children.

At the end of the year, when Dick moved into a rental home in Beverly Hills, darkness engulfed Joan. The combination of a crumbling marriage, neglected children, uncertain film career, June Allyson, and the won't-say-no ardor of a dangerous, enticing man drove Joan to a neurasthenic crisis. She canceled all plans and took to her bed. "Joan Blondell, one of the best-loved actresses in Hollywood, has been lying desperately ill for two weeks from nervous exhaustion," bulletined Louella Parsons. "I talked with her as long as her nurse would permit."

Norman and Ellen were traumatized by their mother's condition. They were instructed to always be quiet if they approached her bedroom. They saw her infrequently, as only Katie and a Swedish masseur were allowed regular entrance. Katie protected her, overseeing family, the press, studios, agents, and friends. When the children were brought in, they noticed their mother had lost some hair, her eyes were cocked outward, and she obsessed on a reoccurring nightmare of being chased by a fireball. She began stuttering again, just as she had during the horrible final days of her marriage to George Barnes. She dissolved into tears without provocation. "What good am I to [the children] in this condition?" she cried before reburying her face in a pillow.

Mike phoned constantly, telling her that his love and the road show of *Something for the Boys* would cure her anguish. She was not ready for the 20 January opening of the show in Philadelphia, and the backers were impatient to recoup, so Merman stepped in for three weeks. Dick meanwhile followed Hollywood wisdom that says a marital split should be accompanied by Dionysian revelry. In the early months of 1944, he was seen with June Allyson at Romanoff's, Ciro's, Chasen's, and Mocambo, then he took a trip to New York. Joan went public with her intentions to divorce, but no legal action had yet been taken. "I am going to file against Dick as soon as he returns from the East . . . and after I have talked the matter over with him. The matter of a divorce is final, however." Radio station news announcements soon followed: "Exclusive! The seven-year 'perfect marriage' of Joan Blondell and Dick Powell is on the rocks! After the divorce, Joan will marry Mike Todd, the fabulous Broadway producer!"

It seemed that everyone, including her doctor, mother, and Mike Todd, was telling Joan to get back to New York and away from LA. Todd's dance-heavy musical *Mexican Hayride* opened in January to great reviews and strong ticket sales. *Something for the Boys* was a boon to Ethel Merman's career, and there was no reason to think Blondell would not triumph with it on the road. Norman and Ellen would be cared for by their grandmother. Joan gave in to the advice and hopped a train to headline *Something for the Boys* in Baltimore on 15 February.

Excitement gave way to jitters. *Boys* was a spirited musical comedy blessed with songs by Cole Porter, but it was created as an Ethel Merman vehicle. Merman's vocal prowess was hers alone, and two of her songs exceeded Blondell's capacity. Despite Mike's continued attempts at boosting Joan's confidence, she was in agony on opening night. It did not help that Merman was front row center for Blondell's bow in the show.

"Do you have to sit in the *first* row?" Todd asked Merman.

"I don't want to miss anything," she said.

Mike pleaded with her to be kind. "You're romancing her, Mike," said Merman, her eyes narrowing. As the house lights dimmed, she adjusted her rump on the seat, faced the stage, and said, "Go fill my costumes, Joanie."

Alas, she didn't, and she knew it. Assuming a role once inhabited by Ethel Merman was a losing game. Blondell "was a beautiful, delightful minx and she couldn't fill Merman's costumes," concluded Art Cohn, writer friend to Mike Todd. "Her singing voice had but a single asset—bravery." Joan endured the constant "she's no Ethel Merman" reviews with grace. In Chicago, she appeared on *The Breakfast Club*, a hugely popular celebrity radio chat program. She traded good-natured barbs with down-to-earth Midwestern host Don McNeill.

Todd was juggling multiple hit plays, war tours of Europe, and romantic ambitions with Joan. He was still married to Bertha, who was in no hurry to rush the divorce. Still the rumblings of a Blondell-Todd union grew louder, inciting Joan to send the press hounds off the scent. "The West Coast radio announcement that I am planning to marry Michael Todd is ridiculous," she said. "I am aware that there have been rumors about Mr. Todd and myself. Although I did not know him until I went East to appear in *The Naked Genius* three months ago, I have found him to be the greatest of considerate friends. I am proud of our friendship. I hope I shall never lose it. But any romantic attachment is emphatically denied."

In March, Joan collapsed during a Chicago performance of *Boys* and was returned to California for recuperation. On this trip home, she was certain that divorce was imminent. Dick had moved out, Mike was hot on her heels, and a showdown seemed inevitable. June Allyson further complicated the romantic geometry. While Joan was touring *Boys* in early 1944, Dick made *Meet the People* at MGM, conveniently featuring his girlfriend in a supporting role. Later she said it hurt to play the heavy in a marital split, telling Dick, "I didn't think I was taking you away from anybody." Granted the Blondell-Powell marriage was taking its last breath, but one wonders how "your wife and the mother of your children" was demoted in her mind to "anybody." According to Allyson, Powell comforted her by saying she "was a chump. Joan came home with a fur coat and she said Mike Todd gave it to her because he couldn't afford to pay her a salary." Joan was not playing a saint. Once again her behavior suggests that she wanted freedom from Dick Powell, who now seemed drab and tightfisted compared to Mike Todd. Whoever was first unfaithful in deed will never be known. Perhaps it does not matter. This marriage was not merely in trouble, it was dead before either spouse cared to make it official.

Amidst so much drama at home came good tidings from work. In the spring of 1944, Twentieth Century-Fox offered Joan a choice role in a prestige movie. When Betty Smith's warm family memoir *A Tree Grows in Brooklyn* became a giant bestseller, Fox grabbed the rights and immediately began fashioning a top-flight movie. The studio sent Joan a first-draft script while she was on tour with *Something for the Boys*, and the fine aroma of a great script was overwhelming. Aunt Sissy, the oft-married glad heart of the tale, was a dream. "I actually lost my breath when Fox offered me a long-term contract—and Aunt Sissy on a golden platter," she said. The terms were not overly generous. Joan was to start with $1,500 per week for the first year, with a $500 per week raise as an option thereafter.

Life at home was getting uglier, though Joan always conceded that Dick made a wonderful father. Such acknowledgment did not stop her from arming herself with lawyers and filing for divorce on 9 June 1944, charging Dick with extreme cruelty. The beginning of the end of the marriage coincided neatly with the beginning of the end of World War II, with the Allied troops landing in Normandy on 6 June.

Joan faced the daunting task of explaining divorce to Norman and Ellen in an age before marriage and family counseling was available on talk shows and in magazines everywhere. Both children were devastated by the wreckage of their home life. Emotionally blinded, Joan told a reporter than Ellen "is too young to understand or be touched by the situation. She is accustomed to her father's absences. He has been away from home before—on location, on personal appearances, on business trips. It isn't as if she had seen him day in and day out all her life. But Normie is old enough to understand. I explained to him as much as was possible. I was cold with fear while I told him what was happening. But he put his arms around me and said: 'Mother, that's the way things are, and don't you cry inside yourself anymore.' Children have far more wisdom and perception than we think."

The matter of Norman's paternity was hidden barely out of eyesight. Joan had done everything to destroy household traces of George Barnes, so as to spare her son a story he was too young to understand. Norman was never shown his well-hidden baby pictures with parents Joan and George. Dick had for all purposes been the boy's father, and for years Joan felt no more needed to be said. But now her allegiance to Dick was gone, and she sought a way to soothe the transition of divorce for her children. In one of the great miscalculations of her life, she told Norman the truth of his father on the eve of her second divorce. She believed telling Norman that Dick was not his "real" father would soften the pain of a split home. This decision was a tactical catastrophe. "The lack of information on good parenting at the time was huge," said Norman years later. "I had no idea until that moment. She was trying to be gentle but that line of reasoning is so distorted, that a child would be comforted by the fact that the divorce doesn't involve a biological father. I had little or no awareness that my mother was married once before. My father was my father."

Norman was losing not only a family but an identity. It was no comfort to learn that George Barnes gave him away. Why had he never seen him? Barnes reached the height of his career during Norman's childhood, winning an Oscar for his great work on *Rebecca*. He remarried and had two other children, but none of this had ever been shared with his son. It all came to light when Norman was nine, too young to seek love and understanding from a stranger. Norman, in effect, lost two fathers simultaneously, the one he loved and the one he did not know he had.

Joan's disclosure was a grotesque echo of the plot of her 1933 movie *Broadway Bad* and her nostrum for divorce. With the split, Norman pulled away from his parents and sister and sought a happier life with friends. Feelings were not shared anymore, and he intuited that keeping a distance from his family was his only salvation. The ripple effect extended to Ellen, a perceptive six-year-old who believed she had lost both her newly withdrawn brother and her now-absent father. Todd was spending time at the Selma house, and whenever Dick intruded, there was screaming and slamming doors followed by the screeching of car tires. As a result, the children spent much of the summer of 1944 with Katie at a rented oceanside home in Malibu, then still a village of farmhouses, horses, fields, and one-lane country roads. The kids were reasonably content there, with only one occasion inciting Joan's ire. When a drunken nanny punished Ellen by throwing her into the ocean, Joan was quickly on the scene to fire her.

On 15 July 1944, Joan went to court to win her freedom from Dick. Dressed in a chic well-tailored black suit with matching wide-brimmed hat and white gloves, she told the judge, "He kept his office in our home. The phones kept ringing and we had no privacy. When I objected, he said 'If you don't like it you can get out.'" Dick did not fight for custody, choosing rather to settle out of court to prevent further hurt to the kids. He agreed to pay one hundred dollars each for Norman and Ellen every month.

Fans of Blondell and Powell were aghast at the divorce. No longer was she the woman who "stole" their idol from Ruby Keeler. Now they were the couple who must stay forever united. Commonly heard were denials such as "It's only a spat," "Don't take it seriously," the guilt inducing "Think of your children," and, finally, the desperately selfish "You can't do this to us!" What the press would not report was a truth known only to those close to Joan. Mike Todd, not George Barnes or Dick Powell, brought about her erotic awakening. So much changed as a result. She rationalized a certain neglect of her children, and a certain burden on her mother, knowing the three were happy together. She agreed to slow the pace of her career if that was what Mike wanted. She denied his jealous rages, his penchant for public violence, and his need to possess by humiliation everyone around him. Mike's effect on her was especially powerful given the ebbed passions of her previous marriages. She marveled at his bedroom stamina. In contrast, love making with Dick had been affectionate but hasty and, for Joan at least, unfulfilling. She all but admitted the lack of heat in their sex life when she said that Dick was "like a brother. He made me feel secure."

In the fall of 1944, the career front was brightening for both Joan and her newly minted ex-husband. Dick was signed for the tough RKO crime drama *Murder, My Sweet,* permanently smashing his nice guy image by playing the hardened Raymond Chandler detective Philip Marlowe. Joan was immersed in the making of *A Tree Grows in Brooklyn.* Her costars, including screen newcomer Dorothy McGuire, James Dunn, and thirteen-year-old Peggy Ann Garner, were as well cast and enthusiastic about the project as Joan. The setting, a poor Irish immigrant neighborhood of 1910 Brooklyn, resembled the environs of Katie's youth.

Despite its respectability as a novel, *A Tree Grows in Brooklyn* had difficulty getting past Joseph Breen at the Production Code Administration. The PCA was still censoring words like "lousy" and telling the makers of *A Tree Grows in Brooklyn* that birthing pains and ladies room stalls would not be tolerated. The first script draft's primary transgression was "the bigamous characterization of Sissy." A second script draft was rejected, again because of Sissy. The Code read: "The sanctity of the institution of marriage and the home shall be upheld. Pictures shall not infer that low forms of sex relationship are the accepted or common thing." Breen noted that "Aunt Sissy is sympathetically portrayed, and her several marital—or extramarital—undertakings are used as a springboard for considerable comedy. All this, in our judgment, constitutes a violation of the Code . . . [inferring] that such low forms of sex relationship are the accepted and common thing." Only after more doctoring by Anita Loos did the script get approval.

First-time film director Elia Kazan, fresh from Broadway hits *The Skin of Our Teeth* and *One Touch of Venus*, adapted well to a sound stage. When the prying eyes of the PCA were elsewhere, Joan loved the working atmosphere Kazan engendered. "There were no big meetings, or going into closets to figure out what your mood was," she said. "You just did it. [Kazan] chose you because you were the right one for that role and then let you go."

As one of the screen veterans on the set, Joan was accorded star status and was given her own dressing room. But she preferred to socialize in the makeup department with her good friend Dorothy ("Dottie") Ponedel, who was also a favorite of Judy Garland, Paulette Goddard, and Marlene Dietrich. If there was an assembled crowd, Joan was in the middle of it with her homemade coffee cakes and sandwiches. When the cameras rolled, she brought forth a splendid performance. Her acting was on fire, her emotions immediately accessible.

Brooklyn was rehearsed like a play, with Kazan spending time with each actor discussing, negotiating, and locating the heart of the character. Fox was willing to invest generously, devoting several acres of the back lot to recreating six blocks and 218 buildings of old Bedford Avenue. Kazan was nervous at having such attention paid to his first outing on film. "Producer Louis Lighton and cameraman Leon Shamroy coached me through step by step and helped me with all of the aspects obviously different from the theater," he said. He won the affection of his movie cast with his respect for their art, which in those days was often belittled in comparison to stage acting. "The camera is like a microscope and will pick out flaws that are often overlooked in a stage production," he said. Motion pictures "make the utmost demands upon an actor's talent."

When Todd left LA and returned to New York on business, Katie, Norman, and Ellen moved from Malibu back to Selma Avenue. Joan had a three-room redwood playhouse built for the kids and their friends, with various experts coming by to teach them the arts of woodcarving, ceramics, and lanyard weaving. "I'm operating on the theory that if parents make a point of finding interesting, constructive things to keep children busy, there won't be any juvenile delinquency," she announced. When Norman's Scout troop went to Big Bear Lake, Joan and Ellen rented a cabin nearby. She even took a turn as Norman's troop den mother. His embarrassment at having a fussed-over movie-star mother led to her quick resignation.

Joan found solace in her family, who mobilized like antibodies whenever a loved one was in trouble. Gloria was establishing herself as a Los Angeles–based radio actress in the Sunday night WABC-Columbia program *I Love a Mystery*. Junie and his wife, Gretchen, were living there as well. They had opened a photography studio in Balboa near the Newport Yacht Club. Junie kept his job as an electrician at Warner Bros., then at Paramount, while Gretchen took on responsibilities at the photography studio. Everyone in the family loved her, and no one wanted to admit that she sometimes drank too much.

When *A Tree Grows in Brooklyn* opened in early 1945, it was met with thunderous critical approval. "Where Miss Smith impinged her printed pages on a vast complex of human love and hope rooted wistfully in tenement surroundings, the camera has envisioned on the screen the outward and visible evidence of the inward and spiritual grace," noted the *New York*

Times. "Joan Blondell is little short of wonderful," proclaimed the *New York Daily News*. Louella Parsons was downright giddy: "You'll be crazy about Joan Blondell as Aunt Sissy. She is great, and great is the word I mean." Much of the enthusiasm was aimed at Peggy Ann Garner, who offered a startlingly honest performance as the young dreamer Francie.

The enduring beauty of *A Tree Grows in Brooklyn* derives from the little girl's growing awareness of the complexities of human relations. There are no villains, only recognizably flawed people struggling for a measure of happiness. No character better expressed the artistic integrity of *Tree* better than Joan's. She is here an irrepressibly warm personality able to crack and reveal hidden sorrows and express an unobstructed love of children. She blows into the movie and nearly steals it, dressed in stripes and frills in an effort to look fancy on a budget. Sissy is an insecure, big-hearted, intuitive woman who mistakes experience for wisdom. She can spitelessly grin and sum up other people's lives, yet on quick glance one notices that hers is in ruins.

For all of the joy of success accompanying *A Tree Grows in Brooklyn*, Joan felt a twinge of sadness. "Thank God censorship has improved since then," she said later when speaking of the strangling atmosphere of the time. "They cut the best scene in the picture, the best scene I ever played, and the best piece of acting I have ever done. Aunt Sissy, who is a very sweet, good woman, worked in a rubber factory. Her profession is kept very quiet by everybody in the family. She takes the colorful tins the contraceptives are placed in—they have girls' faces on them and names like Agnes or Betsy—and gives them to the children to play with. One day she accidentally leaves a rubber in a tin. The little boy asks me about it, and in the most beautiful writing the author, Betty Smith, did, Sissy tries to explain to the children what the rubber is; not by talking about the actual thing, but about love and life itself. It was very simply done, and all of us players hugged each other spontaneously at the end of the scene. It was marvelous and the Legion of Decency made us take it out. Wasn't that stupid?"

The diluting of Sissy's character was noted by the *New York Times*: "Joan Blondell's performance of Aunt Sissy, the family's 'problem,' is obviously hedged by the script's abbreviations and the usual Hays office restraints, but a sketchy conception of a warm character is plumply expanded by her." Film historian Ronald L. Bowers interviewed Joan and stated, "She always felt that if several of her scenes had not been cut from *Tree*, she'd have a good chance at a Supporting Actress Oscar. There was no rancor in this observation. I don't think Joan held grudges. She was always optimistic." When measuring *A Tree Grows in Brooklyn*, Joan's cup remained forever half full, not half empty. "Kazan let me have a moment or two of tenderness, of maturity, that nobody had ever given me before," she said with obvious gratitude.

Joan dutifully took part in Fox's promotion. Norman was her date to the premiere at Grauman's Chinese Theater in Hollywood. On 11 March 1945, she sat down with Edgar Bergen's wooden sidekick, Charlie McCarthy, for a radio spot:

CHARLIE. Yeah! Well, here's one star that will keep you awake—Miss Joan Blondell! (*applause*)

BLONDELL. Thank you, Charlie. You do say such nice things.

CHARLIE. Well, you bring out the best in me.

BLONDELL. What kind of girls do you like, Charlie?

CHARLIE. Oh, redheads, brunettes, and Blondells!

BERGEN. By the way, Joan, we saw you in your new picture—*A Tree Grows in Brooklyn*.

BLONDELL. Oh, how nice . . . and what did you think of me, Charlie?

CHARLIE. The same as I'm thinking now!

BERGEN. You were very good.

CHARLIE. Well, I thought the tree stole the picture.

BLONDELL. Yes—aren't they doing wonderful things with wood these days! Even on the radio!

CHARLIE. I'll ignore that.

BLONDELL. I was happy to play in *A Tree Grows in Brooklyn* because I lived there.

CHARLIE. Oh, happy childhood!

BLONDELL. On the contrary. . . . As a young girl I found life in Brooklyn one continual struggle.

CHARLIE. Where did you live?

BLONDELL. Near the Navy Yard!

BERGEN. Joan, do you know that Charlie took it upon himself to rewrite the story of *A Tree Grows in Brooklyn*?

BLONDELL. Why, Charlie?

CHARLIE. Well, mine is a little different. In the original story the people went through such terrible suffering.

BLONDELL. And how is yours different?

CHARLIE. In my version the audience suffers.

Under the stewardship of Darryl F. Zanuck, who had left Warner Bros. in 1933, Fox became a mature studio dedicated to well-financed quality drama (*The Song of Bernadette, Laura*). Joan saw no benefit from the success of *Brooklyn*, however, and was again saddled with the kind of cheap movies she grew to loathe at Warner Bros. She was announced for the comedy *Don Juan Quilligan* and the drama *Command to Embezzle*, the later reuniting her with *Brooklyn* costars James Dunn and Lloyd Nolan. *Command to Embezzle* never got made, but *Don Juan Quilligan* was rushed into production. It was an oddball outing, with malapropian William Bendix trying to extract humor out of mother obsession and polygyny. As a gesture of new emancipation, Joan displayed her natural beauty mark here after years under pancake.

Though demands on her were intense, Joan never seriously contemplated leaving show business. "I wouldn't know what to do with myself," she said. "I'm not crazy about a career. I gripe all the time when I'm working. The only trouble is, I gripe more when I'm not working." She found happiness in being an attentive mother when her schedule allowed. When the kids were in bed, she could indulge in personal amusements. She enjoyed gin rummy with her mother, sister, and friends. If alone, she would put a record on the phonograph, pull a book off the shelf, then plop into her favorite plush reading chair. In the morning she was up at dawn and off to work, where her professionalism saved menial efforts such as *Don Juan Quilligan*.

The outside world was occasionally felt inside Hollywood. Joan huddled by the radio on 12 April 1945, when the twelve-year reign of President Franklin Roosevelt ended with his death by cerebral hemorrhage. Then on 8 May, the Allies announced the surrender of German forces. Ad hoc revelry broke out all over the country. Gloria came by Selma, scooped up Norman and Ellen, and took them to a packed Hollywood Boulevard to scream with the masses. Their father was not there. He was no longer a part of their daily lives as his romance with June Allyson took more of his attention. Their mother was not there to share the historic moment either. She was already dog tired from *Adventure*, a new movie she was making at MGM between her Fox assignments. Mike Todd was in New York, but never far from a telephone.

CHAPTER 7

Gulag-on-the-Hudson

. . . these pleasures which we lightly call physical.
—Colette, *The Ripening Seed*

Joan began work on *Adventure* in May of 1945 in an unambiguously supporting role. The production was rushed to capitalize on star Clark Gable's decorated service as a pilot flying missions over Germany and his return to the screen after a three-year absence. In *Adventure*, he played a marine as restless as the sea, with Greer Garson as his becalming love interest.

Gable and Garson never liked each other. She was too regally virtuous for him, and he was too coarse for her. Gable much preferred his women to be earthy and animated, so he gravitated toward Blondell, who had the unenviable chore of playing Garson's man-hungry roommate. Blondell and Gable had worked together in 1931 on *Night Nurse* at Warner Bros., but they formed a stronger friendship on the set of *Adventure*. It was nothing more. "Clark adored women—not in a lechy way. He loved beauty," said Joan. "His eyes would sparkle when he saw a beautiful woman. And if he liked you, he let you know it. He was boyish, mannish, a brute—all kinds of goodies. When he grinned, you'd have to melt. If you didn't want him as a lover, you'd want to give him a bear hug. He affected all females, unless they were dead."

Since surviving the war and grieving the death of wife Carole Lombard, Gable was lonely, but Joan found him to be pleasing company. Both of them had no taste for the phonies that infested their profession. During the shooting of *Adventure*, they shared casual dinners with makeup artist Dorothy Ponedel. "He'd go get some steaks," said Joan, "make them himself, and eat with us in the kitchen wearing a towel apron." They sought to lighten the set. Garson held an afternoon tea, Gable delivered fresh milk from his ranch, and Blondell brought coffee and bottles of Coke. The ongoing flow of refreshments incited director Victor Fleming to gibe, "Try to get someone around here to do any work, and you have to bust up a picnic!"

Adventure proved to be an unworthy enterprise, with Joan bringing in the film's best performance. She offered more emotion at a birth than did either Garson or Gable, who played, it should be noted, the baby's parents. Joan's performance here was giddy, flirty, and boundlessly energetic. She was compensating for the two nominal stars, who never appeared convincing as a pair in love. Despite so-so reviews, box office was robust, grossing $4.5 million for seventh-place moneymaker of the year. If Joan had any resentment at her secondary role to Garson, she vindicated herself by stealing the movie and telling the *Los Angeles Times* that she had "a swell job" playing the other woman. While Gable and Garson were routinely trashed, Blondell was praised. *Variety* believed her to be "almost a reborn actress in the role."

Dick Powell was busy emptying the Selma Avenue property of his belongings. Their limited passion in marriage transformed into cool rectitude as he and Joan parted. Frances Marion stopped by and heard Joan's voice in the basement saying "one for you, one for me." She and Dick were dividing their supply of canned goods and supplies hoarded during the war. When they came to the many cases of extra toilet paper Dick had purchased, Joan said, "You can have all of this," thereby finding a polite way of saying "you're full of shit." With that, Dick took his share of the household contents and was gone for good. Joan and the children stayed on at Selma Avenue, even though the house was gutted of just about every reminder that a married couple once lived there.

On 6 August 1945, the *Enola Gay* opened her bottom hatch to drop an atomic bomb on Hiroshima. Nagasaki was destroyed by like means three days later. Japan surrendered on 14 August, and American soldiers came home in droves. The end of fighting in the Pacific coincided with shifting dynamics in a number of households. Dick Powell and June Allyson were married on 19 August. When Ensign Albert ("Cubby") Broccoli was discharged from active duty, he came home to wife Gloria. They both knew their marriage was over. "There was no particular catalyst in the breakdown," he wrote. "I liked her and she liked me, but we weren't suited for permanent life together." They had no children, and no ugly accusations, so Joan's sister enjoyed a relatively amicable divorce.

Seven-year-old Ellen was meanwhile coming unhinged at the loss of her family. Almost overnight she became highly accident prone—she was rarely without bruises, Band-Aids, or stitches. She teased Frances Marion's Great Dane, but the adults hardly noticed. One night she wandered alone into the living room while Joan was upstairs in her bathrobe reading. Ellen opened a drawer next to the sofa and found a silver match lighter with a clamshell disk housing a roll of matches. She struck the entire roll at once on the holder's sandpaper surface, causing a sudden burst of fire. She threw the roll, pinwheeling the individual matches all over the room. One landed in the Steinway, another at the foot of the drapes, and one on the sofa. Ellen cried in sudden fear and ran into the kitchen. Joan rushed downstairs to check on Ellen and the pets and then called the fire department. The living room was charred, and Ellen's right hand was singed, but the pets were unharmed. Still Joan did not or would not see Ellen's behavior as worrisome in itself. Instead, she imagined what might have been. Had there been more furniture in the house, or had Joan been asleep, damage would certainly have been far greater. To Joan, this was a warning, a sign that Selma Avenue had outlasted its use for her and her children.

Joan was uncomfortable seeing Mike at Selma, so the two met secretly in hotels until his divorce was final. He was not, after all, her children's father, who was seeing them once a week by the terms of the divorce. With some able assist from friends at the Warner Bros. wardrobe department, Joan donned several disguises in preparing for her meetings with Mike. Her favorite was as a white-haired old lady. Mike's wife, Bertha, was aware of the charade and grew tired of fighting. On 7 August 1946, she filed for divorce.

This was no civilized split on the order of Gloria and Cubby Broccoli. Bertha was sharing a rental home in Los Angeles with her husband and son when she went into a screaming rage over the disintegration of her marriage. She picked up a kitchen knife and lunged at Mike. The blade pierced the door molding, but her grasping hand slipped and was cut near her two little fingers. She slumped into a nearby chair to avoid fainting while her son, sixteen-year-old Michael Junior, wrapped her bloody hand in his handkerchief and Todd called a doctor. Bertha was stitched up temporarily at home, then admitted to St. John's Hospital in Santa Monica for tendon repair and a complete suturing. She was given cyclopropane gas, but she remained conscious. Then she was given sodium Pentothol intravenously. Then she was given ether. Then she was dead.

The official story claimed her death was due to a collapsed left lung and circulatory failure while under anesthesia. An autopsy was performed, but the Santa Monica coroner ruled it inconclusive. He then ordered an inquest. Todd, meanwhile, had to throw bones to the insatiable press. He announced that the accident occurred while his wife had attempted to slice an orange. But she was right handed, and the cut was on her right hand. In light of revelations in the hospital, the orange story did not arouse enough suspicion to implicate Todd, and no formal charges were made. But the mysterious circumstances of her death, specifically the heavy sedation for minor surgery, are still unresolved. For the present, Todd's very real passion for Joan quashed any uneasiness she had over the circumstances of his wife's death.

After Bertha's remains were sent to Chicago, Todd accompanied his son back to Lawrenceville Prep in New Jersey for the fall term. "Without referring to his unhappy life with mother, or his coming new life with Joan, he indicated that we would now be closer and he would try to build a family life," noted Mike Junior. "Since we were being so honest, I told him he spent too much time and money gambling. He promised that part of his shift in interest to family life would include his giving up heavy gambling."

Todd was described by Damon Runyon as "a short, chunky, dark, dynamic fellow with a big cigar in his mouth." Runyon also called him "the greatest natural gambler I ever knew." Reneging on the promise he made to his son, Todd was soon bingeing again at Hollywood Park and Del Mar. When Todd's Broadway export *Up in Central Park* opened at the Hollywood Bowl, an unseasonable cold fog kept audiences at home and added to mounting financial catastrophe. "I've been broke but I've never been poor," Todd said. "Being poor is a state of mind; being broke is only a temporary situation." As a chronic gambler, Todd played just about every game invented, but he had a particular fondness for gin rummy. According to friend Art Cohn, he did not gamble to win, he gambled to gamble. "He was a psychopathic loser. He had no card sense," he wrote. "Why is it that three of the shrewdest gamblers in show business—Sam Goldwyn, Jack Warner, and Mike Todd—are probably the three poorest card players in town?"

Joan, low profile during Bertha's well-publicized death, had professional obligations to fulfill. She shot her small role in United Artists' *Christmas Eve* in November of 1946. The studio must have known it was a clinker, so they called in Joan to enliven it in a supporting role. She knew her place. She told *Saturday Evening Post*, "I was once described as having a 'busy' face. . . . I have often been pushed into frothy roles in the hope that this facial busyness would instill life into dead-duck pictures." That was also the case with *The Corpse Came C.O.D.*, a movie no better than *Christmas Eve*. It was a throwaway mystery-comedy in which Joan played (please, not again) a reporter, this time following the story of a dead body sent to a movie star.

Through early 1947, Joan and Mike kept testing their affection for each other and the viability of merging her two children with his one. The five of them were practically living together, though keeping separate addresses. Norman and, particularly, Ellen were less disposed to the rearrangement of adults in their lives, but Joan was confident they would adapt.

At least one friend, Frances Marion, saw disaster ahead. She wrote an exceptionally potent letter to Joan on the eve of her marriage to Todd. She never finished it, and she did not share it with Joan for many years:

> Don't rush into this marriage. Search your mind, your heart, and weigh every aspect of what could lie ahead. . . . Mike and you seem as far apart as the two poles. Even the inequality of your social instincts might never be bridged. Analyze this for a moment and see how obvious it is to all of us who love you. What has given you the greatest happiness in life? Your children, whom you adore, your family, and your home. You didn't build one of those phony showplaces, you chose a charming English house with a walled-in garden, and furnished all the rooms to create an atmosphere of gracious living. You enjoyed pleasant evenings with a few intimate friends. As an actress, you never sacrificed anyone to achieve stardom, but accepted your hard-earned success as a blessing which made it possible to contribute to your family and provide the right kind of future for your children.
>
> Now let's look at Mike. What does *he* like? What are *his* tastes? *His* interests? He is happy only in the glare of arc lights. Fawning crowds of sycophants. Crooked games of chance where he can triumph by his wits. Deals involving borrowed millions which he spends prodigally on transient successes and failures. Then there is his gnawing lust for power which may eventually destroy him, for violence sounds its own death knell.
>
> How often he has boasted "everybody has a price." If [you] <u>are</u> afraid of him, in spite of his repetitious vows that after you are married he will overcome his maniacal jealousy, from which you have suffered so much since you fell in love with him. Think of the bitter tears you have shed. How you have been tortured by his false and ugly accusations. And what makes you think that marriage will change him? In every cliché there is a basic element of truth: *The leopard doesn't change its spots.*

Jealousy is a disease. All the empty vows can't eliminate it from its victim. Just review those humiliating scenes we have witnessed: many have seen him revile you, belittle you, strip you of your dignity, and even strike you. A man who is coward enough to strike a woman will do it again and again to satisfy his sadistic craving for the kind of emotional stimuli which reaches an orgiastic climax only when he has completely subjugated her, and driven her to her knees.

While we do not feel that Mike actually will kill you, in spite of his threats, he eventually might kill your spirit, and that's the cruelest phase of a living death.

On 4 July, Mike and Joan prepared their kids for a road trip east in Mike's convertible. "It felt a little rushed as we piled into the back of the Cadillac," recalled Ellen. "[We] placed our pillows and blankets, in case the night air turned cold, arranged the thermos and sandwiches, then made ourselves comfortable for the long ride." With the top down, the drive through the desert was clear, the sky pierced by innumerable stars and constellations. Joan, the front-seat passenger, told of the creepy fireball nightmare she still was having. As her story ended, Ellen saw a small bright light in the rearview mirror that grew bigger as it zoomed toward the car. She asked, "Mom, did it look like this?" just as an unidentified flying object shot silently over the car, filling the sky with a blinding white light before disappearing over the eastern horizon.

Everyone was quiet. Mike was so awed by the display that he stopped the car. Only after pounding hearts calmed did anyone speak. Mike thought it was a comet. Mike Junior believed it to be a meteorite. Norman contributed his appraisal, which led to a discussion on astronomical phenomena. Joan turned to the back seat where her eyes met Ellen's. Neither of them said a word.

Joan and Mike were married in the cavernous banquet hall of the El Rancho Vegas, the oldest hotel on the Strip, on 5 July 1947 just before midnight. Joan was lovely in a flowered afternoon dress with an orchid corsage.

Mike was in a tux, his hair gelled into a raven black skull cap. Reverend R. V. Carpenter officiated as the hotel owner and manager witnessed. Mike Junior and Norman were fidgety and wished they were somewhere else. Ellen, tired and uncomfortable in a formal dress, was more interested in sleep than in ceremony. She had just a nibble of the heavily frosted white wedding cake before Joan put her to bed.

Soon after the wedding, Todd flew east on business in New York, then rejoined Joan and the kids in Los Angeles. Joan had been signed to Fox's *Nightmare Alley* three months before the marriage and was needed on the lot to begin production. The script was mesmerizing, all about a carnival hustler who claws his way to the top as a spiritist, only to fall when his fakery is exposed. Every role in the drama was unsavory, including Joan's as a counterfeit seeress. The script needed rewrites to pass the censors, but it was approved to begin production on 14 July.

Joan knew immediately that she was involved in something rare. She found the story morbidly fascinating, and star Tyrone Power was "a darling." The film was close to his heart as he hungered to overcome his bedroom swashbuckler image. With a plot that twists like a pretzel, *Nightmare Alley* proved to be one of the most memorable films of his or Joan's career. As she did in *A Tree Grows in Brooklyn*, Joan showed her age to advantage, looking slightly looser at the seams. She possessed a new mature beauty on screen as the world-weary Zeena, tethered to a wasted drunk of a husband. He was played with great distinction by Ian Keith, a rawboned actor who would costar with Joan on stage in the coming years.

The artistic success of *Nightmare Alley* was something of a happy accident. Its tawdry source novel should have been off limits to filmmakers during the era of the Code. It should never have been produced by ex-vaudevillian George Jessel, financed by a first-string studio, or directed by Edmund Goulding, an astute Englishman with a taste for elegant romanticism. With his playing of women's scenes during rehearsals, short attention span, and affection for afternoon tea and evening scotch, Joan referred to him as "that nut." But there's no denying the excellence on the screen, from Joan and everyone else. "That nut" served her as well as any director ever had, including Elia Kazan.

In its own way, the role of Zeena fit Joan as well as that of Aunt Sissy. She had cultivated a toughened, streetwise image for years, but she had never found her way to a carnival before. The match was ideal. Blondell "reveals herself as a dramatic actress of considerable power," the *Hollywood Reporter* noted. But even with a string of great notices, Joan did not change her outlook. "Mom didn't talk about her work," said Norman. "She didn't bring it home. The job was important to her, but it wasn't her passion. It was a way to make money."

Meanwhile, Mike was discontented. This was not what he envisioned for his new life as repentant family man. Since Joan was less driven to pursue her Hollywood career, and Mike was a Broadway producer, it made sense to settle in New York. At the completion of *Nightmare Alley*, Mike nullified Joan's Fox contract with one of his persuasive phone calls. Joan then negotiated with Dick to sell the house on Selma. With ties to the recent past severed, and Mike waiting for her in New York, she boarded the Super Chief with Norman, Ellen, collie Sandy, and twenty-five pieces of luggage for a first-class cross-country trek.

The new family lived briefly in Mike's apartment at 1040 Park Avenue, a sumptuous penthouse with a panoramic view of Central Park. Mike and Joan accompanied the kids all over town, to museums, theaters, parks, and nightspots like Lindy's and the Stork Club. But the outings grew tiresome to the children. They were more excited by Mike's television, a true domestic novelty in 1947. Joan and Mike knew they would be happier in suburban environs, so they sought a place that would fulfill all their wishes: big kitchen, gardens, room for animals and recreation, and good schools.

Since Mike had suffered losses with recent producing ventures, it was Joan who bought the family a new home in Irvington, twenty miles up the Hudson River from Manhattan in Westchester County. The seller was an insurance company that had intended to use it as headquarters, but backed down and sought to unload it quickly. At $27,500, the property was a steal even by 1947 standards. Built by a railway developer, it was by any criteria a mansion that contradicted Joan's basic unpretentiousness. It had four stories and twenty-seven rooms and was done in red brick English manor-style under a stone slate roof. The twenty-two-acre estate included vegetable and flower gardens, pastures, a stable and greenhouse, two orchards of apple and pear trees, a decorative pond, herb garden, lilac trees, and a dog kennel. There was a quarter-mile winding driveway leading to a courtyard with two five-room apartments on each side, completed by a six-car garage and a tool and tractor shed. The views on the grounds took in Nyack, High Tor State Park, and Tappan Zee, the widest part of the Hudson. The Palisades were to the south, and on a clear day the view extended all the way to the George Washington Bridge linking Manhattan to New Jersey.

The main house construction included hand-hewn hardwood timbers and hand-wrought iron. Hardwood floors ran throughout most of the ground level and up the grand central staircase. The living room, dining room, sun room, and pale yellow breakfast room had French doors opening onto a deck overlooking the river two hundred yards down a gently sloping meadow. The spacious kitchen was fully modernized and had an attached pantry. At bibliophile Joan's insistence, the library with fireplace was filled with leather-bound first-edition books. The master bedroom was at one end of the second floor, and at the other end was Ellen's bedroom with an adjacent playroom with carousel horse, a bathroom tiled entirely in little white octagons, and maid's quarters. Norman and Mike Junior had the third floor to themselves, and they could come and go via a staircase in a turret. They had a workout room, separate bedrooms and bathrooms, and a sitting room. The attic was converted into a rec room lined with the autographed movie-star photos that once hung in the den on Selma Avenue.

Joan immediately set about making this great brick behemoth warm and livable. "Joan generated tremendous enthusiasm for our new home and tried to instill this feeling into Norman and Ellen," said Mike Junior. She "worked tirelessly at getting us settled. I was crazy about her." The feeling was mutual—Joan, Norman, and Ellen all grew to love amiable, forthright

Mike Junior. Before matriculating at Amherst, he became Norman's big brother mentor and got him started weightlifting. "Joan didn't spend extravagant sums on herself, but was a free spender fixing up a house and catering to everyone else's comforts," he said. "Few women ever had a stronger nesting instinct. She made no use of decorators or pretentious furnishings, but whatever she purchased was of the finest quality. Any room she decorated looked lived in. There were no fragile antiques, but large comfortable sofas and arm chairs—books, flowers, and chintz, lots of sturdy polished wood and the smell of furniture wax."

Joan domesticated her husband, insisting that he forego late-night parties and gambling. He obeyed, and the two increased family togetherness. They took regular weekend trips with the kids to the lovelier beaches on Long Island. Norman, growing into lean and handsome adolescence, got a job at a local drug store, joined sports teams at school, made friends, and started to notice girls. Joan volunteered at Ellen's PTA until the others in the group were too distracted by a movie star in their midst. Mike enlisted at the Irvington Volunteer Fire Department. Katie moved into one of the courtyard apartments, joined a bridge group, and caught up with her Brooklyn relatives. She kept a low profile in Irvington, venturing into the main house only when asked. This was in part to avoid burdensomeness on her daughter, but also because she detested Mike Todd.

Soon enough the premonitions of Frances Marion came true. Both Joan and Mike tried to hide the fact that neither had enough money for their palatial spread. On top of the house payments, Joan had lent Mike eighty thousand dollars for one of his stage ventures that went bust. With that handout, Joan's divorce settlement money was spent. Despite her efforts to fill Irvington with the effects of former residences, the house was never completely furnished while the Todds lived there. Entire rooms went empty.

With Joan's career attenuated, the family had to rely exclusively on Mike's earnings as a producer. Unfortunately, his brand of showmanship was beginning to wear; he hadn't had a moneymaker in two years. On

Joan's parents, Ed and Katie Blondell, in costume for *The Lost Boy* vaudeville act, circa 1908. Courtesy of Ellen Powell.

Joan "Rosebud" Blondell at the dawn of her show business career, circa 1909. From the Norman S. Powell Collection.

Fourth from the right: Rosebud Blondell is Miss Dallas of 1926. From the Norman S. Powell Collection.

An early publicity shot of Joan Blondell at Warner Bros. Author's collection.

Three on a Match (1932), with Bette Davis, Joan Blondell, and Ann Dvorak, is a tough-as-nails little movie that ages well. Author's collection.

Joan Blondell and James Cagney had fantastic chemistry, as demonstrated here in
Footlight Parade (1933), Warner's splashy Busby Berkeley musical. Author's collection.

Joan comports herself very much as the glamorous movie star, here with dapper husband George Barnes at a movie premiere in 1933. From the Norman S. Powell Collection.

Joan Blondell and Glenda Farrell made a delightful screen team, even in lackluster efforts such as *Kansas City Princess* (1934). Author's collection.

Joan and her brother, Ed
Blondell ("Junie"). From the
Norman S. Powell Collection.

This happy scene at Lookout Mountain in 1935 of mother Joan,
father George, and baby Norman masked deep problems in the
Barnes home. From the Norman S. Powell Collection.

Wedding aboard the *SS Santa Paula*, 19 September 1936. *From left to right*, mother of the bride Katie Blondell, best man Regis Toomey, Joan, Dick, maid of honor Ruth Pursley, the Rev. H. W. Tweedie, and father of the bride Ed Blondell. From the Norman S. Powell Collection.

Joan Blondell in a publicity still from *The King and the Chorus Girl,* 1937. Photo by Elmer Fryer. Author's collection.

Joan Blondell sits for a portrait, circa 1940. Photo by A. L. Schafer. Author's collection.

Dick Powell and Joan Blondell in Paramount's *I Want a Divorce* (1940), which was more successful as a radio series than a feature film. Author's collection.

A radiant threesome: Ellen, Joan, and Norman in 1941. Courtesy of Ellen Powell.

Joan Blondell messes with the troops during her exhausting tours in 1942. From the Norman S. Powell Collection.

Joan Blondell was at her best as tart and tender Aunt Sissy in Elia Kazan's *A Tree Grows in Brooklyn* (1945). Author's collection.

Norman, Joan, Ellen, and Mike Todd at the Stork Club in New York soon after Joan and Mike were married in 1947. Author's collection.

Adoring young father Norman and first-time grandmother Joan with a sleepy infant Sandy in 1957. Courtesy of Ann McDowell Traub.

Joan Blondell with Siobhan McKenna in a dramatic pose from *The Rope Dancers* on Broadway in 1957. Courtesy of Ellen Powell.

All three together again: Joan, Bridey, and Fresh on "The Joan Blondell Tour" of *The Dark at the Top of the Stairs*, 1959. From the Norman S. Powell Collection.

With Ellen on her wedding day, 28 May 1960. Courtesy of Ellen Powell.

Letting loose. *Left to right*: brother Junie, sister Gloria, Joan, and sister-in-law Gretchen celebrate Junie's birthday at Gloria's Pacific Palisades home. Courtesy of Ellen Powell.

Joan Blondell as the smart and moral businesswoman Lottie in *Here Come the Brides*, airbrushed for this publicity shot for the ABC television series. Author's collection.

Joan Blondell with costar Bridget Hanley on the outdoor set of *Here Come the Brides*, which was heavily watered to resemble the muddy streets of nineteenth-century Seattle. Courtesy of Bridget Hanley.

Joan Blondell enjoys a warm embrace from stepson Mike Todd Jr. backstage on the opening night of *The Effect of Gamma Rays on Man-in-the-Moon Marigolds* in New York, 27 September 1971. Courtesy of Ellen Powell.

Joan Blondell in *The Champ*, her last big-budget feature film. Author's collection.

Gloria Manon gets masculinizing makeup while a deathly ill Joan Blondell reads the script of *The Woman Inside*, her last film. Courtesy of Gloria Manon.

19 September 1947, three creditors filed an involuntary bankruptcy against him. His liabilities were tallied at over one million dollars, while his assets came to just over a quarter million. Mike was adjudged bankrupt in a New York court on 23 September, a mere ten weeks after he and Joan were married.

With money woes came violence. Todd was truculent, manic, and physically aggressive. He attempted control in his life by converting Joan into a "Jewish fishwife" and beating her for any supposed transgression. Then he would cry, fall to his knees, beg her forgiveness, and promise never to do it again. For her part, Joan made a mistake common to abuse victims everywhere. She tried to reform her attacker, and for a time it seemed to work. "She remodeled him completely," wrote Art Cohn. "The new Todd won't even play gin rummy for a tenth of a cent a point. He is seriously considering starting an organization to be named Gamblers Anonymous. He even resigned as Abbot of the Friars Club because his duties might tend to keep him out evenings."

The first round of abuse in the fall of 1947 abated to make way for the holidays. Snow came before Christmas, covering the grounds in heavenly white drifts just as a semblance of happiness came over the family. Mike had an aerial shot taken of the estate with the message "Seasons Greetings from *Jemmen-on-the-Nut.*" *Jemmen* was *J* for Joan, *E* for Ellen, double *M* for the two Mikes, *E* for "an added starter," and *N* for Norman. "On the nut" is theater slang for lost production expenses. The pile of holiday gifts could not fit under the fragrant tree in the living room. Everyone could languish at the estate for the first time, try out the snow tractor, string decorations around the sparsely furnished living room, learn how to truss a turkey, and reach for a loving existence as a newly defined family. Joan's commitment to cooking meant that great plates of delicious, rich holiday food filled the dining table. Ellen noted that, despite the employment of a live-in servant and groundskeeper, her mother seemed forever to be waiting on someone.

The joy of the holidays gave way to fear and dread. A new round of beatings commenced in 1948. "She tried to keep us protected, but I remember waking up to screams and saying 'I'm going to get my BB gun and kill him,'" said Ellen. On one occasion the bathtub in the master bathroom overflowed, causing Joan to scurry madly for a mop and towels. Ellen thought it was funny, no one was hurt and nothing was damaged, but Joan was frightened of Mike's reaction. "Quick, quick, let's clean it up," she told Ellen before Mike knew what had happened. Mike Junior said his father was gripped with an irrational possessiveness, perhaps because fluctuating professional success threatened his identity, self-esteem, and manhood. He and Joan still generated tremendous passion; a casual glance could trigger a blood rush to the loins. But she dreaded having a child by him. In contrast to the George Barnes days of multiple abortions, Joan was diligent in practicing conventional birth control, wearing a gold IUD recommended at the time.

Todd applied his energies to business. Efforts at Hollywood deals were stalled, so he tried to renew his standing on Broadway. He schemed to produce *As the Girls Go*, a show for veteran funny man Bobby Clark as the "First Gentleman" of the first woman president of the United States. Joan put up a large portion of the front money for the production, all the while not earning an income but playing the role of sacrificing mother, stepmother, and wife. With the show still in planning by the summer of 1948, Todd had various actors, directors, and backers flowing in and out of Jemmen-on-the-Nut for meetings. Housewife Joan was dispatched to fetch lemonade and cookies for Mike and his collaborators.

Joan's professional activities that year barely registered in tiny squibs. She endorsed Tangee Queen of Diamonds lipstick and was considered for roles at United Artists and Warner Bros. She passed on the radio comedy *Our Miss Brooks*, all about a fast-talking high school teacher, before Eve Arden took the role and made it forever hers. Instead of working, Joan accompanied her husband to ringside seats at Madison Square Gardens as Joe Louis knocked out Jersey Joe Walcott for the heavyweight title. While Mike shouted and punched the air in mock participation, Joan buried her face in his shoulder, sure this was the most gruesome spectacle she had ever come upon.

When *As the Girls Go* had an October tryout in Boston, the theater was nearly empty. Backers were getting nervous and the Todds were in debt for $750,000. Mike, unshaven and insomniac, made panicky trips back and forth to New York to pacify the money men. He collected $15,000 from Mafioso Johnny (Blue Eyes) Aiello just before the show moved onto New Haven. While Joan and Mike checked into the Taft Hotel, the sheriff was at the back door of the Shubert Theatre ready to impound the scenery and costumes just six hours before opening-night curtain. Investor Bill Richardson had to hand deliver cash before the sheriff withdrew. Joan cried from relief when she saw Richardson, giving him a bear hug and a big kiss. To everyone's glee, the show had been jury-rigged sufficiently to look good and the New Haven reviews were exceedingly positive. Business was strong, and the Boston expenses were recouped. When *As the Girls Go* opened at the Winter Garden Theater in New York, reviews were mixed, but public demand turned it into a hit.

President Truman, basking in his "Dewey Defeats Truman" moment, was amused by the premise of *As the Girls Go* and invited Mike and Joan to a White House ball. At the black-tie affair, Mike avoided the president, wishing to spare him the embarrassment of not remembering the name of Joan Blondell's husband. As the Todds were dancing, Mike felt a tap on his shoulder. It was Harry Truman. "What's the matter, Mike? Why don't you say hello? Are you stuck up, now that you have another hit on Broadway?"

Joan returned to Irvington and continued decorating, adding furniture to the dining room and library. The kids were often on their own, enjoying astronomical weekly allowances of fifteen dollars for Norman and ten dollars for Ellen. Still, there was rarely a moment when everyone was happy. Norman was given a .22-caliber pump-action rifle and a motor scooter by Dick Powell for his fourteenth birthday, and he couldn't help but wonder if he was supposed to use the rifle on his stepfather then flee on his new set of wheels. He had grown attached to steady girlfriend Ann McDowell, a sweet-natured Westchester County native. She was from a blue-collar family, her father worked in the nearby Chevrolet plant, and they lived in an apartment over a plumber's shop. They welcomed Norman, who was drawn to the warmth of a guileless, unpretentious family far removed from the madness of theater or filmmaking.

There was a strike in Hollywood, leaving Joan's studio electrician brother, Junie, out of work. Todd gave him a job as stage manager on *As the Girls Go*, with Junie occupying the second Irvington guest apartment with Gretchen and their eight-year-old daughter, Kathy. To Joan's delight, Junie's congenial demeanor won him admirers on the East Coast. "Ed Blondell was a goodhearted extrovert who liked to have a few drinks at neighborhood taverns," recalled Mike Junior. Kathy struggled against a hatred for Todd Senior, and her parents shared her feelings. They actively prevented her contact with him.

Neither the presence of the Blondells nor the success of *As the Girls Go* made for a happier life in Irvington. Joan managed to get out of her duties as a "Jewish fishwife" long enough to guest star on *Studio One* and *The Ford Theater*, two radio anthology shows. An exchange with film director Robert Wise, RKO executive Sid Rogell, and studio owner Howard Hughes points to Blondell's waning marketability and the high price of her marriage to Todd. Judging from Joan's terrific performance in *Nightmare Alley*, Wise and Rogell wanted to cast her in their tough, low-budget crime drama *The Set-Up*. When the idea was pitched to Hughes, he said, "What's wrong with those two guys? Blondell looks like she's been shot out of the wrong end of a cannon now!"

As the Girls Go did well into the early months of 1949, but business fell precipitously by summer. It closed for the season, then reopened in September at the smaller Broadway Theatre, where it barely met its payroll. Concurrently, Mike and Joan did not mingle with the Westchester crowd. Joan socialized only with already established friends, including actresses Betty Bruce and Glenda Farrell. She was still close to Gloria in California, they talked at least once a week, and she was thrilled when her sister met, courted, and wed handsome ad man Victor Hunter. But Joan's world was narrowing. The problem was fame; whenever she went into town she was approached for conversation and autographs. She had never been so exoticized while living in the show business capitals, and the experience was unsettling. Church, grocery stores, and school functions were out of the question.

Work pressures, the never-ending debts, and the exile to Irvington all led to Todd's continued mental deterioration. He became irrationally jealous when Joan spent time with others. "He would hear Joan laughing on the telephone with her family or friends, or she would casually refer to one of them in conversation, trying to cheer him up with an amusing incident, and this would only irritate him," said Mike Junior. "Joan was scrupulously careful never to force their company on him, and later, catering to his paranoid jealousy, she kept her contacts with them out of his sight and hearing. Her sensitivity to his feelings was wasted. At first he made little jokes. These soon degenerated into snide remarks, until finally he was provoking vitriolic arguments about the attention she paid to them."

By 1949, Todd's rages were occurring at least once a week, and the children were witness. "I am sure he never struck her, but his verbal abuse was so loud and profane that it seemed more vicious and intimidating than a physical assault," wrote Mike Junior. "Joan put up a minimum of defense and quietly tried to reason with him. When it became apparent that there was no deflecting his anger, she simply endured his abuse as long as she could. When she was no longer able to hold back her tears, she would lock herself into the sewing-sitting room next to Ellen's bedroom." Joan often made excuses. "Michael had another nightmare," she told her children over breakfast. She said he was like "a pathetic child sometimes" who woke up sweating and hysterical, haunted by his first wife.

There were ongoing humiliations as well as assaults. When Todd lost a pair of cufflinks and accused Joan of misplacing them, she searched all over the house and into the garbage cans. When that failed, she degraded herself by scrounging through the city dump to no success. "She seemed to spend a lot of time picking up his used linen handkerchiefs, monogrammed imported silk underwear, cashmere socks, and $500 suits from wherever he had thrown them," wrote Ellen. "Some nights I would awaken when Mom and Mike's fights left their bedroom and spilled into the hall. It was usually a terrified voice saying 'don't wake the children, Michael,' that woke me up. I would listen in the dark and root for Mom until my heart slowed down." Norman remembered a fight one night: "[it] went out into the hall and my mother was screaming to me to please come help, that Mike was trying to kill her. She had a toy gun and was trying to pull the trigger. There was a lot of adrenaline pumping. I think my mother thought it was a life or death situation." When Norman came down from the top floor with his .22 in hand, Mike backed off.

When in the presence of other men, Joan was not wholly a tremulous victim. *As the Girls Go* company manager David Lawlor noted that she did not always negotiate Mike's temper. He said, "In my book each gave the other the devil's due." Lawlor was in the Irvington kitchen before a Broadway opening when the Todds had a huge altercation, and Joan finished it by shoving her homemade cheesecake, which was reputed to be delicious, into Mike's face. She then plastered the mess into his dress shirt and tuxedo. She left the room, he followed, changed, and then got into a waiting limousine with Lawlor but without Joan.

Author friends Frances Marion and Anita Loos visited Irvington, voicing a desire to write a stage play for Joan to get her back in business. They were upset by the Todds' domestic scene, described by Marion as "clap trap bedlam." The house was forever occupied by one or another creative type who was working for Mike at the time. "This kept [Mike] winging in all directions, his body a network of coiled springs," wrote Frances. "He paced back and forth, snapping out orders or else sprawled on a sofa, cigar in one corner of his mouth, a telephone in each hand, calling London, Hollywood, Miami, or Rio until he practically had girded the earth."

Joan slid into the Old School expectations of a woman sacrificing her professional life to take care of her man, and this troubled Frances. It wasn't that dutiful wife was an unseemly role, but here it was given to the wrong man for the wrong reasons. "Joan was whizzing around the high English house catering to Mike's guests," recalled Frances. "Trays were constantly being shuttled from the kitchen in the main house to the beehive in the guest house by the 'short order cook,' as Joan called herself. She looked desperately tired in the midst of this hard work and confusion, but managed to give the impression that she was happily married to that volatile madcap, Mike. 'He's a genius,' she said proudly. 'There's no showman comparable to him. His mind is like a string of firecrackers, a new idea pops every moment.' "

Joan could act the part of happy homemaker through the worst storms of her marriage. She never tried to divide Mike from his son, nor speak harshly of Mike to her children. "Joan was kinder and more affectionate than he had ever known her to be," wrote Art Cohn. "She massaged his feet and back, which were aching from the physical and emotional strain."

"You're a pro," Mike said admiringly.

"After all, I was the star of *Model Wife*," she replied through her toothsome smile.

Another fight spilled from the master bedroom into the dark second floor hallway late one night. "I'll show you, you fat ugly slob!" said Mike as he hauled Joan out of the bedroom in her robe and slippers. A growl accompanied the threat, with Joan saying, "No, Sandy, no!"

"Get him off of me! Get him off of me!" screamed Mike, as the collie leapt. "He's trying to kill me! That dog attacked me, he tried to kill me! I'll kill him, your dog's vicious, just like you! Get him outta here."

Soon after that Sandy disappeared. A distraught Joan called the police and nearby kennels, then ran newspaper and radio ads offering a one-hundred-dollar reward for his return. A few weeks passed before Sandy's collar and decaying corpse were found. The incident occurred in the summer when Norman was in California visiting his father. Sandy was his dog, and when he got off the return train at Irvington, there was a black-faced boxer puppy ("Booberboy of Yankee Place") waiting there as Sandy's replacement. Joan tearfully informed Norman that Sandy had been hit by a car on a quiet stretch of road leading out of town. Norman believed this story for years until Ellen told him that Mike had poisoned Sandy, then thrown his body into a swamp at the far corner of the estate.

Sister Gloria and her husband, Victor, were living in Los Angeles and expecting their first child in 1949. When the pregnancy was in critical trouble, Katie left Irvington and sped cross country to be with her daughter. To appease Mike's jealousy, Joan stayed at Irvington but was thoroughly distracted. Wearing the brown tweed coat of Mike's that reminded her of her father, she paced the grounds between the terrace and the Hudson. She alternated prayer with tears as Katie reported that Gloria was nearing death from blood loss. Katie raged and prayed over Gloria, who survived. Gloria's child did not. Before the little girl was cremated, and her mother had a hysterectomy, she was named Joan.

The dynamics of a complex sister relationship were now established for life. Both would love each other absolutely, but each would long for what the other had. Gloria had a sweet, devoted, handsome life partner in Victor Hunter. He loved Gloria and they teamed up for good. Joan could never understand why they fought. "If I had a man like Victor in my life, I'd never get upset," she used to say. But Gloria never had a surviving child, and never adopted, so the glorious burden of motherhood eluded her. She was emotionally and physically destabilized by the hysterectomy, which in the late 1940s came without hormone therapy. Gloria also took no pain killers, since she had many allergies. The sum results made her frequently choleric, even violent on occasion. She would not know the implacable bond of parent to child, but she kept her rollicking sense of humor as she exercised her talent at painting and sculpture. Both Joan and Gloria were imprinted with what they had and did not have in their lives and what they perceived the other to be. They worshipped each other, they would die for each other, and they raged at each other.

Anita Loos never got around to writing a vehicle for Joan. But she did give her blessing to Joan essaying the lead in her stage play *Happy Birthday* in the summer of 1949. Milton Stiefel, longtime producer at the Ivoryton Playhouse in Connecticut, assembled the production, then sold it as a package deal to his colleagues. From Ivoryton, *Happy Birthday* moved to various Northeastern hamlets such as Fairhaven, Lakewood Park, Coonamesset,

Marblehead, and Fitchburg. Joan, in her first stage appearance since *Something for the Boys,* was luminous.

It was in Princeton that a well-publicized incident exposed the tensions of the Todd marriage. According to one account, theater manager Harold J. Kennedy scolded Joan for using foul language in earshot of others. This enraged Todd, who lunged at Kennedy, while Blondell struck union deputy Richard Bowler with a hand mirror. Kennedy and Bowler then allegedly lodged a complaint against Blondell to Equity. "The original story was that Mike Todd had beaten me up for reprimanding Miss Blondell," said Kennedy. "Then there was a story that Miss Blondell had hit me, and a counter story that I had hit her. In trying to slough it all off, Miss Blondell told the *New York Times* that she had merely thrown a piece of Kleenex at me and that was how the tabloid dubbed the story 'The Battle of the Kleenex.' What actually happened was that through a weird chain of circumstances Mike Todd hit Miss Blondell."

Joan was unsuccessful in quieting the press. Nobody bought the line about Kleenex. Blondell's, Todd's, and Kennedy's mugs were spread over the front pages of the scandal sheets. Kennedy asked Equity to suspend Blondell from playing summer stock and filed assault and battery charges against Todd. "Miss Blondell used foul and abusive language on my cast and hurled a mirror at me," charged Kennedy. "Todd hit Miss Blondell twice and choked me. I managed to get away but Todd chased me down the aisles of the theater and hit me over the head with a chair."

Todd had a different story, saying Kennedy greatly exaggerated the incident.

"Did you strike Joan?" asked a newspaperman.

"*I* hit Joan? I'd be afraid," answered Todd.

"What did happen?"

"A girl in the cast was canned. Joan didn't want her to leave until the end of the run because she didn't want to rehearse a new actress. Kennedy came to me and changed the whole thing around. I jumped down his throat. He locked himself in his office and called the riot squad. Then he hired a six-foot-six bodyguard."

"Did Joan curse the cast and throw a mirror at Kennedy?"

"Positively not!" avowed Todd. "She might have said 'gosh' or 'darn it,' but that's all. She started to throw a wadded paper at him but I told her not to. If she threw it when my back was turned, I'm sorry. She positively did not hit him with a mirror. That would have been bad luck."

After the *Happy Birthday* contretemps, and when Mike was out of town, Joan had dinner with Clark Gable. He knew Joan was unhappy and advised her to leave Mike for the sake of her mental and physical well-being. He then surprised Joan by proposing marriage. In a halting voice, he told her she had always reminded him of his late wife. "You're the only woman I know who could replace Carole in my life," he said. Joan was moved by the display, but gently stated she did not want to replace his wife and doubted she ever could.

Life at Irvington continued to disintegrate, mostly due to tempers and inattention. Once Joan began to work again, she fell into the familiar routine of being gone from home for long periods. Jemmen-on-the-Nut was emptying. Junie had moved back to California with Gretchen and Kathy when television work became available. Katie was living on the West Coast with Gloria and Victor, trying vainly to pull her daughter out of the depression of a late-term miscarriage and sterilizing operation. She was also smarting from a spat she had with Joan that left them estranged. Katie believed that Joan wasted her affections on Mike, and she had told her so.

Joan's great reception in *Happy Birthday* led to a touring production of the darker play *Come Back, Little Sheba* in late 1949. Ellen traveled with her and had a walk-on delivering a telegram. She was awed at her mother's talent and commitment. Joan arrived a full two hours before curtain to prepare and insisted on absolute quiet in her dressing room as she got inside her pitiable, destructive character. "She never gave the same performance twice," said Ellen. "When her drunken husband, Ian Keith, chased her across the stage with an axe, the audience always gasped and would sometimes even scream. No matter how many times I watched that violent scene, her terror would raise the hair on my scalp."

Christmas 1949 and a January holiday to Golden Beach, Florida, were the last times the family was united. The holiday was festive, and Florida was a welcome relief from the Northeastern winter, but the Todds were on borrowed time. Frances Marion wrote a eulogy of sorts to their marriage: "Mike was the most driven and demanding human being I had ever met, a megalomaniac, a schizophrenic Don Quixote, and a showman extraordinary. Yet he was a fascinating man in many ways, most of them hard to fathom—or to forgive at times. For eight years Joan followed Mike's blazing trail through success and failure, through high hopes and utter despair. She still loved him when she could no longer endure living with him while trying to bring up her own two children."

In early 1950, after the Florida trip, Joan and Mike flew to Paris to do reconnaissance for *Peep Show*, a new Todd musical concoction with a "French flavor." Owing to her paralyzing fear of flying, Joan combined Nembutal and sherry one hour before takeoff, then knocked back three slugs of whiskey. The results were sublime: Joan reported that she "did not open even one big blue eye till [they] arrived at Orley Field, Paris!!" Checking into the Ritz, the Todds surveyed Paris as tourists for the first time. Joan was dazzled by its "great beauty," but she was candidly unflattering in a letter to Gloria. "I was sick as a dawg the whole trip," she wrote. "After about six days in Paris, when things started erupting from all ends I had to have a doctor. Docteur said I was no sicker than most Americans are for the first few weeks." When Joan wasn't wobbly, the Todds wandered through the streets and were amused to come across the Rue de la Blondelle in the Red Light District. Joan loved Paris, but she reported miserable conditions still present five years after D-Day, whereby "the beauties lucky enough to be 'kept' *all* take to the streets or else they'd have nuttin' to feed themselves with—very pathetic!" She did not suffer guilt bred from privilege, telling Gloria, "Oh Lovey—what things they have. Nowhere in America do you see such linens, silver, laces, perfumes, dresses, hats, jewelry."

The flight from Paris to London was short but gruesome. A plane just one hour earlier than the Todds' crashed and killed twenty-eight, while theirs was lost in the fog over London for three hours and running out of fuel. To heighten her displeasure, Joan was "peed over, interviewed, and photographed the clock around for the three days we spent in London. Took Churchill right off the front pages! You'd think I was, at least, Cary Grant!" Finally she started home without Mike, who went on to do business in Germany, Italy, and Belgium. As if the fates conspired against Joan, storms delayed the return passage by twenty hours on a six-day return voyage. She docked in New York on 10 February 1950, happy as never before to be on dry land. Mike was due home on 2 March.

If the trip to Europe was meant to realign a destructive marriage, it did not succeed. The early desire to be an intact family collapsed as Joan and Mike traveled frequently, Mike Junior went away to college, and Norman spent days at a time with his girlfriend. Ellen's most frequent companion was her horse, and her abhorrence of Todd compounded the alienation everyone felt. "Ellen and I both loved our mother a lot in very different ways," said Norman. "When all of the agony she brought with her spilled over to her kids, it was overwhelming. The turmoil that surrounded her was too much to bear. As a kid, you either let it envelop you or you get up on higher ground."

With hundreds of painful moments swirling in Joan's mind, the actual end of the marriage came quietly. There were no broken dishes, no bruises, and no firearms. Mike simply crossed an invisible line that signaled to Joan that her children, particularly her daughter, might be in danger. Mike had never directly abused Norman or Ellen, but Joan no longer felt assured that he would keep his distance. Joan believed she caught Mike fleetingly leer at Ellen's newly adolescent body, and at that moment she knew it was time to leave.

CHAPTER 8

Solo Rites

An actor's life is finally one of rejection. If you're bitchy and talented and have had, let's say, a break, you can sail along for quite a few years. But then, no matter how many service stripes you have and no matter how smoothly you've transferred yourself into character roles, rejection, depression, panic, hurt, bewilderment, even fury is "your treat."
—Joan Blondell, *"Tick Tock, an Actor's Life"*

Joan moved quickly toward a premeditated escape. She packed mostly clothes and costumes, then stored the trunks and suitcases in a tarp-covered trailer with her Uncle Ernie and Aunt Mae in Brooklyn. Norman was spending extended time at a friend's house, but Ellen would be leaving with her mother. The night was animated by fear, as everything had the potential to wake Mike and alert him to Joan's flight: the firing ignition, rotating tires on gravel, moonlight, and the low tree branch that made a scratching sound on the hood of the Cadillac convertible. Joan did not turn on the headlights until the car faced away from the house and was many yards down the drive. As planned, she drove to Brooklyn, hooked up the trailer, and headed west with a sleeping Ellen spread on top of more suitcases piled in the backseat.

The trip was a noxious mix of deprivation and jangled nerves. Joan soon found that she could not drive over fifty miles an hour or the trailer

153

would sway dangerously. In a moment of obvious symbolism, she also discovered that the wobbly trailer prohibited her from backing up. When she hallucinated a monkey on the road and screeched to a stop, she knew she had to sleep. Joan's rest in a seedy motel was interrupted by Ellen screaming. She had almost swallowed a potato bug that dropped out of the faucet and into her drinking glass. "Let's go," said Joan, and soon they were back in the car and on the road again. With affected voice and downcast eyes, Joan went unrecognized when they stopped to eat or fill the tank. They arrived in Las Vegas in five days and checked into a dark corner room of the Twin Oaks Motel. Ellen was enrolled in school, but Joan had to stay hidden so Mike could not find her.

Joan was in Las Vegas for six weeks, long enough to qualify for residency, endure sunstroke, and be awarded a divorce. Through it all, she was unnerved by despair. "The things that hurt my personal relationships were the things that were most devastating, not the ups and downs of my career," she said in summarizing the lowest moments of her life. There was creeping self-doubt to consider as well. What was wrong with *her* that three marriages ended badly, this one worst of all? "I was ashamed of divorce," she said. "After my third divorce, I knew I couldn't go through it again." In court, Joan originally sought payment by Mike of one hundred thousand dollars in cash which she claimed to have loaned him. By 8 June, when the divorce was being finalized, she no longer asked for alimony, a cash settlement, or property. Charging mental cruelty, emotionally and physically spent, she just wanted out. With dwindling money, Joan and Ellen moved on to LA, staying with Gloria and Victor for a week.

The Hunters offered an emotional oasis of sorts as Joan set about finding a place to live. Ignoring every rule of public image maintenance and drawing on the memory of a childhood without privilege, she rented two trailers at Paradise Cove off Highway 101 in Malibu. The setting on a bluff high above the Pacific was spectacular, though conducting business at the lodge pay phone was inconvenient. If a trailer park represented extreme downsizing from Irvington, at least Todd was far away and unable to do immediate harm.

Joan and the children quickly grew to prefer their new way of life. Ellen marveled at her mother's low-cost decorating. When Norman visited, he learned to surf. Dinners (their favorite was chili and garlic bread) on the outdoor picnic table with an ocean view were more casual and less tense than anything at Irvington. Lizards and jack rabbits were frequent guests. "I like a trailer better than a mansion in lots of ways," Joan told a reporter after her fear of Todd's reprisals abated. "It's easier to take care of. There's not so much to dust." She even came to appreciate the unique culture of this new kind of living. "We have big [gossip] sessions in the showers and the laundry room. They're all talking about one of the women who sees her boyfriend while her kids are down at the beach. Just like Hollywood."

She retained Hillard Elkins, a William Morris agent whose job in part was to make sure Mike Todd did not further harass Joan. Todd called Elkins several times each day, trying to find her. "It took a long while for that business to calm down," recalled Elkins. "She was a very strong personality, and very certain that she must keep away from Mike. Some of her quotes when she was trying to avoid him are colorful but not printable." Mike was slow to face the inevitability of Joan's lost affections. His good friend Eddie Fisher said, "A lot of people believe [Joan] was the real love of his life. I could understand that. As Mike would say, she was a great dame."

Forty-three-year-old Joan was eager, borderline desperate, to find work. She had gained weight, and that plus her age meant romantic leads now went to younger stars. She had been off the screen for three years, certainly enough time for audiences to abandon interest in an actress so associated with bygone times. Roles were not immediately forthcoming, but in the summer of 1950, Elkins secured her fifth-billed participation in a bit of whimsy at Fox called *For Heaven's Sake*, starring friend Joan Bennett. For her efforts she was guaranteed four weeks' work at twenty-five hundred dollars per week. Joan was beguiling in her small role as an urbane playwright. In the intervening years since *Nightmare Alley*, she had acquired a knowing intelligence tempered with an attractive new maturity in her face. Due in part to her cigarette habit, her voice took an appealing descent into lower registers. Too bad, then, that *For Heaven's Sake* was largely ignored by audiences.

In the fall of 1950, Joan was in New York to attend to business, including the sale of Irvington. On 20 October, the estate was sold to real-estate developer David Bogdanoff. Two days later, there was an auction of much of the contents. Joan's collection of early American glass, furniture, oriental rugs, and continental porcelain all went to the highest bidder. In between these grim events, Joan agreed to meet with Mike, which gave him the opportunity to pour on the romance as ardently as he had during *The Naked Genius*. Brazen even by his standards, he took her to dinner and theater *à deux*, introducing her as "the former and future Mrs. Todd." When Mike Junior joined them at the Stork Club, the former Mr. and Mrs. Todd appeared happy and relaxed. What was going on? "The whole situation struck me as perverse," wrote Mike Junior. "Why hadn't they achieved this kind of serenity and developed such confidence in each other during their marriage? Now, when all our lives had been disrupted and our marvelous home sold, it seemed a little late for a reconciliation. . . . How dare they disrupt my life, and Ellen's and Norman's and then get back together as if nothing untoward had happened." Mike and Joan came to see the effect their behavior had on their children, and they finally ended all romance.

An impecunious Joan had to scrounge for any work. Unfortunately for her, she returned to a changed industry. A 1948 Supreme Court decision forbid Fox and others to own chains of exclusive theaters, delivering the death blow to the studio system that nurtured (or entombed) Joan before the war. Television and Joseph McCarthy's red baiting further destabilized the movie business. With no prestige offers forthcoming, Joan did a battery of guest spots on early television shows beginning in the fall of 1950. There was *The Colgate Comedy Hour* on NBC with funny man Bobby Clark, former star of *As the Girls Go*. Todd produced, while Joan was given little to do but be decorous. She did *This Is Show Business* with Rudy Vallee on CBS. On *Penthouse Party*, a New York TV variety show, she whipped up a casserole on camera. She appeared on the game shows *Kollege of Musical Knowledge* and *What's My Line?*

She looked unrehearsed in her skits on the live variety show *Don McNeill's TV Club*. Being ill-prepared in the knockabout world of early television was more comically rewarding on *The Frank Sinatra Show*, where studio audiences loved seeing actors flub their lines and break character. Such was the case in a skit with Joan as lovely Princess Black Root of the Peroxide tribe.

Jerry Wald and Norman Krasna, the producer-screenwriter team that had established an independent production unit at RKO, sent Joan a script called *The Blue Veil*. Wald was an old friend, having collaborated on the screenplays of a few so-so Blondell pictures at Warners. But *The Blue Veil* was different; in the script, Joan's character was labeled "faded." She recoiled. "When I saw the word it turned me off," she said, "but I could see the 'faded' just around the corner. I knew my cute little glamour girl days were over. I quickly went into character roles and beat them to the punch." That one bout of pragmatism may very well have ensured Joan's tremendous career longevity. She was now somebody's mother instead of somebody's cookie. Time and the searing Todd years had rearranged the molecules of her face. "The only right thing I ever did was when I looked at myself in the mirror in 1951 and the rosebud lips weren't quite as upturned and there was that line between the eyes," she later said. "I told my agent to get me anything that said 'aged.' I'm not going to have anything lifted so, why not, I might as well play the fallen-faced dames."

In April of 1951, she undertook her "faded" supporting role in *The Blue Veil* as the neglectful show-business mother of twelve-year-old Natalie Wood. As a saccharine, episodic yarn, *The Blue Veil* boasted impressive *dramatis personae*, including Jane Wyman, Charles Laughton, Everett Sloane, and Agnes Moorehead. Joan's numbers were choreographed by none other than Busby Berkeley. Wald's bouquet of roses in Joan's dressing room, and the gift of a meaty role, further enamored Joan to the experience. So, too, did great notices. "Miss Blondell dazzles as the fading star—her best part since *A Tree Grows in Brooklyn*," wrote *Variety*. "Miss Blondell wows the audience with a parade of songs while her portrait of a show business wheel horse is enchantingly mannered," wrote the *Hollywood Reporter*.

The Blue Veil was quite an eyewash. Wyman played a self-sacrificing nanny who softened families lacking in tenderness. Joan added needed vinegar to a movie drowning in molasses, but she was not merely a diversion from sentimentality. She invested her downward-spiraling character with a barely contained panic and fear. Wald and Krasna were so pleased with her performance that they announced plans to cast her as a beauty-parlor operator for *High Heels*, their upcoming musical film.

High Heels was never made, and despite raves for *The Blue Veil*, Joan did not appear in another movie for five years. Her strategy of embracing age would find rewards later on the screen, so for now she turned to theater. Immediately after *The Blue Veil*, Ellen accompanied her mother on an encore tour of *Happy Birthday*. Joan called its author, Anita Loos, and asked if she might write in a role for Ellen. Loos graciously added a character, giving Ellen three lines, a laugh, and her Actor's Equity card as a result. Still, Ellen's interests were elsewhere. While appearing at the Redmond Arena Theater in Birmingham, Alabama, she fell in love with a hackney pony named Little Black Imp. Joan had an aversion to anything equestrian, but she faithfully took Ellen riding every day before the performance.

Joan's desire to offer stability to her children accounts for yet another cross-country move. Through contacts with friends, she met a builder who was a big Joan Blondell fan, and he helped her get a small house on White Birch Ridge in affluent Westport, Connecticut, for next to nothing. There was a birch forest with glades and swamps behind the backyard and a good school nearby for Ellen. Once again she tried to make a home for Norman and Ellen, but smoldering bitterness and the rage of young adulthood prevented it. Ellen played hooky and fell behind in her courses. Her and Joan's happiest chore was caring for a Shetland sheepdog named Lucky, while Norman enrolled at the elite Lawrenceville Prep in New Jersey, where Mike Todd Jr. had recently graduated.

Joan's frustration with men, or the depressed state of her career, may explain a destructive night early in her residency in Westport. With Gloria visiting at Christmas, seventeen-year-old Norman threw a blowout party with girlfriend Ann. He got drunk and trashed the downstairs rumpus room, leading to altercations with the reunited buddies from his high school football team. Norman threw one fellow so high he left heel marks on the ceiling. Then Norman passed out, and when he came to his aunt Gloria was kneeling over him, pounding on his chest. She was in the midst of one of her postoperative tantrums, screaming, "You've got to decide whether you're going to be with your mother or that bitch! We know you're fucking her!" Joan was more subdued, but made no effort to calm her sister. Both agreed Ann could not see Norman. Believing his mother's and aunt's behavior was irrational and unfair, Norman predictably enough sided with his girlfriend. "The greatest tragedy of our relationship is that we lost our sense of humor," said Norman. "There was a distance." He returned to Lawrenceville, and the episode was never spoken of again. Joan did not torture herself over the occasion, nor did she labor to shield her children from the harsh realities of life. "They grew up in Hollywood," she reasoned. "Fruit ripens awful fast there. They practically start dating the minute they are potty trained."

In early 1952, Joan wowed full houses in another tour of *Come Back, Little Sheba*. The drama's mewling Lola Delaney was arguably playwright William Inge's most indelible creation, and Joan was magnificent in the part. Sadly, her acting gymnastics went largely unnoticed among journalists and producers, while the 1952 film version won an Oscar for its star, Shirley Booth. Joan, meanwhile, "had come the familiar route from ingénue to leading lady to character parts," wrote Art Cohn. "Few came to interview her anymore. Her name was in lower case." Even a Best Supporting Actress Academy Award nomination for *The Blue Veil* failed to generate interest. "Nothing pleased us more than your getting that nomination for *Blue Veil*," cabled Jerry Wald and Norman Krasna. "We are certainly going to do everything we can to win for you but in the meanwhile we couldn't be happier." Joan was on tour with *Sheba* when the Oscar ceremony was held in March, and Bette Davis was at the Pantages Theatre to accept on her behalf. Davis applauded politely as the Oscar went to Kim Hunter in that penultimate hothouse drama *A Streetcar Named Desire*. Joan had no jobs confirmed after the tour and wondered if *The Blue Veil* was a benediction to her film career.

Since Joan was not maintaining sufficient employment in New York, Westport became an impractical base. She returned to LA with Ellen, where she found a sun-drenched apartment on Olympic Boulevard in West Los Angeles, closer to the studios than the trailers in Paradise Cove. Ever the domestic wizards on a dime, she and Gloria went shopping at Acron for inexpensive furniture. While Norman was away at Lawrenceville, Ellen grew closer to Joan and alternatively played her daughter, adviser, and long-suffering best friend. "My life was locked to hers when the divorce came. After that, we didn't have much of a home, we traveled a lot, and lost friends," she said. "I later realized that we had an unhealthy, interdependent relationship, nothing ill-intended, but out of mutual need. She always did the best she could and it was impossible to ever get angry at her. She tried so hard to make everything wonderful for me, but the over-sheltered confinement and the very limited social exposure eventually drove me a bit nuts."

Joan was an itinerant worker through much of the 1950s; the latest move to LA did not secure ongoing film or television work. What she landed was often dreary, as when she appeared in a revue for employees of the Bell Telephone Systems. A short stint in Clifford Odets's *The Country Girl* at Quarterdeck Theatre in Atlantic City followed. She became one of many name actors to perform in the summer playhouses dotting the eastern seaboard. During a surge of interest for live theater, dozens sprang up in tiny hamlets, from Surrey, Maine, to Cherokee, North Carolina. Though quality varied, world premieres as well as revivals were traveling with the hopes of being tagged for Broadway. Loyal fans were not dissuaded by granite-hard seats, weird acoustics, overpriced lemonade, and ravenous mosquitoes. The bigger threats were rain, hurricanes, and television, but most theaters turned a profit by the end of the summer and kept the cottage industry alive. As one manager put it, "They can sit in the living room and watch Berle, Toscanini, and Pinza for free. It's going to take more than Myrtle Hammerschlog in *Camille* to get them to come to my theater and pay."

Joan was happy to be tapped for the national tour of the musical version of *A Tree Grows in Brooklyn*. She was top billed as Aunt Sissy, just as Shirley Booth was in the original Broadway staging. With the emphasis now on Sissy's multiple attempts at marriage, this version was considerably lighter than Elia Kazan's movie or Betty Smith's novel. With Ellen as assistant stage manager, the show opened at Chicago's Shubert Theater to good reviews and robust business. Joan sang "Love Is the Reason" and "He Had Refinement," among other ditties, and had discovered how to sell a song on charm instead of vocal skill. She maintained that Sissy was a role close to her heart, and the production more than justified the top-end ticket price of five dollars. Still, life on the road came with ample challenges. "Home is where I hang my mother," Ellen once joked.

On 5 October 1952, less than a week after she appeared to advantage on *I Love Lucy*, Gloria woke up in the middle of the night. Somehow she knew that something was terribly wrong. She stood at the top of the stairs, screaming for Victor to get an ambulance to mother Katie's apartment down the street. Gloria was in her nightgown as she ran down the block, where Katie was doubled over from a heart attack. She was driven to St. Joseph Hospital in Burbank, where she told Junie not to worry, that where she was going "it's beautiful and I'm going to be happy." Her last breath, at age sixty-eight, came soon after. For the open-casket service, her body was prepared beautifully, as if sleeping, her hair and makeup done by Gloria.

Katie's last attack was most certainly not her first. Her frequent "heartburn" and her avoidance of doctors may well have hastened her death. When Joan began developing rheumatoid arthritis in the 1950s, she was similarly discreet about her condition. Her reasons may have been more practical, as she feared losing work. As for the role of Christian Science, Joan was less dedicated than her mother in practice. She called on her Christian Science background and summoned a practitioner whenever pain struck, but the second call was always to the doctor.

Joan was inconsolable at Katie's death, in large part from guilt suffered at their estrangement since the Todd marriage. Whatever they fought over seemed so meaningless now, but only in private would Joan allow herself to weep like Niobe and ask forgiveness. There was no time to mourn, for she had nightly responsibilities. *A Tree Grows in Brooklyn* played Chicago, Bridgeport, and Boston before, during, and after Katie's fatal heart attack. If she wanted to support Norman's private education, she could not relinquish her performances and paycheck to the understudy.

Former husbands were never far from Joan's thoughts. Mike Todd was in the midst of a grand movie experiment in widescreen projection called *This Is Cinerama*, which became the third-highest-grossing movie of all time and made Todd a multimillionaire. Dick Powell was enjoying success on an equally high level. He was one of the founders of the pioneering Four Star Television Production Company and was living in show-business splendor in Bel Air with June Allyson. Joan was currently unemployed, visiting New York after the *Brooklyn* tour and apartment-sitting for a friend. It was an unusually hot May night, and she was having trouble falling asleep. She swore that she woke from a half-dream state and faced the spectral image of George Barnes beside the bed. He was trying to speak to her, and as she reached to turn on the lamp his image moved to the other side of the room and disappeared.

Joan was too stirred to sleep that night. Early the next morning Gloria telephoned to tell her that George Barnes had died that night. He was sixty years old and had been admitted to St. Joseph Hospital in Burbank, where Katie had also died. With his death following abdominal surgery, he left four children in various combinations with seven wives.

In September of 1953, Joan was in Texas rehearsing a comic production based on Alfred Kinsey's recent book on female sexual behavior. With such racy material, the Houston mayor barred it from opening in his city. "That kind of entertainment does not meet the esthetic requirement of the city as a precedent to leasing of the city's premises," he said by way of refusing the producer's request to play the public Music Hall or Civic Auditorium.

Oklahoma City, Fort Worth, New Orleans, and Dallas were no more wel-coming, and the show died before it ever saw an audience.

After the Kinsey debacle, the ever-peripatetic Joan took her measly rehearsal paycheck and made preparations to leave Los Angeles as a home base and move to Manhattan. She found an apartment with a terrace for $395 a month on the nineteenth floor at the corner of Sutton Place South and East Fifty-seventh Street along the East River. It was in a large and weighty building, with a facade of red brick and pseudo-classical detailing of the quoins. She gave Ellen the master bedroom and bath, while Joan's wardrobe, makeup, business file folders, and various other professional necessities were well organized in the cramped, airless second bedroom. The contraction of space from Irvington to Sutton Place via Paradise Cove, Westport, and Olympic Boulevard was not alien or overly distressing to Joan. Her childhood life on the road taught her how to reduce material possessions. And still she provided for Norman and Ellen. "She was the milk cow of the family," said Ellen. "She gave and gave and gave and gave." She afforded Sutton Place by the skin of her teeth, traipsing off to Vicksburg, Mississippi, to raise money for tornado relief and coming home overjoyed at having one thousand dollars in her pocket. When the rent was paid, the rest went to a new dress for niece Kathy, Norman's tuition, or a "loan" to one or another needy friend or relative. She despaired when her nephew Sonny announced his engagement and she could not afford a proper gift. In 1954, to help cover medical bills for her Uncle Ernie, Joan hocked the mink coat given to her by Mike Todd.

Dogs were Joan's remedy for loneliness. Norman had taken his boxer, so Joan brought home a stout English pug she saw caged at a farmers' market. She named her adoptee Bridey Murphy, in honor of the fabled nineteenth-century Irish woman who allegedly spoke beyond the grave through a hyp-notized Coloradoan. Joan also found a captivating group of friends and companions. There was talk of marriage to millionaire sportsman and archi-tect Hal Hayes, but nothing came of that. She was seen repeatedly in the com-pany of lawyer Charles Mintz, and was delighted when he secured more child support from Dick Powell. There was dapper, well-read restauranteur Michael Pearman, with a demeanor both delicate and kind. Some of her companions were gay, some were not. Though Joan and her sister would laugh with each other about "fags," she maintained a liberal attitude about sexual orientation. She knew from her ill-advised marriages that the heart wants what it wants, and she judged her friends by character, not by whom they slept with.

Social life in New York kept Joan busy, if not happy. She went out with the great *New York Post* sports columnist Jimmy Cannon, occasionally double dating with heiress Gloria Vanderbilt and Frank Sinatra. Vanderbilt recalls the conversation was always all about Sinatra, leaving her and Joan to do little but smile over their cocktails and cigarettes. Cannon's open adoration of Joan was not returned. "Jimmy Cannon has a big crush, but I haven't," Joan wrote to Gloria. "Talks an ear off me and is a short fat bore—but a gent in good standing around town, so I go out to dinner with him a couple of times a week." Frances Marion stated that "Judy Garland and Joan Blondell were close friends, and though they both had gone through tragic experiences they had a zest for fun and laughter. They used to entertain us by recounting stories of their days in vaudeville, and once they made their entrance at one of my parties, arm in arm, chanting a line familiar to old vaudevillians: 'Here come the actors—laughin' and scratchin'.'" They also shared a deep friendship with makeup artist Dorothy Ponedel. When her precious Dottie was stricken with multiple sclerosis, Joan bribed the hospital staff with chocolate to get her special attention.

Joan also counted actress Norma Crane among her intimates, as well as Mrs. Virginia Zanuck, journalist Adele Rogers St. John, and socialite Liz Whitney Tippett. Nancy Sinatra, first wife to Frank, was "wonderfully kind and generous to a fault, a very dear friend. A most down-to-earth person." But New York society proved to be an inadequate milieu for happiness. Joan was fearful of Mike Todd, forever worried he would hurt someone she loved. She confronted death so many times, and he ingrained such trepidation in her, that she gave up romantic intimacy.

In the summer of 1954, Joan was touring the Northeast with *Happy Birthday*. Looking every day of her forty-eight years, she was in heavy war paint these days: makeup, eyebrows, and lipstick were all thickly applied. Ellen and Norman, now a student a Cornell, were in St. George, Utah, for the filming of *The Conqueror* under the direction of Dick Powell. Their father put them to work: Ellen was in charge of a horse that took her out into the desert to prepare for location shots. Norman worked on the set and dug holes in the sand made radioactive by recent atomic testing. He also doubled as an actor. John Wayne as Genghis Khan says, "You were fortunate to have escaped death." Norman, as an unnamed soldier, replies, "Truly, fortunate, Lord. We had drunk much." He is then hauled off to be executed.

Joan was hurt when Ellen announced her wishes to live at the huge Mandeville Canyon ranch of her father and stepmother. Ellen could exercise her love for horses there, but it was excruciating for Joan to let her go. She was most afraid of Todd's anger, but her second greatest fear was June Allyson's potential to undermine her mothering. Ellen's departure was also a demonstration of an unhealthy dependence Joan had acquired for her daughter. If they were apart, Joan would call daily, express her worry, and unwittingly instill guilt in Ellen for developing independence.

Joan's prolonged career slump of the 1950s was compounded by the unfamiliar anxiety of living alone. She wrote to distract herself, but rarely shared the results. In addition to short stories and poems, she left her thoughts in a spiral, loose-leafed binder. There were pages and pages of biblical quotes in longhand, mostly to do with forgiveness, strength, and God's abiding love. Words from Christian Science founder Mary Baker Eddy were there, too. Most telling were Joan's own writings, which managed to convey familiar thoughts in personal ways. "Home is not merely a house, a flat, a hotel," she wrote. "It is not merely something that can be bought or sold or leased. Home in reality is a mental state, a divine idea in consciousness provided for man by God." Angels are "God's thoughts passing to man," while hatred is "mental gangrene." She believed that "as you think God-like thoughts you will begin to see the world as it is; a place of security, beauty, opportunity."

Joan had particularly bad professional luck when beginning rehearsals in June of 1955 for *A Palm Tree in a Rose Garden*, a dramatic play set in a Hollywood boardinghouse. The tour began in a mouse-infested theater in Mountainhome, Pennsylvania, then moved to Ivoryton, Connecticut, while rising costs and small audiences forced its rustic impresario to get gimmicky. When Joan was to appear at Westport Country Playhouse, the theater offered an $8.80 package deal for out-of-towners including round-trip transportation from New York, a steak dinner, an orchestra seat to the show, and a post-performance highball at a local tavern. The whole deal was moot when a flood canceled the show midweek. When Joan was offered another tour of *Happy Birthday*, the decision to leave *A Palm Tree* was easy.

A flurry of short-term television work did not ease Joan's bill-paying burdens, and she decided to make a vigorous effort to get more lucrative jobs on the big screen. When she heard that June Allyson was to star in *The Opposite Sex*, a glossy remake of the all-female 1939 classic *The Women*, Joan asked June, via Ellen, for a part in the movie. Joan found herself tenth billed, playing a gluttonous, always-pregnant gossip. Shot in early 1956, this was Joan's first movie-screen appearance in five years and her first MGM title since *Adventure* ten years earlier.

Headliners Allyson, Joan Collins, and Dolores Gray did not light up the marquee as did Norma Shearer, Joan Crawford, and Rosalind Russell in the original. In retelling Clare Booth Luce's story of female schadenfreude, producer Joseph Pasternak added men, musical numbers, and widescreen MetroColor. None of these upgrades put the movie over. Joan was the frump of the bunch and was denied the jewels and sexy gowns of her costars. Even so, it was perversely enjoyable for her to play in a movie that had June Allyson's husband being romanced by a scheming young chorus girl. In another inside joke, Joan and Ellen giggled at any mention of "Whimpsy-Poo," their private nickname for Allyson.

On Sunday, 22 July 1956, Norman married longtime girlfriend Ann McDowell in a ceremony attended by twenty-six at Joan's Sutton Place apartment. Since that appalling episode in Westport on New Year's Eve of

1951, Joan had grown to love Ann and see her as another daughter. Gloria had made peace with her nephew and his wife as well. Joy was compounded with the news that Ann was pregnant. Anger at Norman and Ann vaporized when their sex life was consecrated by marriage and parenthood. Joan gave the couple a new car, a coupe with "Ann and Norm—Just dunn it!" sprayed on the back hood. They drove away from the small well-wishing throng near the front doors of Sutton Place to their honeymoon in Myrtle Beach.

Immediately after the empty champagne bottles were collected, Joan went into a touring production of *The Time of the Cuckoo*. As Leona, an American spinster in Italy, she interpreted a third character that had been originated on stage by Shirley Booth. Ellen was living with her mother again and traveled with *Cuckoo*, gamely essaying a small role requiring an Italian accent. When the tour was over, Joan reported to the Sheraton-Blackstone Hotel in Chicago for a Democratic gala for Adlai Stevenson. Harry Truman was there, but Joan did not mingle with him as she did when accompanied by Mike Todd following the success of *As the Girls Go*. Now she was the hired help, telling jokes to the party elite as the opening act of a fund-raiser.

Joan's appearance in *The Opposite Sex* sparked a mini-revival of her film career. To her considerable delight, she was given back-to-back offers for strong supporting roles. In the fall of 1956, she played Eleanor Parker's scabrous whiskey-guzzling aunt in the modestly financed *Lizzie*. It was directed by Hugo Haas, an early independent director-producer-writer-actor well acquainted with shoestring budgets. There was not a shred of vanity in Joan's performance as she shuffled around in an unflattering house robe or dowdy print dresses. She was an authentic drunk, her liquor breath wafting off the screen. She was pleased with her performance in *Lizzie*, calling it her best since *A Tree Grows in Brooklyn*. Unfortunately, the script performs an exorcism in the last reel, turning her into a mealy, sincere caregiver for the convenience of a tidy ending.

She was used to slicker advantage in *This Could Be the Night*, done in black-and-white CinemaScope at MGM. Joan played a bellowing stage mother, but passed through the movie so incidentally that one wonders if the world forgot that she was ever a star. At least one participant remembered. "I grew up with Joan Blondell," said costar Anthony Franciosa. "She was in just about every movie I saw. What I remember of her on *This Could Be the Night* were those wonderful eyes. From across the set I was looking at her, and she was looking at me. I was wondering if I should go say hello. Movie sets can be very cool, not like the theater. No one was paying attention to the fact that we had not met. But something about her demeanor was extremely welcoming. She was very present, a very alive person."

During the shooting of *This Could Be the Night*, Joan went to producer Henry Ephron's New York suite to audition for a prominent role in a topical comedy for Fox called *Desk Set*. The movie's two stars, Spencer Tracy and Katharine Hepburn, were present, and both took an instant liking to her. She was told to report to the set the day after completing *This Could Be the Night*. Money considerations landed the production in Hollywood instead of New York as originally planned, and Joan's twenty-five hundred dollar weekly paycheck was no higher than it was when she made *For Heaven's Sake* for the same studio seven years earlier.

Joan was not well, her newly diagnosed rheumatoid arthritis was flaring, but Hepburn fought to keep her in the movie. Hepburn even arranged for a dog sitter to take care of Bridey Murphy at Sutton Place. Of Tracy and Hepburn, Joan said "I loved working with the two of them. . . . It was a terrific experience to be with them—and no effort at all." She reserved special praise for Hepburn. "I really don't have envy in my gut but I admire Hepburn a helluva lot," she said. "She'll lay into you if she thinks you're not doing the right thing, but we had a good feeling going between us and I have great respect for her." In *Desk Set*, it is not Hepburn's femininity being challenged, as it was in *Adam's Rib* and *Woman of the Year*. This time it is her job that is at risk. The threat comes from Miss Emmy, the Emmarac computer designed to rule the Federal Broadcasting Department's research department. The moral of *Desk Set*, if there is one, is strikingly modern: Robots will never fully replace humans because their brains are ruled by mechanical hearts.

Reviewers decided that Joan Blondell "shines" in her role and was a "fine and earthy counterpart to Miss Hepburn's more intellectual approach." *Desk Set* publicity offered some musing by fifty-year-old Joan on her life thus far: "I don't remember ever taking one (a vacation). I don't plan to. I wouldn't enjoy it. I'd be lost. I only have a holiday when I'm working on a part I like, and I haven't had any other kind in recent years." Of marriage she said, "I'm a three-time loser. My only romance is with my work, and that's a completely satisfactory one. Here I am working with Spencer Tracy and Katharine Hepburn, the two I've always been a fan about, but never worked with before. I haven't a complaint in the world. Who says it's tough for an actress to grow older? Not me! I may have lost my girlish slimness—let's face it, I'm plump—and I'm getting to the bags under the eyes stage, but the parts keep getting better and better, so here's to the onslaught of age!"

This moment in Joan's life was a happy one. She enjoyed professional fulfillment and her children's lives were on track. Ellen was enrolled in animal husbandry classes at a community college, then got a job in the Casting Department at Four Star Television at her father's urging. On 23 February 1957, Norman became an overjoyed father when Ann delivered a girl at Cornell University Hospital. Joan's first grandchild, named Sandra Lynn Powell, was born pink and hearty.

Good fortune followed Joan with the movie she made immediately after Sandy's birth. Shot in March of 1957, *Will Success Spoil Rock Hunter?* proved to be a zesty satire of just about everything modern, loaded with commentary on advertising, consumerism, blondes, television versus the movies, celebrity, sexual politics, breast obsession, executive washrooms, Technicolor, and pampered canines. Joan played Jayne Mansfield's demure secretary, which on paper sounds like the most thankless job in the history of motion pictures. Joan does not have many lines, as most of her scenes are taken up with pithy reactions to the star's misuse of simple English. Considering Mansfield's acting consisted of animal squeals, respiratory affectations, and mammary displays, Joan's command of attention is impressive. She has one highlighted scene in which she delivers a soliloquy on her lost love, a milkman. She deftly balances comedy and drama in barely contained hysteria for the man that got away. When she says she goes to pieces at the sight of half and half, she's funny, but when she suggests that she knows a thing or two about love, she's poignant. It is, in its own quiet and succinct way, a bravura turn.

Hardly anyone noticed. "I have to show them my wares," she said. "I'm taking anything that comes my way. One of these days I'm damned sure somebody will have a mature, important role . . . and I'm going to be ready." Joan's flurry of movie work in 1957 ended as quickly as it began; she would not appear on the big screen again for four years. Meanwhile, however, she boarded a train to New York to meet her first grandchild the moment *Rock Hunter* duties were complete.

Joan was gracious when Mike Todd married Elizabeth Taylor in a small ceremony in Acapulco. She had given up trying to recoup her loans and fought bitter thoughts with biblical quotes when every newspaper in the land reported on the Rolls Royce, the one million dollars worth of jewels, the yacht, and the hundred-thousand-dollar private plane christened *Lucky Liz*. Blondell showed no rancor for Taylor. "She didn't take Mike away from me," she assured, perhaps alluding to the contrasting reality of June Allyson. "Mike and I had been divorced for five years when Elizabeth and he fell in love. I thought he was a very lucky man to have won her. She is probably the most beautiful woman in the world, and a fantastic actress. She is *the* movie star, the last of the great ones." Todd owned a majority interest in *Oklahoma!* and produced the hugely profitable *Around the World in 80 Days*, two films made in the sumptuous widescreen Todd-AO process that he patented. At the 1957 Academy Awards, he was at the pinnacle of earthly success, squeezing his ravishing wife with his left hand and a gleaming Best Picture Oscar for *Around the World* with his right.

Joan had to make do with quieter pleasures, as new father Norman graduated from Cornell with a BA in government and a minor in drama. She was pleased when he and Ann moved to Pacific Palisades in Los Angeles after graduation. She and Gloria put together a cozy apartment to get them started in Southern California. Norman began working as an assistant director before landing a job at his father's Four Star Television Company. When she was not cooing over her new granddaughter, Joan was back at work in the original stage musical *Copper and Brass* with squat comedienne Nancy Walker. The story, written by Walker's husband, David Craig, served as a vehicle for Walker to play a rookie cop out to purge juvenile delinquency from a jazz club. Joan was cast as the mother, a vaudeville hoofer living in the past. The show tried out badly in New Haven, then Philadelphia. When one director was replaced with another, Joan's part got pared down. Morale was low, audiences stayed home with their televisions, and she saw no dignified option but to leave the show following the 3 October performance in Philadelphia. It was a wise move. *Copper and Brass* was a risible flop even before it limped into New York, where it died after thirty-six performances.

Few occasions in Joan's career offer a reminder of the vagaries of show business better than *Copper and Brass* followed by *The Rope Dancers*. Written by radio and television writer Morton Wishengrad, *The Rope Dancers* was a strange, confining drama of a troubled Irish-American couple (Art Carney and Siobhan McKenna) living in a fifth-floor tenement in 1900s New York. Their shame comes from the sixth finger that juts out of their daughter's left hand. Her stern mother refuses surgery, calling the apparition "the finger of God's wrath."

Joan was cast as the sloppy neighbor Mrs. Farrow, a warm creature, all curves and no edges, happily removed from the tormented family's inner circle. The play had a superficial resemblance to *A Tree Grows in Brooklyn*, with its embittered mother, affable but self-loathing father, and tender, sensitive young girl. But it is ultimately more despairing, with the girl's deformity symbolic of a deep sickness. "You know that there's something wrong," said theater historian Miles Kreuger of the experience of watching *The Rope Dancers*. "It was a fascinating, engrossing evening of theater. Joan was fat, blowzy, vulgar, and delightful—the exact opposite of Siobhan."

After previewing in Princeton, Philadelphia, Boston, and New Haven, *The Rope Dancers* had its New York premiere at the Cort Theatre on 20 November 1957. In her first Broadway appearance since *The Naked Genius*, Joan was praised to the heights. "She expresses the sentiment of the part without sentimentality and the vulgarity without cheapness," wrote *New York Times* critic Brooks Atkinson. "[It is] a wonderfully exhilarating and at times affecting performance." Atkinson did not hold back on his enthusiasm for the entire production. "*The Rope Dancers* makes the theater look like a palace of truth again," he wrote.

Even though Joan was on Broadway, and Sutton Place was a quick cab ride home every night, the run of the play was difficult. The Cort Theatre, where Joan appeared in *Maggie the Magnificent* twenty-eight years prior, was in need of refurbishing. Its Louis XVI–inspired marble and plaster work were dulled by a matte of fine dust. Backstage, Joan had to climb two flights of stairs to her tiny dressing room with its cracked water basin and smell of mildew. Not that she made a habit of complaining. "She was very good, utterly professional," said Theodore Bikel, who played a kindly doctor. "This role was a breeze for her. Strip away Joan's fame and affluence and what you got was a simple girl from a simple family and she did very well at that." Bikel came to see Joan as the emotional savior of the production. "She was always a lot of fun, lively, raucous," he said. "She was able to bring conviviality to a play that was frankly very dark. If it hadn't been for Joan making the work environment more palatable, we'd have been overtaken by the mood of the play. Largely because of Joan, we didn't succumb to that. She gave parties, we drank wine, we laughed a lot."

Miles Kreuger remembers the night he saw *The Rope Dancers*: "I went backstage to see Siobhan. I was asked if I'd like to meet Joan Blondell. 'I would *love* to meet Joan Blondell!' I said, knowing her to be one of the most underrated actresses in the United States. We went into her dressing room. She was so sweet. We started talking about her movies. I told her that I loved her in *Gold Diggers of 1933* and *Colleen*. 'I never saw *Colleen*,' she said. 'I'd finish a movie on Friday and begin another one on Monday.'"

The biggest show-business circus of the 1950s was Mike Todd's marriage to Elizabeth Taylor, until Todd bested his own publicity by dying on the hills of New Mexico when the *Lucky Liz* crashed on 22 March 1958. Todd's death was shocking front-page headlines all over the country. NBC-TV's David Brinkley held a special news event with footage of the plane's wreckage. Tuning into the breaking news before a performance of *The Rope Dancers*, Joan could hardly believe Mike was dead. She honestly thought it was one of his publicity stunts.

Much has been written and said of Taylor's magnificent stoicism. She completed her screen performance in *Cat on a Hot Tin Roof* while grieving Todd amidst a media firestorm. In contrast, almost nothing has been noted of Joan's reaction or her quiet fortitude and dedication to performances of *The Rope Dancers*. She offered public condolences to Taylor and canceled an appearance on *The Ed Sullivan Show* scheduled that Sunday, but otherwise kept to business. Too much attention on a previous wife might complicate the myth of an absolute love between Todd and Taylor. Not that Blondell sought the attention or suddenly manufactured tender feelings for her abusive late ex-husband. Indeed, she spent the rest of her life keeping a distance from his memory.

The Rope Dancers was an artistic success, but not a commercial one. Consistent with its critical reception, it was nominated for several Tony awards, including Best Play, Director (Peter Hall), Actress (McKenna), Supporting Actor (Bikel), and Supporting Actress (Blondell). It won nothing. The Best Supporting Actress trophy was scooped up by young Anne Bancroft in *Two for the Seesaw*. *The Rope Dancers* was still playing when the awards were handed out in April, but just barely. Great ticket sales were never expected. Running concurrently on Broadway were tuneful mainstays *The Music Man, My Fair Lady,* and *West Side Story* as well as the acclaimed dramas *Sunrise at Campobello* with Ralph Bellamy, *Look Homeward, Angel* with Anthony Perkins, *The Entertainer* with Laurence Olivier, and *The Dark at the Top of the Stairs* directed by Elia Kazan. Considering that dazzling lineup, it might be said that *The Rope Dancers* is a forgotten and worthy gem produced at a time when serious theater *mattered* in the cultural life of America.

The Rope Dancers struggled to get an audience and closed after 189 performances. Joan was grateful for the praise, but the production weighed upon all cast and crew. "It was beautifully written but it *was* sad and I must say that both Art and I were happy when it was over," she said. "It was an awfully damned depressing play to do." Its lasting benefit was the friendship sealed between Joan and Art Carney. On closing night, 3 May 1958, he wrote, "Dear Joan — I want to say a lot of things—but I don't know how to. So—I'll be brief and to the point—*I LOVE YOU MADLY!* I'm going to miss you and pray that it won't be too long before we'll be working together again. We have had a lot of laughs together. . . . Love, Art." Joan was touched by his words, but at present she was distracted. Two days after closing, Norman's wife, Ann, gave birth to a boy, Scott Powell, in Los Angeles.

Ellen met tall, chiseled stunt man Chuck Hayward in 1959. Seventeen years her senior, Hayward was respected in his trade, having worked regularly for John Ford. Soon Ellen and Chuck were dating. Norman became production manager of *Zane Grey Theater*, another TV show produced by Four Star. June Allyson starred in Four Star's aptly titled *June Allyson Show*. Joan was once again cursed by bad timing. If she and Powell were still married in 1958, no doubt there would have been a *Joan Blondell Show* to revive her flagging career. Instead, she did an unsold TV pilot called *The Jacksons* and toured the Northeast in a tent production of *New Girl in Town*, a musical based on Eugene O'Neill's *Anna Christie*. It had lasted on Broadway barely more than a year, but it offered a showy role for Joan as a lovable dockside sot. She was able to steal a few scenes, but the show itself was a failed effort to musicalize a somber play. The chorus loathed the Bob Merrill score and sang off-key renditions of some of the sappier songs backstage as they got into costume and makeup.

New Girl in Town was followed by *Crazy October*, a gothic comedy about an indomitable West Virginian (Tallulah Bankhead) set in a seedy roadhouse. Joan was cast as a middle-aged waitress clinging to the semblance of youth. She had labored heroically to keep an alcoholic Art Carney dry during the run of *The Rope Dancers*, and she faced a similar assignment with Bankhead. It seemed to Joan that Bankhead was always drunk and argumentative with director-writer James Leo Herlihy. To keep Bankhead from getting flummoxed, Joan made her an apron with labeled pockets. It was a gesture meant to lighten tensions backstage, and it worked. Stage manager Ed Strum found the actresses most agreeable to work with. He called Joan "Mother Earth" and said, "If you met her, in two minutes you'd be telling her your life story."

Joan had a marvelous time, though the production never ran smoothly. "My part was better than hers," said Joan, "and I grabbed at it. At first Tallulah really bothered me—I didn't think she was professional. . . . I was very nervous when we started and kept away from her. But after we'd played a half dozen cities and I'd gotten the applause and the notices I realized she never complained . . . even though she was billed above me and Estelle Winwood. In fact she'd often say, after a performance, 'I think I moved on your line,' or 'I don't think I did it right, you didn't get the solid laugh you did before, let's rehearse and see.' She was fantastic. Her sarcasm, drunkenness, and misbehavior in public were all something she put on so as to be talked about. She was a sensitive, lonely woman and I think she wanted to die."

The first performances in New Haven and Washington did not go over well, and 25 October was the announced final performance of what was labeled another road casualty. But Herlihy did a few rewrites while the producers secured a reopening in Detroit. Whatever was lost in its first performances was found over time, and *Crazy October* began a modesty successful national tour. It ran at the Huntington Hartford Theater in Hollywood during holiday season for almost a month. Box office was buoyed by strong word of mouth. One observer during the San Francisco run noted that the production had been "chased by saddened reviewers and not saddened audiences wherever it went. Along the line, Bankhead became more Bankhead, Blondell became more Blondell, and Winwood became more Winwood. They are completely wonderful on stage, to the point where the audience laughs not only at unfunny lines but, from time to time, even before the lines are delivered." Just as the production hit its stride, and all three women were in perfect harmony with each other and their audiences, the show died. Talk of going to New York dried up, and for all its improvements, *Crazy October* was fated to be another road casualty—twice.

While Joan was on the West Coast, she and Bridey Murphy (her dog) visited Norman, Ann, and their two children. Gloria and Victor lived nearby, and Gloria was so enamored of Bridey that she and Victor adopted a male pug named Rocky. Joan wanted Bridey to experience motherhood, and Rocky was the obvious stud of choice. "It was Sunday and the setting was Gloria's house, her lovely den," wrote Joan. "The local veterinarian had given her instructions. Sister and I set the scene. The fireplace was blazing, 'People Will Say We're in Love' was on the stereo, and puffs of steam seemed to be coming from pug nostrils." Alas, it just wasn't happening. After Rocky and Bridey failed at coitus, the vet intervened with artificial insemination.

When Joan and Bridey were back in New York, Joan was told by her vet that Bridey was pregnant. Joan was a mass of anxiety, even canceling work to oversee the bitch's delicate condition. She prepared the closet floor of her guest bedroom with a new cotton quilt and an infrared lamp, while an old playpen was repainted and made ready to house Bridey and her children. The vet made a house call and oversaw delivery while an overwrought Joan paced, alternating consumption of a tuna sandwich, Bloody Marys, and cigarettes. "I itched," she said. "I cried on the terrace, I mourned and banged on the elevator door, I bawled in the bathroom, the dining room, the living room, the bedroom." At final count, Bridey delivered seven healthy pups.

Then came the taping of an Edward R. Murrow *Person to Person* interview, with the host speaking to Joan via a television connection into her apartment, 19D at Two Sutton Place. With his avuncular manner and ubiquitous cigarette, Murrow opened by saying that "Actress Joan Blondell, in reviewing her long Hollywood career, insists she has played the role of a chorus girl in just about every way but standing on her head." It was 10 April 1959, and Joan was reclining serenely on a comfortable chair in her living room, stroking new mother Bridey. As herself on camera, Joan combined smiling girlishness with a backbone of granite. "I think you need an awful lot of flops to have the joy of success," she said in her assessment of the rigors of show business. She then rose to conduct a tour of the artwork hanging on her walls. There was a childhood drawing by Ellen and a painting Joan did of a horse's head on a man's body that she signed "Go Van Go." There was a portrait of Ed Blondell in his *Lost Boy* costume and face makeup. Gloria's portraits of Ellen and Joan were hanging, as were photos of Ellen with her horses and Norman graduating from Cornell, his diploma in one hand and his infant daughter, Sandy, in the other.

Into this home tour came Gloria in a tight black dress with ruffled collar, present in New York to assist at the Blondell kennel. They moved into the side room, where Bridey's seven squirming whelps were fed with tiny milk bottles. Joan finished the twelve-minute appearance in front of her full bookcase discussing the manuscript she wrote, she said, about "people that I understand, I hope." It was not autobiographical, but it combined "love and a little murder and chase. I think it's box-officy." As herself, she appeared almost shy and nervous, but amused and engaged, seemingly delighted at this strange intrusion.

"The pugs received more fan mail than I ever did for all my sterling performances laid end to end," said Joan of her appearance on Murrow's show. When she was offered a role in an episode of the well-respected *Playhouse 90* TV show in Los Angeles, she insisted on taking her entire canine brood with her. Thankfully, Gloria, who had recently completed a long stint as Honeybee Gillis on NBC's sitcom *The Life of Riley*, was there to make the trip with them. With the seven asleep on their backs, their little paws jiggled to the rhythms of the train. Finally, Joan and company checked into Hollywood's dog-tolerant Knickerbocker Hotel.

On 14 May 1959, after *Playhouse 90* opened with its familiar announcement, "Live from Television City in Hollywood," Joan was again seen to great advantage. "A Marriage of Strangers" was a kitchen-sink drama with Joan as an over-aged, abandoned mother-to-be. In offering advice to a young neighbor, her voice broke as she talked of a lost marriage and about the giving and sharing inherent in any successful union. Her extended speech is one of her very loveliest acting feats. Her training in the arts of diction, pitch, and carriage are faultlessly united with the internal emotional style that colored much of the best American acting of the 1950s. There is so much raw, unearthed pathos in "A Marriage of Strangers" that watching it feels like peeking through a keyhole.

The late 1950s were creatively fulfilling for Joan. At first glance, her work appears modest, varied, and underreported, the efforts of a former star struggling against the autumn of her career. But *Lizzie, Desk Set, Will Success Spoil Rock Hunter?, The Rope Dancers*, and *Crazy October*, done within a two-year period, illustrate the dazzling range of Joan's ripened talent. She felt the new power in her work, saying that she was now "serious about acting" after giving it secondary importance behind husbands and children. But she was taken for granted by 1959, and her skills were so conclusive that inductive reasoning guaranteed good to great Joan Blondell performances in whatever she was doing. Her excellence had become a foregone conclusion that hardly merited comment anymore.

Though Joan declared a new dedication to her craft, her priorities had not changed so much as they had discreetly shifted. She was still eager to dandle the grandchildren at every occasion. And there were her pugs to consider. She turned down work in England since it meant quarantining them. When the time came to return East, two of them had found new homes. Three others were picked up by good parents in New York, leaving two females, Tulip and Freshness (Fresh for short), still in mother's custody. By now, of course, Joan was madly in love with both but knew that practicality required she keep only one. Tulip went home with a police officer, leaving Joan, Bridey, and Fresh a trio for life.

CHAPTER 9

Love, Matey

To look backward for a while is to refresh the eye, to restore it, and to render it more fit for its prime function of looking forward.
—Margaret Fairless Barber, *The Roadmender*

Playwright William Inge, who served Joan advantageously with *Come Back, Little Sheba*, thought she was a brilliant actress and personally selected her for a seven-month, 110-city national tour of his *The Dark at the Top of the Stairs*. The story of a troubled Oklahoma family in the 1920s featured loquacious, slatternly Lottie Lacey, a character perfect for Joan's colorful theatrics. "It's the kind of role I love," she said, "nice and juicy." When the production managers told Joan she could bring Bridey or Fresh, but not both, she made the wrenching decision to give Fresh to a willing new owner. She wept copiously at her decision and swore that Bridey did, too. Her dependence on those two was extreme and caused the speculation that a pair of canines became surrogate children. Social life offered few rewards, and she reserved any purging for her sister. She wrote to Gloria, "[I] had a night out with Merman, Natalie Wood, Bob Wagner, Jimmy Van Heusen, and my escort Mel Denneli (the wop fag writer). I don't know which is duller, being alone or surrounded by celebs in eye-burning joints. Ya can't win!!"

Little mattered but her dogs. She was so miserable at the loss of Fresh that she told the management she would either take *both* dogs on tour or they could find another Lottie Lacey. Joan got her way. Fresh was reclaimed, and she and Bridey were asleep backstage in their padded brown wicker bed when the *Stairs* company opened in Providence, Rhode Island, on 21 September. The troupe then wound its way though Worcester, Sioux City, parts of Tennessee and Texas, San Francisco, and Seattle into the dawn of 1960.

It was a no-frills tour. The scenery traveled in two trucks in advance of the cast, which was assigned one chartered Greyhound. With Bridey and Fresh reunited, Joan was her usual sanguine, uncomplaining self. "This is the way to see the country," she said. "I've got it easy anyway. They've partitioned off my part of the bus, though the partition is always down. I've got my own bed from home, an easy chair, a desk. I'm even raising plants and flowers. . . . Of course, it's nothing new to me, the road. I feel like I've been on it all my life." Now, as she phrased it, she was a "grandma on the lam." The stop in Seattle brought a torrent of memories. The host theater was the same one Ed Blondell and Company played in vaudeville. "I felt I was a kid—I was little Rosemary again," she said. "Had the devil of a time—nearly blew my lines." She fought the blues for a few days when she learned that the film version of *The Dark at the Top of the Stairs* was being shot during the tour and that Eve Arden was playing Lottie.

Joan was performing *The Dark at the Top of the Stairs* in Los Angeles when Junie had a severe heart attack. Family members shared hospital vigils, and he survived, but the crisis was the culmination of some hard luck. He had gone up against the edge of poverty, and Gretchen had become a heavy drinker, but his sense of humor was still intact. He was currently working as Liberace's lighting director, which was the source of much laughter among the Blondells. Illuminating Liberace, Junie used to say, was no more complicated than lighting a candelabra.

Joan was unbowed by setbacks or the demands of touring. "They tell you the road is dead but this is nonsense," she said. "If you've got a good play, they love you. Everywhere we've gone, they've loved us because they've loved the play. It cuts across all classes of society—audiences in dress clothes and audiences of farmers, they react the same." Joan enjoyed one line in particular that inadvertently commented on her life. In addressing the character of a tormented Jewish teenager, Lottie's tactlessness was fully summarized: "You know what you ought to do?" she asks. "You ought to join the Christian Science Church. Now I'm not a member myself, but I know this Jewish woman over in Oklahoma City, and she was very, very unhappy. . . . But she joined the Christian Science Church and has been perfectly happy ever since." If only happiness was that easy for Joan to find.

When the epic *Stairs* tour at long last ended in April at the National Theatre, Joan immediately set about to prepare for Ellen's upcoming wedding to Chuck Hayward. On Saturday, 28 May 1960, they exchanged vows in an afternoon ceremony at the Sportsman's Lodge in North Hollywood. The family was happy at the union and showed Ellen the proper disrespect. Gloria presented her niece with a huge diaphragm on a doily at her wedding shower. Positioning herself as an expert on marriage, Joan gave Ellen an original poem called "Do's and Don'ts for the Bride-to-Be." Hand written in clear block letters, with margins decorated with sketched flowers, cherubs, and hearts, it was Joan's primer for success. The self-identified "three-time loser" warned against monotony in the bedroom, refusing sex, or holding grudges. Husbands must be reminded when it is time to give household expense money. A wife must smile through menstrual pain and develop thick skin when her husband does not notice how pretty she is. Do not be jealous, and do cultivate feminine mystique. Laugh until you pee. Remember that he will always want a comfortable chair, a place for his pipe, and a book to read. Learn to like his friends, even if you don't. It is not necessary to share politics, but it is necessary to share God. Do not forget to praise his looks and skills in bed. Hold your head high, because you've got a *man!* And, above all, do not fart before the third year.

By 1960, the world came to realize that motion pictures had a history, with the 1930s already referred to as "The Golden Age." Joan found herself a part of that awakening as audiences looked fondly backward. *The King and the Chorus Girl, The Corpse Came C.O.D.,* and *Cry "Havoc"* were all staples on the Late Late Show. *Gold Diggers of 1933* was shown by New Yorker Film Society as "one of the representative Warner Bros. musicals of the depression era." *Blonde Crazy* played at the Museum of Modern Art, and *Dames* at the New School.

Writer Seymour Krim lusted after the Joan Blondell of yore, noting that she "had slung that marvelous ass and those fantastic breasts around long enough on celluloid to enter every straight American male's mental nightlife." He met her at a party in New York, and their association became a short-term friendship. He later drew a melancholy portrait of what her life had become. Krim found her withdrawn, removed, and somewhat unresponsive to anything more than dancing on her terrace to Guy Lombardo tunes. She might drop endearments ("You're dreamy") pulled out of one of her Warner Bros. scripts. "She was a very scared and lonely woman when I knew her in New York," he wrote, "her life was narrow and barren." She had grown obsessive with Bridey and Fresh, feeding them filet and calling the vet every time one of them so much as sneezed. Krim noted that they had the run of Sutton Place, their nails forever clacking on the wood floors. He stopped by late one morning to find a kimono-clad Joan drinking coffee. She was on the phone to LA, trying to secure a job, even though "the part [w]as a stereotype that brought up her puke juices." "Yes," she said, "will you please leave a message that Joan Blondell, the actress, called. Mr. Fiegleman has my number."

There were precious few reasons, professionally or personally, for Joan to stay in New York. In 1960, she left Sutton Place and returned to California under the reliable assistance of Gloria and Gretchen. The Sutton rent was going up, and the majority of her family—Junie and Gretchen, Gloria and Victor, Norman, Ellen, and the grandchildren—were in greater Los Angeles. She found a spacious apartment in a seven-story building called Colonial House. It was Old Hollywood to a tee, with high ceilings, wrought-iron fixtures, a terrace, and a secluded swimming pool. Her apartment had captain's chairs in the dining room with red velvet seats and backs and a big, cushy sofa in the living room that was primarily used as a destination for Bridey and Fresh. But the real draw of Colonial House was its occupants. Longtime friend and former neighbor Frances Marion was living there. She and Joan became part of an informal woman's salon, enjoying drinks every afternoon at five in the company of newspaper columnist Jill Jackson, publicist Maggie Ettinger, and stockbroker Flora Marks. For Joan, it was a most congenial and advantageous group to fall in with. Flora took pity on Joan, whose finances were in a mess. She organized her pensions and stocks and guided her toward sensible investments. At fifty-four, Joan learned how to balance a checkbook.

Soon after moving into Colonial House, Joan did back-to-back TV guest stints at Desilu Studios in Culver City. She played a rich widow who meets an unnatural death in a strong episode of *The Untouchables*, then a vengeful psychopath in the short-lived anthological *Barbara Stanwyck Show*. When Joan was called out of town to shoot a movie, Jill Jackson agreed to feed and walk Bridey and Fresh. "Her life was those two ugly dogs!" said Jackson. To her consternation, "those damn dogs" only agreed to evacuate their bowels on the lawn of the nearby Christian Science church.

While Jackson coaxed her charges to defecate, Joan went to Homestead, at the southern tip of Florida, to make *Angel Baby*, her first movie since *Will Success Spoil Rock Hunter?* in 1957. Inspired by thick humidity and a ripe script, she went over the top to play a sodden preacher woman with visions of the Lord coming through a whiskey bottle. *Angel Baby* is superficially akin to *Elmer Gantry*, made at a time when fundamentalism was perceived as a fringe cult concentrated in America's backwater towns. It veers from realism to camp, with its cast of veterans (Henry Jones and Mercedes McCambridge alongside Joan) and newcomers (George Hamilton, Burt Reynolds, and Salome Jens) never forgetting that the subject is well served with overacting. The seedy revival tents, cheap trailers, and white trash onlookers recall *Nightmare Alley*, but its documentary-like capturing of Southern poverty is all its own. *Angel Baby* is more successful at flavor than character development, but it is stylistically audacious and filled with dialogue so feverish even Tennessee Williams would blush.

Back in LA in March of 1961, Joan began rehearsals for the national tour of the popular musical *Bye, Bye Birdie*. She was never happy with the production or her role, though both were loved by audiences and critics. She played querulous Mae Peterson, and the part ate at her disposition. She was concerned about how to interpret her, and director Gower Champion was not offering much help. "In New York, the mother was played with a thick Bronx accent, and I started out playing her that way," she said. "But with me they don't believe it. You feel it. The audience laughs wrong. So I'm playing it me now—just Grandma Blondell." "And," said cast member Bill Hayes, "the laughs rock the house." "You should see the cast gather backstage to watch you work," said actress Elaine Dunn to Joan. "But that's when you know you're in a good show," said Joan, "when the cast likes it so much they watch it from the wings." Joan was the most experienced member of the company, and her presence was cherished. "I wouldn't have been half as good in the theater without Joan Blondell's help," said Jesse Pearson, who played the Elvis Presley-esque title character, Conrad Birdie.

The *Birdie* tour went south from there. A new bit of stage business instituted by Champion gave Joan a slipped lumbar disc, landing her at St. John's Hospital in Santa Monica. Her general health was also in decline. In addition to the back trouble, she was overweight, in part from steroids for rheumatoid arthritis. Her joints, particularly her knuckles, were stiff and swollen, and she tired easily. Depression had also set in.

Financial necessity put her back on the road with *Birdie* for most of the rest of 1961. When she wore a back brace on stage underneath her costume of a dress and full-length fur, she was struggling against too much weight, causing her to move in slow motion. Finally, she wore the brace only during the day, with back pains accompanying her performances. "I did it for seven months," she said. "Well, it was seven months of *torrrrture*. It was too unbearably long to be miserable and sick to your stomach and hide out all day long because you knew you had to go to that theater. And they would *not* let me go, even though I wasn't accepted in the part. . . . I got no help from the management at all, [so] each night I cut out another line that was unfunny. By the time we got to LA I had about four lines and they were four funny ones and the notices were great." She hated the tour so much that it soured her to theater altogether. "I'm going to try desperately not to do a play," she told Hedda Hopper. "It's a zillion to one shot if you get a good one. In choosing a play, you almost have to choose management first, at least you get it properly produced."

Several hours before dawn on 24 August 1961, the end of Ellen's seven-month pregnancy was preceded by excessive bleeding. Luckily for his wife and unborn child, Chuck Hayward was home from location when Joan Ellen Hayward was delivered by emergency Caesarian, weighing just four pounds, eight ounces. Joan was in Dallas enduring the agony of *Bye, Bye Birdie* at the time. When she heard that her newborn granddaughter was in an incubator, she told the *Birdie* production manager to call her understudy. She then took a cab to the airport and boarded the first plane to Los Angeles to join Norman and Dick in celebrating the new parents and their baby.

Following assurances that Ellen and her newborn were out of danger and recovering well, Joan rejoined the *Bye, Bye Birdie* tour, then raced back to Colonial House as soon as she had fulfilled her contract. With some money saved and her health compromised, she scaled back work. She made an appearance on a daytime game show, but otherwise did not walk into a studio or theater for months. As if ruled by the precepts of a matrilineal clan, a needy Joan took charge of her daughter's child just as her mother raised Norman and Ellen. The access to her daughter's daughter was immediate, the baby was her namesake, and Joan assumed a control of Joanie that she never attempted with Norman's children. She cooked incessantly and promoted her family nickname "Matey" as an alternative to the more standard moniker "Grandma." She paid for Baby Joanie's redecorated nursery, showered her with dolls and toys even before she could play with them, outfitted her exclusively, and hired a nanny without consulting Ellen. Ellen accepted her mother's well-meaning generosity, but later realized that such grasping attention dislodged her relationship with her own daughter and also angered her often absent-on-location husband.

In the summer of 1962 Dick Powell was diagnosed with cancer of the lymph glands. When he resigned as president of Four Star and accepted the less demanding post of chairman of the board, it was common knowledge in Hollywood that the cancer was inoperable. He was ashen but cheerful when Ann and Norman visited with their infant daughter, Stephanie, born on 26 September. During his decline, he and Joan enjoyed a convivial if not close relationship. Old animosities were retired. He scribbled a note to her on Four Star stationery: "Dear Joan: Loved your card. . . . You know somethin'?—I'm gonna fool 'em and make it! Best as ever, Dick." Three days later, he wrote to her again: "Dear Joanie-Poo, . . . the doctors tell me the tumor in my chest has shrunk about 85% and that in two more weeks I'll be just as obnoxious as ever. Lots of love, Dick." As a favor to Joan, he cast her in an affecting episode of *The Dick Powell Show*, even though her role would have been better served with a plain-faced actress.

Joan delivered homemade food to Dick, but there was the presence of June Allyson to consider. "It was a thoughtful thing to do but I couldn't appreciate it," June wrote of Joan's soups, casseroles, and salads. Both Dick and June had entered into affairs, and no doubt Joan's presence caused further marital stresses. "Joan was a standout during the long days and nights," June wrote diplomatically. "Once she stood talking to Norman . . . sobbed and said, 'I should never have divorced Dick.' The words cut like a knife."

Now he was dying, and June dictated the terms of how, when, and where Dick could see Joan. She accommodated Joan's visits for a time, but eventually barred her from their apartment. When Ellen called to tell her that Dick was approaching death, Joan was distraught. On New Year's Eve, when June was out, Joan reportedly enlisted Jill Jackson to drive her to the Powell's Westwood apartment and park in the alley. Joan, dressed entirely in black, then scaled a fire escape and entered through a back door into Dick's bedroom. Jill waited in the car while Joan said her goodbyes, then drove her weeping friend back to Colonial House. Joan never saw Dick again.

On 2 January 1963, Dick's pain finally abated when June's brother, a doctor, closed his eyes and declared him dead. Joan grieved at his death. Whatever animosity or ambivalence she had for him was gone. She was reawakened to his basic decency and love of family. His passing allowed her to ponder the three husbands she had outlived. "They were different types but I loved every one of them. . . . I didn't change. They did." She softened over time. "I had put so much into each one of them," she said. "I can't tell you the blood that ran out of me with their deaths."

Joan's eyes were red and teary during the service at All Saints Protestant Episcopal Church in Beverly Hills. Eight hundred mourners attended, including James Stewart, Walter Pidgeon, Ronald Reagan, Barbara Stanwyck, and then former vice president Richard Nixon and his wife, Pat. Dick's body was cremated and inurned at Forest Lawn in Glendale. His will left the bulk of his wealth to June and the two under-aged children that resulted from that marriage. Norman and Ellen each received five hundred shares in Four Star, which when released from probate were worth about fifteen thousand dollars.

Soon after Dick's death, Joan began a reoccurring role as busybody Winifred Jordan on the popular television series *The Real McCoys*. The ancestral rural comedy had been on the air for more than five years and was showing signs of wear. This was not the first time Joan was hired for the expressed purpose of energizing an anemic TV show. She could be counted upon to supply wit, charm, and energy to the home screen just as she had to Warner Bros. programmers in the 1930s. Her participation in *The Real McCoys* was a case in point. When series regular Kathy Nolan left the show, it was shuttled from ABC to CBS. CBS made a tentative pact with Blondell to write her in a few episodes and possibly enlarge her role if aging Walter Brennan made good on his threats to leave. Joan was hired the following

February, but her warmly rendered character could not salvage the show, which folded just weeks after she came aboard.

On Hedda Hopper's radio program, Joan excitedly revealed that CBS had talked to her about a possible series of her own as "the mother of Hollywood" who runs a little restaurant on Hollywood Boulevard. Nothing came of that or of television producer Aaron Spelling's vague plans to use her in a series. Promises by low-budget horror director William Castle seemed more binding. In early March of 1963, while she was still reporting to *The Real McCoys* set, Joan awaited her starring role in Castle's new shocker, *Strait-Jacket*. She was not put off by the demands of the part, in which a woman allegedly hacks her husband and mistress to death with an ax, then is locked away in a mental hospital. "It's a fantastic acting role," she said. "So far we have had only a handshake on the deal. But I would like to do it." There were reasons to believe the role was secure when Castle went on record saying this will give Blondell a *Whatever Happened to Baby Jane*–style tour de force.

Joan had costume fittings and was ready to shoot, but when Joan Crawford encountered Castle at a social gathering, she arrogated the starring role. Castle "then proceed[ed] to turn his picture upside down to please her," according to Blondell friend and sympathizer Bette Davis. "It stinks, I tell you," she fumed. "There is an unwritten *law* in this town. Once an actor is signed for a part, it's *his* until they die or drop out voluntarily. Miss Crawford *knows* this and should be ashamed of herself." Blondell showed more sangfroid in her retelling of the tale. She withdrew because of a horrible accident that left her scarred. "I stepped through a glass partition in my home and had to have sixty stitches in my leg," she said. "Nothing was said in the newspapers, because of the insurance, but Joan Crawford did not steal the role. Someone had to do it." Blondell's entry into the Grand Guignol parts given to actresses of a certain age would have to wait. *Strait-Jacket* or no *Strait-Jacket*, she occasionally despaired at the conditions of her employment in the 1960s. "The sets are depressing," she said. "No more team work or gaiety. . . . Now it's all so rushed; every moment it's ticking money!" This is from a woman who made ten movies in 1932.

Joan became a staple on TV in the early 1960s, but rarely was she in the same place twice. She became a sought-after guest star, commanding five thousand dollars per appearance. Her high price was justified repeatedly by her stellar work. She played the termagant wife of cantankerous William Demarest on *The Twilight Zone*. Exposing her two beauty marks and sporting outrageous false eyelashes, she was called upon to do some roughhousing with Demarest that left her bruised. She was seen to less advantage in the short-lived series *The Greatest Show on Earth*. Jack Palance directed and starred in the episode, in which Joan, trout-mouthed Joe E. Brown, and Buster Keaton play circus has-beens. Blondell's character was once a champion lassoer but is now demoted to seamstress. Keaton played a mute, white-faced Pierrot named Pippo. It is painful to watch, as their characters unavoidably reflect on the status of their careers. There was relief of a sort that Joan did not have to consider a carefully groomed image as she did in the 1930s. Now, she was purely an actress for hire. "It isn't ambition that drives me on," she said. "It's just good sense. . . . [T]he thing that matters now is I need something to do."

Wedged between TV spots was a small role in *Advance to the Rear*, a summer drive-in entertainment in which a Civil War spy for the South (Stella Stevens) moles as one of the "girls" in Joan's whorehouse. Jesse Pearson, her admiring costar of *Bye, Bye, Birdie*, was in the cast. So was Melvyn Douglas, her well-matched compatriot in three Columbia comedies of the late 1930s. On the first day of shooting, he gave her a bear hug on the set. "So you're in the picture, too?" he asked. "What role?" Swirling a pink feather boa around her neck, she answered "I'm the boss lady, what else?"

Joan's broad, fleshy shoulders were exposed to good effect in strapless, frilly costumes befitting her profession, but *Advance to the Rear* was a labored effort relying too heavily on laughs from slide-whistle sound effects and men in long johns. The MGM set did allow Blondell to engage in a bit of wistful reflection. She brought Bridey and Fresh to the lot, along with the food and squeak toys necessary to content them in her trailer. Every three hours, she excused herself to walk them "through back lots with fronts of green cottages and mansions encircled by park-like grass. Once in awhile I get a strange feeling, and they seem to share it with me. I get it when we walk along the deserted Andy Hardy street where Judy Garland and Mickey Rooney spent their childhood. At Metro too, we come to the tree where the beautiful Garbo stood waiting for her car that long ago day. When we pass Stage Eleven, Clark Gable's voice comes back to me. 'Don't marry that guy, Joanie, he's too jealous, too violent—marry me, Joanie.' Sometimes we walk in Warner's Sherwood Forest where Errol Flynn glee- fully told me untold tales of his youth, during a picture we were making. I see a dilapidated carriage that proudly transported George Arliss and Bette Davis. At Fox, Shirley Temple and Bill Robinson danced before my eyes."

Current reality lacked the warm glow of remembrances. In 1964, Joan's working fortunes tumbled with a low-paying Straw Hat tour through New Jersey's outback in *Watch the Birdie*, a new play by *The Blue Veil* coproducer Norman Krasna. Then came the fustian comedy of the nos- talgic "Hooray for Hollywood" set in the 1920s. As an episode from *Vacation Playhouse*, a series comprised entirely of unsold pilots, it was the television equivalent of sausage. She was back in southern Florida for the feature *Big Daddy*, this time battling alligators, voodoo, swamps, and Victor Buono. The low-brow realities of *Big Daddy* did not pull Joan toward self- pity. Pregnant costar Tisha Sterling found her to be compassionate and warm, even spearheading a baby shower on the set for the expectant actress.

Joan's work had nowhere to go but up, and, indeed, it did through a fortuitous sequence of events. Sam Peckinpah was hired to direct MGM's *The Cincinnati Kid*, a tale of a hotshot young poker player who challenges a veteran bigwig. Peckinpah shot for two weeks in black and white, never hit his stride, and was fired by the studio. Young Norman Jewison was hired and started all over again, reminding the producers that diamonds and hearts are red, and color would allow the cards to be recognized quickly. For the master gamesman, Spencer Tracy was in, then out, only to be replaced by Edward G. Robinson. The location was changed from St. Louis to New Orleans to take advantage of the ambiance of the French Quarter.

Joan's films of the 1960s were a déclassé lot, with the lone exception of the talent-laden *Cincinnati Kid*. Richard Jessup (author of the original novel), Paddy Chayefsky, Ring Lardner Jr., Terry Southern, and Charles Eastman contributed to the script. Future Oscar winner Hal Ashby was editor. Blondell and Robinson joined an extraordinary collection of actors: Steve McQueen, Tuesday Weld, Karl Malden, Ann-Margret, Jack Weston, Cab Calloway, and Rip Torn.

Joan appears in a small role an hour into the movie. For her first entrance, she sweeps through the room like she's auditioning for *Hello, Dolly!* As "Lady Fingers," dealer extraordinaire, she's got a "high style of playing," according to Robinson, and, indeed, we believe him. The climax of the film is a stud poker duel between McQueen and Robinson, but still Blondell stays in focus. Jewison felt blessed to have her in his movie. "When she entered and had a few lines here or there, there was this great energy, this strong presence on camera," he said. "We had lots of fun together. She was worried about the part. 'I'm not good with cards,' she said. 'Look at these hands—I've got arthritis.'" She knew nothing about poker, much less dealing. Jewison solved the problem by hiring a hand double who was nimble with cards, painting his nails to match hers.

"She had a tough side to her which I loved," said Jewison. "But she had a twinkle in her eye, and she could always make me laugh. Whether it was a kind of self-mocking thing she would do, it was very cute. And I thought she was terrific in the film. She was absolutely convincing as one of the top dealers, known by everybody, an artist with cards who can stand up to all of those guys. We were lucky to get her, and I made sure she was treated like a star. I had great respect for her." He also appreciated the fantastic rapport between *Bullets or Ballots* costars Robinson and Blondell. "There was an old star/new star dynamic between Robinson and McQueen, and I encouraged Joan to play on that," he said. "So there's a scene where she says to Robinson, 'He's good and you're a has-been.' There was wonderful sparring."

Joan was giving one of her best performances, but like some replay of *A Tree Grows in Brooklyn*, much of it never left the editing room. "The sad thing about [making *The Cincinnati Kid*] was that they cut [the] stuff [between Robinson and me]," she said. "The pictures now run so long, and they had to cut something, so they cut our meaning to each other, which had made the thing interesting." Still, she was pleased with the leavings. "I loved Eddie Robinson in *The Cincinnati Kid*," she said. "He called me up one day and said, 'I want to ask you something. When I was young at Warner's, was I a bastard?' I said, 'Yes, you were.' He said, 'I think so, too.'" Jewison did not express regret at Joan's pared-down role. "Hal Ashby and I had so much fun editing that film," he recalled. "In the climactic card game, there are a lot of close-ups of Joan, even though she's not the center of the action. Hal and I said, 'When in doubt, cut away to Joan or Eddie.'"

Joan was practical in her self-assessment. Her sparse work on the big screen of late was attributed to a current unfamiliarity about who she was. Before old movies were videotaped, digitalized, and readily available in the home rental and retail markets, only an aging population knew of Joan Blondell. Her tremendous stage work in the 1950s did not regain her widespread recognition. "Unfortunately these plays were done when the new movie group did not see them," she said. But she was confident that her gifts had not abandoned her. "There's nothing wrong with being ripe—and that's what I am—ripe. . . . Wine is better mellowed. Cheese. You go down the list. I consider myself in that category—a hunk of cheese."

In May of 1965, twenty-six-year-old Ellen filed for divorce and took up residence in Marina Del Rey with three-year-old Joanie. Joan stated that "one of life's biggest heart aches is divorce," and she was "miserable" that her "wonderful Ellen has to go through it." Ellen's happiness came with horses. She bred, raised, conditioned, and trained competition performance animals, often winning blue ribbons. But horses were expensive, and Ellen began looking for ways to make money. With the divorce settlement, inheritance, and additional help from Joan, she founded a Los Angeles music, electronic sales, and service business called Stereo to Go and Blondell Stereo. The move unwittingly contributed to a downward arc in Ellen's life. She literally and figuratively got off horseback and turned away from her life's great passion. Now she was deep into the myriad details of running a business. Because of Ellen's long work hours and Joan's increased responsibility for Joanie, every corner of Ellen's life included her mother. "That's when Ellen first got on drugs," said longtime family friend Rose Lundin.

Joan had her own encounter with 1960s drugs at a party in Marina del Rey attended by Norman and Ellen. The hostess passed her a marijuana cigarette and said, "You haven't tried it yet and it's about time." Joan took three deep hits, then, as she said, "My heart started to pound so fast that I became terrified and started to cry in front of all these people. They looked like a frozen tableau to me, so I ran out on the beach, crying and then suddenly laughing, and there were some kids playing a little radio and it was playing 'Born Free' and, I'll never forget it, I kept screaming 'Louder! Louder!' and then I decided 'Born Free' meant we'd be free of disease and I started to make speeches and I want to tell you I haven't been within blocks of marijuana since."

Lucille Ball's perennial second banana, Vivian Vance, had recently quit the *The Lucy Show*, leaving Ball in need of someone to glorify her comedic talents. Enter Joan. She was a type roughly equivalent to Vance, another well-rounded dirty blonde wisecracker. She was contracted to tape two back-to-back episodes to test the chemistry. While the on-camera results were pleasing enough, Ball and Blondell behaved like anything but the friends they had been in their studio days. "Lucille was intimidated by Joan Blondell, because she was so strong," said episode director Maury Thompson. "Joan showed up in an awful dress to wear in the show that made her look like a streetwalker. Lucille approved it and dismissed Joan. I tried to broach the subject, but Lucille cut me off. 'Stick with the money,' she said. 'Forget about her, just make sure that *I* look good!' I said, 'Honey, I want the *whole show* to look good. That way, *you'll* look better.'"

According to Herbert Kenwith, a director and friend of Joan's who was on the set for the taping of the second episode "to offer moral support," relations deteriorated from there. He recalled that "while they were rehearsing together, Lucille said, 'I thought you were a comedienne. Can't you turn any of those lines to be funny?' And Blondell said, 'If they were written in that vein I could do it, but these are straight lines. There is nothing I can do except feed *you* the lines.' Ball didn't accept that. When their scene ended and [Thompson] yelled, 'cut,' Lucille pulled an imaginary chain in the air as if flushing an old-fashioned toilet. 'What does *that* mean?' she demanded. Lucy said, 'It means that stunk!' Joan looked her right in the eye and said, 'Fuck you, Lucille Ball!' and left. The studio audience was stunned. You didn't hear words like that in those days." The search for Vance's replacement continued. Joan was crying when she told the story at the Colonial House hen party that night. "I've *never* been treated so badly," she said between wiping her nose and gulping her vodka and tonic. She had an extra belt that night and went to bed drunk.

Joan was meanwhile getting award recognition for *The Cincinnati Kid*. Her "Lady Fingers" was nominated for a Best Supporting Actress Golden Globe, and on 9 January 1966, she was announced as the Best Supporting Actress of 1965 by the National Board of Review. The joy of professional recognition was offset by family woes. Norman had grown restless in his marriage to Ann, his high school sweetheart, and in 1966 he declared his intention to divorce. Joan was discountenanced, fearing that he was making a huge mistake. Sweet Ann was being wronged, another woman was involved, and no one in the family liked her. According to Norman later, Sue Zan Palmer delighted in using her beauty to get what she wanted. She had already been married and divorced, but Norman saw only the excitement of the new. Ann moved out with their three children and found employment in a clothing store that utilized her education in fashion merchandising. Joan was aching. She was more sympathetic and supportive of Ann than she was of Norman, believing her son to be making an enormously bad decision.

Back at work, there was *Ride beyond Vengeance,* a violent, not-good Chuck Connors western in which Joan played Mrs. Lavender, an over-aged prostitute with a taste for brandy. It is in efforts such as this that Joan's enduring professionalism shines. She made a vigorous attempt to give Mrs. Lavender humor and humanity, providing a back story that was absent from the writing and directing. She taped two episodes of *The Man from U.N.C.L.E.* as Mrs. "Fingers" Stilletto, an adenoidal old gun moll to a Sicilian mafia don. In November 1966, she explained a few secrets of comedy to a columnist on the Mojave Desert set of *Waterhole #3,* a brawling western starring James Coburn. "Comedy is as elusive as a waiter's eye when you're in a hurry for the check," she said. "There is no sure formula although some elements are basic. After all my experience in vaudeville, radio, television, stage, and movies, I've developed a strange theory that laughter is just dry tears. . . . [Chaplin, Keaton, and Laurel and Hardy were great because] they kept reminding people of things they dream of—and making these dreams come true in some degree . . . like giving the bully his comeuppance. And when one of those comedians threw a pie in the villain's face or placed a well-directed boot in his other end, there wasn't a single viewer in the audience who didn't visualize himself doing the same thing to a guy who'd been pushing him around for a long time."

She had a few minor gigs, including an appearance in a fantasy installment of *Bob Hope Presents the Chrysler Theatre,* in which she was turned into a talking horse. She was a saloon keeper in her first TV movie, *Winchester '73,* a lunkheaded remake of the 1950 big-screen western. She attended the Academy Awards at the Santa Monica Civic Auditorium in 1967, declaring, "I still like motion pictures best of all and a good role will always prevail over pressure-cooker TV." Or pressure-cooker theater. Joan spent the next eight weeks with *Come Back, Little Sheba* at Chicago's Ivanhoe Theatre. She broke house records and shared her triumph with Bridey Murphy and Fresh nearby in her dressing room and hotel. A short story by Joan called "A Tale of Two Dogs" reveals the extent of her dotage: "After thousands of miles of travel, Summer Stock, Winter Stock, television, guest appearances, National Companies, pictures, I learned about the Pug Dog. . . . They are fastidious eaters. Giblets boiled slowly and long, with carrots, celery, and garlic—the meat cut in small pieces, the juice strained before serving—Monday and Friday. Beef hearts and kidneys—Tuesday and Thursday. Steak broiled Wednesday and Saturday; chicken every Sunday. Most times we split these meals."

Waterhole #3 opened while she was on tour in Chicago. Joan was every inch the good-time hostess/madame, done up to the gaudy limit in neon yellow and pink. Once again the contrast of roles, the comedic one in a rambunctious western and the pathetic one in *Come Back, Little Sheba*, points to Joan's exceptional range. Her gifts would have to wait for wider recognition in nobler efforts. If *Angel Baby* sought to capitalize on *Elmer Gantry*, *Waterhole #3* attempted the same trick with *Cat Ballou*. Both failed.

In August of 1967, Joan traipsed off to Hawaii with ten-year-old granddaughter Sandy to make a TV pilot called *Kona Coast*. Joan played Kittibelle Lightfood, tough-talking manager of an island home for reformed drunks, while grizzled Richard Boone executive produced and starred in the lonely-man-against-the-world drama. Joan was one of only seven professional actors, the rest of the cast peopled with authentic Hawaiians. The idyllic location did not compensate for Joan's dislike of Boone. Without reporting details, she told Ellen that he was "crude, impolite, and cruel. He was mean and degrading." She did enjoy costar Vera Miles, who remembered Blondell as "a dear, dear woman. She hadn't a mean bone in her body. Working with her was fun and rewarding."

Joan's short run of bad movies in beautiful locations continued with *Stay Away, Joe*, an Elvis Presley vehicle shot amidst the gorgeous Sedona landscape of northern Arizona. *Joe* spends much of its time wandering the desert in search of a plot. The high point involves a May–December seduction between Presley and saloon keeper Blondell. She later guards her backward daughter's virtue, becoming a rifle-blasting smother mother with extremely bad aim. Joan performed some kind of miracle in making *Stay Away, Joe* watchable. Indeed, the movie demonstrates that with better writing she could have been a great comic villainess. Otherwise, *Joe* is nothing but fist fights, roving cattle, off-road car rides, and quaintly mod party scenes.

Junie's daughter Kathy Blondell was twenty-eight, divorced, the mother of three, and thriving as a movie hairstylist. She had done a few publicity shots for her aunt, but had never been on a set with her before *Stay Away, Joe*. "I loved working with her, but I had to control myself," said Kathy. "I'd want to do such a great job that I'd overdo her. I had to keep telling myself that I'm doing a character, not my aunt. As she was sitting in my chair one day on the set, I started talking about my grandmother Nana, her mother. When I looked at her face I could see she was crying. I was so sorry; I ran and got her a Kleenex."

Kathy got an up-close appreciation for her aunt's strength and a new understanding of family dynamics during the shooting of *Stay Away, Joe*. "She had bad arthritis by this time, but she wouldn't take medication while working," she said. "Nothing would deter her from giving the best performance she could. She was so fantastic that way, so trained. Nothing would get in the way. When I made her cry, I felt horrible. I went to her house in Sedona at the end of the day. I told her how badly I felt and asked her what I had said. I found out that Joan and her mom hadn't been speaking when her mom passed away. They had an argument and Joan got very mad and they never made up. I spent the last year of my grandmother's life with her, and I was thrilled. 'Nana loved you,' I told Joan over and over again, which was true. 'I'll tell you that right now. We had great conversations about you.' That helped Joan a lot. She told me that later she opened letters from Nana to her that she had never read before."

When the dire *Kona Coast* went unsold as a TV pilot, Richard Boone extended it to ninety-three minutes with scrap footage and sold the distribution rights to Warner Bros. Like *Stay Away, Joe*, it was a box-office miscarriage. Joan was given a more promising script called *Mrs. Thursday*, in which she played a cleaning lady who inherits $100 million. That TV project, however, sat on the shelf. In late 1967, she finally broke the cycle of TV work that went straight to nowhere when she played the salty and wise Carlotta ("Lottie") Hatfield in a pilot for series television called *Here Come the Brides*. When ABC bought an entire season of the Screen Gems production, a reporter asked Joan if she was ready for the stresses of a weekly series. She threw her head back and let out a chesty laugh. "Are you kidding?" she asked, her eyes drilling into him. "Honey, I know what work is all about."

The series was populated largely by young newcomers. Joan was the spectacular exception, her work history exceeding the combined experience of all other cast regulars. The producers honored her with a solo title card and the coveted "and" spot at the end of the opening credits ("AND JOAN BLONDELL AS LOTTIE"), falling just short of the "And Starring MISS BARBARA STANWYCK as Victoria Barkley" royal decree afforded Joan's friend on *The Big Valley*. She was offered the most deluxe trailer on the set but gave it to Robert Brown, an actor with more responsibilities on the show.

Shot largely on Stage 29 at the Columbia Ranch outside of Burbank, *Here Come the Brides* was billed as a comedy set in tiny post–Civil War Seattle, but it was not laugh-out-loud funny. At the pilot episode, the muddy outpost is without females, save for Lottie and a few scattered old maids. On a bet, the three virile Bolt brothers embark on an epic journey to New Bedford to find one hundred marriageable young women willing to relocate. But if any of them leave within the first year, the Bolt's lumber business will fall into the hands of resident nemesis Aaron Stempel. Pilot writer N. Richard Nash was inspired by the true story of Asa Shinn Mercer and his two brothers, who coaxed eleven women from the East Coast to relocate to Seattle in 1864. Similarities to the 1954 musical *Seven Brides for Seven Brothers* or the Rape of the Sabine Women were nearer to coincidence.

With its fine-line drawings, granny glasses, hand-stitched quilts, and stereopticons, *Here Come the Brides* was awash in images from the 1870s that few had memory of in 1968. But America was reeling from unprecedented cultural shifts, allowing the show to evoke an "innocent time" while engaging in retrograde sexual politics. The men of Seattle were beasts; one of them assaults the schoolmarm in the premiere episode, but he is explained away as a victim of his own unsatiated libido. "The show is the opposite of hip, and in this day of the protester that's unique," said Screen Gems studio chief and former child star Jackie Cooper. "What the heroes are so lustily protecting is the old fashioned morality the Bible Belt holds so dear."

Once again Joan became a role model, this time in her performance rather than in her private life. Lottie is the lone self-sufficient and self-assured woman in the series. As bar owner, hotelier, and cook, she is capable and smart, the sage of the Northwest. "It's a marvelous part," Joan said. "Lottie is surrounded by men all the time—and what woman doesn't like to be surrounded by men? [They] are either flirting with her or seeking her advice on how to court the girls who've arrived from the east. It's almost a pivotal part and you can almost hear the viewer saying, 'well, will that guy take her advice or not?' 'Will he get the girl or won't he?'" In the pilot episode, the Bolt brothers plan to snag "fancy ladies from San Francisco," but it is Lottie who sets them straight. "Real men want real women, not floozies," she informs them. From the beginning, Lottie is established as the surrogate mother and moral arbiter for all of Seattle.

That was not by accident. "When we came to talk about character, to her credit she never talked about Lottie solo," said *Brides* story consultant William Blinn. "She always talked about her in conjunction with the other characters. I very rarely felt she tried to be protective of Joan Blondell. She might have been protective of Lottie, but not Joan Blondell. She was very much a team player, though she hated those scenes where she had to be there for four hours to say a line and a half. She was a good old broad, and she had an edge to her."

Brides provided steady income, which allowed Joan to buy a house after so many years of renting. With the help of stockbroker friend Flora Marks, she bought on the Whitespeak Drive cul-de-sac in the Santa Monica Mountains above Sherman Oaks. Her new place came with two bedrooms, a wide, curving patio surrounding a pool, a lattice fence along the front walk, and a stellar wrap-around panorama of the San Fernando Valley. Joan described it as "homey, poolish, bookish with a view."

She placed a Tiffany lamp on her desk and put down bright hand-made throw rugs and a green sofa. Family photos and paintings by Gloria hung on the walls. A stained-glass rendering of the word *Love* was attached to the sliding glass doors to prevent a repeat of the bloody accident at Colonial House that cost her *Strait-Jacket*. Joan liked Whitespeak immensely and so did Bridey and Fresh. They were old dogs now. When their hind quarters gave out, Joan had special ladders built so they could still get onto the bed or sofa. During heat waves, Joan swathed them in wet white towels so they resembled two whiskered old men wrapped in dough. The attention they came to expect weighed on Joan. "Sometimes I'd like to bathe, just once, without two black faces peering at me over the edge of the tub," she said. "I'd like to go to the kitchen, dining room, bedroom, living room, or bathroom just once without the patter of eight feet following me. Just once I'd like to enjoy a gentleman-caller without two squat bodies sitting in front of me weaving, blinking, yawning, letting me know they're bored with him and it's time for us girls to go to bed—alone."

Gloria stopped by frequently. "We've never been apart," she told a reporter. "We talk two or three hours a day on the phone. Girl talk. Joan's pendulum swings are very great but she does a good job of warding off the downs." Her technique involved an egg timer. She allowed herself six and a half minutes to be lonely, and if depressed, twenty-two minutes to feel sorry for herself. When time was up, she took a shower or went for a walk or swam or cooked something. "The best thing I'm good at is love," Joan said. "I'm a staunch lover in every sense of the word—I love people, husbands, children, grandchildren, dogs. I'm a great appreciator of good things—the veins in a leaf, roses, the look of a morning, the smell of babies. I try to forget the bad things. There's a lump inside you always, lumps of sorrows, griefs, and failures. But with a little effort you can make them stay in the background. And I'm proud of myself. I've lived in dignity. I've made *beaucoup* mistakes and have come out of them without shame. They weren't deliberate or thought-out mistakes. They were sheer stupidity and I think women can be stupid if they want to be." To granddaughter

Joanie, Joan was "the most generous person [she had] ever met. Always bringing gifts and shopping down at the mall." There were squabbles between Ellen and Joan over Joanie, particularly when Joan suspected Ellen of using drugs, marijuana most regularly. The stereo business took much of Ellen's time, and when Joan was in charge of Joanie, she tended to be indulgent, letting her eat candy or watch TV. When Ellen and Joanie lived with her on Whitespeak, Joan would seek out girls in the neighborhood for pool parties. With unwavering patience, Joan helped Joanie overcome a terror of the water after a bathing accident. For all of the grandchildren there was an open tap of pleasures, including Disneyland, skating lessons, summer camps, and new clothes. Granddaughter Stephanie remembers bouts of supernatural generosity. They were once perusing a toy store when her Matey was seized by the spirit of giving, insisting that she buy every nearby child a gift. Even young Stephanie did not find this gesture entirely welcome, as it came with the insistence that everyone be happy at that moment.

Of course Bridey and Fresh accompanied Joan to the *Here Come the Brides* set, but the grandchildren were repeat visitors as well, occupying themselves with toys and crayons in Joan's trailer. Joanie, like many Americans, had a crush on Bobby Sherman, who played the boyish stutterer Jeremy Bolt. He enjoyed a brief run as a bubble-gum singing sensation, which virtually guaranteed a repeat audience for the series. Joan and Henry Beckman, who played the mutton-chopped old sea captain Clancey, got along like old friends. In keeping with the romantic shadings of their characters, they flirted on the set, and she christened him with the nickname "Fish Face." Barrel-chested Robert Brown as alpha brother Jason Bolt was the very personification of Paul Bunyan; Joan found him to be the choicest slab of beef since Errol Flynn.

Joan was the popular attraction on the set, with a starry-eyed cast and crew literally sitting at her feet to hear stories of old Hollywood. "She was so easy to work with and never played the star," said Brown. "She was still engaged in the work. She would watch scenes that she wasn't in.

Everybody loved her." Bridget Hanley, as the leading bride and love interest for Sherman, stated that "it was the coup of the century to get Joan
Blondell." Executive producer Robert Claver said, "Based on time in service and grade, she's entitled to be the chief complainer but she doesn't
complain. I remember only one complaint: She said her stand-in wasn't
making enough money and wondered if we could find some more work
for her." Robert de Roos of *TV Guide* wrote, "In a world of plastic flowers,
'genuine leatherette' and ersatz emotions, the lady is real. Real and realistic and alive, warm and tremendously generous; flesh and blood and experience, and some unschooled wisdom." That last insight flared when Joan
admired Robert Brown's Volvo. She bought one for herself, then enthused
to a reporter about her "beautiful new vulva!"

With survival tactics honed in vaudeville and at Warner Bros., Joan
developed coping strategies during the run of *Brides*. She was up every
work day at four to be ready for makeup at five thirty. "I read a little first,"
she said. "I've always got a book within reach. Then I make breakfast and
drive over to the set. When I'm through I come home and have a snort,
then dinner, ready my lines for the following day and then I go to bed. When
I'm alone, it's because I want to be. Parties? Nightclubbing? Openings? You
can have them. I'm bored with all that jazz." She stayed quiet about her
worsening rheumatoid arthritis, painful enough to require Percodan to get
through the day. When she had a yen to cook, aching joints could not stop
her. Nothing else mattered until she had prepared fifteen ham hocks and a
gallon of beans. Then she would load her pugs and her victuals in her
Volvo and make the rounds to friends, dispensing home cooking to the
unexpecting.

She never lost an appreciation for her fans. *Here Come the Brides*
brought her to the attention of a young generation, and she relished their
affection. "Funny thing about a series," she said. "A little girl came up to
me the other day. 'I know you,' she said. 'You're Lottie.' You know, she
was right. Joan Blondell no longer exists. I'm somebody named Lottie.
That's—what do these kids say?—where it's at these days on TV."

Here Come the Brides played on Wednesday nights against *Tarzan* on CBS and the long-running *The Virginian* on NBC. Corny, far-fetched, and anachronistic, *Brides* also charmed with its gentle sentiment and spirited characters portrayed by an earnest and well-chosen cast. A varietal score and outdoor shooting at Franklin Canyon Park and Angeles National Forest added to the show's production values. Though hardly a ratings giant, it performed well enough to be renewed for a second season just as Emmy nominations were announced. *Brides* might have expected several nods, but it received only one. Joan vied for Best Actress in a Dramatic Series against Barbara Bain's femme fatale in *Mission: Impossible* and Peggy Lipton's cool hippie chick in *The Mod Squad*.

Joan was genuinely surprised at being nominated. "I don't know why they singled me out," she said modestly. "I do so little in the show." Lottie was underwritten as charged. She spent inordinate time commenting on other characters' travails or silently reacting to the prevailing action from behind the bar. Lottie was the kind of character who threw her arms in the air and shouted, "Drinks on the house!" whenever a celebratory moment was called for. On those occasions when she was highlighted, as when her former beau shows up and she melts at his touch, audiences were hit hard by Joan's seasoned talent. Most often she had too little to do, yet Joan made Lottie a great broad.

Certain she would not win, she took a suite at the Miramar, hired a makeup man and limousine driver, and decided to have some fun. She saw her effort as a tribute to her fans. "I know how disappointed I am when I watch an award ceremony and someone hasn't shown up," she said. When Barbara Bain took home her third consecutive Emmy, Joan could not deny her chagrin—for Peggy Lipton's loss.

CHAPTER 10

I Hear Voices

I don't know what the secret of longevity as an actress is. It's more than talent or beauty. Maybe it's the audience seeing itself in you. I reminded secretaries, waitresses, reporters, chorus girls, and now fading anybodys that a girl who didn't get the best of everything could eventually reach some of the goals in life.
—Joan Blondell, 1972

Soon after finishing season one of *Here Come the Brides*, Joan picked up some extra cash doing a brief turn in Warner Bros.' *The Phynx*. It was a supposed comedy about a rock band rescuing kidnapped "world leaders" Xavier Cugat, Johnny Weismueller, Butterfly McQueen, and Busby Berkeley from imprisonment behind Iron Curtain Albania. Joan played the American-born first lady, living in palatial opulence while being served thighs in a bucket by Colonel Sanders. *The Phynx* combined pop culture misdates with "now generation" references to James Bond, the Beatles, the generation gap, racial stereotypes, the draft, Vietnam, and swinging London. But the problem with *The Phynx* was that it was light-years away from being funny. Joan was among a cadre of old-timers resuscitated for camp value, but *The Phynx* was so bad it was pulled soon after release and, apart from a few television airings, has been moldering in film canisters ever since.

By the 1970s, Joan was an antediluvian actress and a genuine show-business survivor. Even as the quality of her offers declined, she was given respect as expected for someone who has been around and seen it all. She attached herself to the old guard, declaring her disdain for campus protesters and the disrespect shown President Nixon. She rejected any serious thoughts of plastic surgery. "I feel if my heart lifts, my face will go with it," she reasoned. She had little interest in current cinema, preferring to spend free time with her family. She did allow an occasional glimpse into her past, catching *Bullets or Ballots, Lady for a Night,* or *Topper Returns* on television when Joanie was visiting. They would watch on Joan's cushy double bed, snuggling up with popcorn or eating dinner on silver TV trays. Their cozy pleasure was interrupted only when the phone rang or Bridey and Fresh needed hoisting onto the bed. Matey and Joanie stayed up late one night to catch *A Tree Grows in Brooklyn* but were disappointed. "They cut my scenes out of it," said a melancholy Joan. "I was hardly in it a'tall. . . . I wanted my granddaughter to be *prrrroud* of me. And here was a hunk of nothin.' "

Joan's fashion sense of the 1970s veered toward loud. She painted her fingernails bright pink, applied fly-swatter eyelashes, and smoked Benson and Hedges through pearl-white filters. She occasionally wore mod black pumps and bellbottoms under diaphanous blouses. She had given up on dieting, hiding the details of her figure under the cerise, yellow, and green caftans that comprised what her grandchildren dubbed "Grandma's hippie outfits." With her gently sloping double chin and crow's feet etched in her temples, she gained both a self-awareness and resignation that come with age. "For the first time I can just be what I am, really," she said. "Would I marry again? Oh my God! No. I don't think I can face any more pain. I don't mean to sound bitter about husbands. Out of three I had, bits and pieces of each made one perfect man. And most women don't have that. That's enough. I live a quiet life now; I've earned the right to live the way I want to. I can relax and enjoy my $34 set of silverware, and every time I see a gorgeous hunk of silver, or a painting, I can think, I've had all that. I don't have it now, but I *did* have it, and the hell with it."

As *Here Come the Brides* began taping its second season, Joan found the grind was diminishing her enjoyment of the work. "It was an uphill thing, that series," she said. "You turn into an absolute phony." Even she, the workhorse of Warner Bros., tired of the routine. "I think a series is a dangerous thing to do," she said. "You have to keep hyping yourself up. Because there's such a sameness to it. You're never nervous—it's not like the theater. But you think: 'I read that line last week and the week before that. Isn't there something new I can say?' And then morale gets low. Temperaments can go up and down to a ridiculous extent." On one occasion, a full-of-himself young assistant in a silly hat knocked on her trailer door and said, "Joan, you're late and you're needed on the set." No one, least of all a disrespectful greenhorn, was going to impinge on her professionalism. Joan emerged seconds later, fully prepared to shoot. She looked straight into his eyes and in a normal pitch said, "It's Miss Blondell. And take off that fucking hat and say 'please.' "

During the run of *Brides* there was an executive shuffle at ABC, and word came down that the show needed less comedy and more typical western action. This plus a time change from Wednesdays at 7:30 to Fridays at 9:00 proved lethal. The show had been a magnet for young audiences, due in no small part to the pop-culture phenomenon of Bobby Sherman. Now he, hunky lumberjacks, and fair maidens could not compel enough viewers to stay home at the commencement of the weekend. Still, *Brides* never embarrassed itself. Plot lines were often mature, addressing arranged marriages, anti-Semitism, women's suffrage, and racial prejudice. Occasionally, it drew on history. One second-season episode featured no less than showman P. T. Barnum, soprano Jenny Lind, and the admittance of Washington Territory into the Union. Another combined the Anglo settlers, Yakima Indians, and Big Foot. Yet another highlighted Joan brilliantly, as Lottie's former life is unhappily brought forth with the introduction of a long-lost husband, played by Robert Cummings.

In fulfilling the directive from the network front office, the show had lost a bit of what made it special. "It began as a comedy that wasn't a sitcom, and a drama that wasn't action, so it was a bit of an odd duck," said story consultant William Blinn. "When it worked, it worked very well. But we weren't cast for conventional action drama, and so the show suffered." When Joan earned her second Emmy nomination, momentum was not with her or the series. At the June awards ceremony held simultaneously at the Century Hotel in Hollywood and Carnegie Hall in New York, she lost Best Dramatic Actress to Susan Hampshire for her role in the acclaimed public television series *The Forsyte Saga*. Then *Here Come the Brides* was terminated after a run of fifty-two episodes. In a kiss-off reply to grieving fans, ABC noted that "it is very unfortunate for everyone concerned when favorite programs are canceled from a network schedule. But after having been on television for two years, it seemed a great many of the people who had followed the program lost interest." Teary phone calls spread throughout the cast and crew. The announcement of *Brides'* cancellation was sad for all, as Joan found herself in the closest show-business family she had known since Warner Bros. And time has proven ABC's dismissive statement of "lost interest" wholly inaccurate. Though short lived, *Here Come the Brides* has been fondly remembered by many ever since it left prime time.

On 25 July 1970, Norman married Sue Zan Palmer in a small ceremony at the Beverly Hills home of a Four Star executive. The divorce from Ann in 1969, followed by this marriage, sent Joan into maternal despair. She accompanied Norman's son Scott, then eleven, to the wedding. She was sobbing behind the wheel of her car when she told him, "I want you to cry, too." Scott, an obedient boy, began tearing, as much out of Matey coming apart as for his father's matrimonial status. It was not the only time that Joan had involved Scott in adult business as she had done similarly with her own kids. As a teenager later in the 1970s, he would smoke cigarettes and drink champagne with her.

After *Here Come the Brides*, Joan felt the actor's familiar uncertainty of what comes next. She hired puckish, theatrical gay man Ted Hook as her secretary. He immediately took charge of her affairs as he had with his former employer Tallulah Bankhead. Joan had been writing her life story on notepads in longhand. As her typing skills were strictly hunt and peck, Ted began pounding her words into a Smith Corona typewriter. He also distributed a Joan Blondell fact sheet to casting agencies that shaved six years off her age. Her birth was no longer in 1906, or 1909, but 1912. There was no spectacular payoff for Ted's efforts, but Joan was sent a script of the cryptically titled new play *The Effect of Gamma Rays on Man-in-the-Moon Marigolds*. She was repulsed by the lead character, a sadistic mother saddled with long monologues. She caught a performance of the play at the Huntington Hartford Theater in Los Angeles, but still she failed to sympathetically connect.

Then Bridey Murphy and Fresh died within a few months of each other. Joan suffered pitiable grief over her two squat companions of nearly twenty years. "They went everywhere with me," she said. "The children had grown up, I didn't have a husband any longer, and everyone has to have something close, to love. They were all I had in the world. I loved those pug dogs with all my heart. . . . Bridey almost pleaded to die. I saw her look up at me as she lay in my arms, then she closed her eyes, and that was it, forever. The other little one didn't last much longer. I felt an overpowering weakness. I couldn't stand that house, or that car, or anything. I could see my dogs' eyes everywhere, their sounds, the little trick we had of lying all curled up together, and suddenly it had gone."

To save money for her stereo business, and to afford private schools and summer camps for Joanie, Ellen and Joanie moved into Whitespeak. The living arrangements brought joy to all. For Joan, it helped her overcome grief. For Ellen, her long hours necessitated sharing responsibilities for Joanie. As for Joanie, the dual attention of mother and grandmother meant opportunity and indulgences. Joan saw to it that Joanie learned to swim, gleefully practicing water ballet in the Whitespeak pool with the dancerly Ted Hook. Friction between Ellen and Joan arose over the candy Joan freely gave her granddaughter.

Joan got on the nostalgia bandwagon that fall with a huge farewell bash for a retiring Jack Warner, glowing again in the company of Ruby

Keeler, Edward G. Robinson, Bette Davis, and actor turned California governor Ronald Reagan. As for her current work, she was growing increasingly depressed over perfunctory guest spots in pictures and on television. In early 1971, she took a small role in *Support Your Local Gunfighter*, probably the best of her latter-day comic westerns, where many shots are fired but no hits are made. When writer David Johnson mentioned he'd seen it on a flight from California to New York, she said, " 'Oh, God. Who was that with?' 'James Garner, Suzanne Pleshette, and Marie Windsor,' he answered. 'Oh yes,' she said tentatively. 'Was it any good?' "

There were occasions that reminded Joan she was not entirely forgotten, nor was the public indifferent. American choreographer James Waring staged a dance called "Purple Moment" for the Neatherlands Dance Theater and dedicated it to her. In April of 1971, Joan was asked to give out the Scoring Awards at the Oscars in the unlikely company of Glen Campbell, warbler of "Witchita Lineman" and other blue-collar hits of the day. After the two bestowed honors on *Love Story* and *Let It Be*, Joan repaired to the Dorothy Chandler Pavilion bar, deciding the view of the proceedings was better on the overhead television. Her only consumption of current film occurred when a friend persuaded her to see *The Last Picture Show* later that year. She did not expect to be so stirred: "I thought [it] was beautiful, and so moving. The way it was done captured so well the loneliness of that Texas town, and those people's lives."

Prolific film historian John Kobal interviewed Joan and urged her to contemplate the arc of her career. She rewarded him with a fertile response:

I'm sane enough to know that if I had taken myself more seriously—and by that I don't mean that I didn't work as a professional, just as hard as I could, as hard as anyone—I still feel that if I had fought for better roles as, say, Bette Davis did or a lot of those gals and guys that walked out and fought for better roles or stayed on suspension and all that business, I think maybe I might have been a damned good dramatic actress. I know I'm able to be. But I didn't get it because I just . . . a peculiar thing with me, I was always conscious of throwing people out of work, which is something kind of silly when you're young. But I feel that way, very conscious of the crew. If they had set up a picture for me and I fought against doing it, I think of the almost forty people who'd be out of work. At least. I couldn't do it. I have no idea why I felt that way. Well, there's one thing: I saw vaudeville through to its downfall, and we knew what it was to suffer through that, to be stony broke and hungry and everything else in our profession, and maybe that had something to do with it. It's funny to think about it now, because people like Davis or Cagney didn't throw people out of work when they fought roles, because *more* people worked when they came back in *better* roles and in their step higher as a star. But it was just *my* way; I don't think I ever had the security of feeling confidence in myself, really, ever. I used to think, "I'm just lucky to be here!" You know, I've been in the business since I was four months old.

By the summer of 1971, Joan was idling. She cranked out an episode of the treacly hit series *Love, American Style*, but work was both spotty and laborious. Whitespeak became a place of loneliness. Ellen and Joanie had moved out. Norman and his second wife had moved to Scottsdale, Arizona, where he was associate producer and director of *The New Dick Van Dyke Show*. The deaths of Bridey Murphy and Fresh kept Joan grieving. There were lovely memories of the hilltop home, but it was painful to be there alone. It was there that Joan, with quiet diligence, penned her autobiography, newly reworked as a *roman à clef* called *Center Door Fancy*, by "Timathea Scott," Joan's pseudonym. After Gloria added her editorialisms and Ted typed the final draft, Joan scrawled *wheeeeee!* on the manuscript cover, Joan and Gloria's expression for excitement and relief. But all that was in the past, and Whitespeak seemed like a haunted cage rather than a home breathing with love. There were other reasons to leave. She was getting damn tired of the birds that kept slamming into the sliding-glass terrace doors with nuclear force. And then there were the horrible memories, most notably Ted's sleeping pill overdose in Joan's bathroom following a failed love affair with a sailor.

Once she was resolved to get out of town, Joan single-mindedly disentangled herself from Whitespeak. "I called my agent and said, 'Can you find me something play-wise that would take me to New York for three months to get over this agony?' " She found the offer of *The Effect of Gamma Rays on Man-in-the-Moon Marigolds* still open. Overriding her misgivings, she learned the part in two weeks and found her acting muscles getting a workout. "I'd done nothing on stage for five years," she said. "You begin to wonder if you can still act. So I decided—Wow!—it's time to make a change! This [*Marigolds*] is a three-month experiment to see if I had turned into an amateur." Joan found a tenant for Whitespeak, then traveled by train cross country with Turt and Squirt, her two little dime-store turtles. Once again she could play mother to a pair of animals, feeding them lettuce and little balls of hamburger while eyeing the heartland vistas streaking by. "I wanted to make a quick change," she said. "Y'know, there comes a point where you must always make some *wild* change—even if you don't want to. I was in rutsville."

Joan arrived in New York and promptly sat down with Johnny Carson on *The Tonight Show*, where she expressed her hope that *Marigolds* would be a worthwhile enterprise. Van Johnson sent a huge pot of marigolds to the New Theatre on East Fifty-fourth Street on 27 September, Joan's opening night. Patsy Kelly, Penny Singleton, Ruby Keeler, and Mary McCarty were there. Adored Mike Todd Jr. was also there and came backstage for hugs, kisses, and photos with his beloved stepmother.

Marigolds won a Pulitzer prize, but Joan was not impressed. She thought it stunk, and she said so. The last thing she expected was good reviews, but she received a handful. The *Village Voice* found her "rich and complex . . . [but] a Blondell warmth softens the character. She is now pitiable, bizarre, mean—and human." Then came the hard part: playing this sulfurous harridan over and over. "It was very, very painful to do every night," she said. "I walked the floor of my small apartment all day long. I was so exhausted when I got to the theater I hardly knew what was going on. Twenty-four hours a day I was trapped inside that terrible woman, fighting to get out. I said to the producer, 'Can't we say she's insane?' But the author did not want that written in." Beatrice's repeated threats to chloroform a pet rabbit were agony for Joan, the softhearted animal lover. Her character does eventually kill it, but Joan insisted that she take her bows holding the live rabbit as a way of discharging the toxins of the play.

When Turt and Squirt grew lethargic and cloudy eyed, Joan kept them alive with milk baths, eye drops, and various home remedies recommended by other turtle lovers. But nothing worked, so she called a reptile expert at Columbia University, who offered the winning remedy. "One day the little fellows' eyes suddenly reopened, bright and shining, and I was so happy," she said. Then Joan became sluggish as her face swelled. She was diagnosed with mumps, the one childhood disease she averted in her youth. She had to do some artful camouflage for a taped interview with David Frost, but she largely *enjoyed* her malady since it kept her away from the New Theatre. "I was never so grateful for anything in my life," she said. "Maybe I got it from kissing too many dogs on the street. People sent me kid things, teddy bears, dolls; it was wonderful." She recovered by early November and dreaded her return to *Marigolds*. "That woman would never have caught the mumps," she huffed.

Marigolds was playing while Ruby Keeler was enjoying a flurry of nostalgic interest in a popular Broadway revival of *No, No Nanette*. Joan went four times and was overjoyed at the reception: "The entire audience rocked the house with a bellowing BRRRRRRAAAAAVO!! And I couldn't help but feel terribly proud for Ruby and Patsy [Kelly]." Keeler and Blondell both appeared at the Musical Theatre on St. Marks Place to put their signatures and footprints, with shoes, in wet cement. In newspaper photos, Joan was scowling, perhaps in response to the role she was playing nightly. She said she was caught in a memory of Grauman's Chinese Theatre with Dick Powell all those years ago. She said she tried not to look backwards: "All of that stuff is painful to me. Nothing you do couldn't be done better and I pain inside when I look at myself." When duties at the

Musical Theatre were over, she hurried into her chauffeured car with Ted Hook. As they neared Sheridan Square, she saw a dog on a stoop and rolled down the window. "Hello, you beautiful thing," she said loudly out the window. "What are you all tied up for? Don't be depressed. Put your head up. You're a pretty dog. I wish I had you."

When her three months of *Marigolds* were up, an ecstatic Joan declared herself through with live theater. "I'm not a night person anymore," she said. "I don't go for pacing the floor all day until curtain time. I'm used to getting up at dawn and going to work." She kept her professionalism intact despite her distaste for the play, and so won the affection of the cast. She was presented with a green-eyed orange tabby named Shadow on closing night. Joan got teary and fell in love on the spot.

Joan returned to Southern California and Whitespeak. Ted Hook remained her Boy Friday, and soon enough she was looking for work, though the offerings were not rewarding. When asked about an appearance on the drama series *McCloud*, Joan agonized: " 'Uhhhh. Ohhh. the mother of—uhhh—a guy—uhhh—who—uhhh—I don't think I read the script.' She laughs. *'Oh dear*. Well, you're liable to see it some day and then maybe you'll understand why I don't remember it.' " She kept tinkering at her manuscript. She was modest in her self-appraisal, and so triply delighted when Random House showed interest. "I write at night. I mean, what else do you think I'd be doing at night—dating?" she said, smiling to a reporter.

Despite much interference, Ellen was a good mother, saving money to give her daughter opportunities at education and recreation. They divided their time between an apartment in Venice and a trailer on two and a half acres of country land abutting the Angeles National Forest in Saugus, California. Joan helped with the down payment, while Rose Lundin and her family, friends with a working horse ranch, lived across the street. Saugus, for a time, was a place to escape urbanity, breathe fresh air, and run horses. But trouble began when Ellen was taken in by a Rasputin-like self-proclaimed psychologist who used LSD in a "guided session" to put her through a personal transformation. From there, as Ellen wrote, "My life had no anchor in reality." She spent increasing time in Saugus with this violent man, and the stereo business suffered. The store co-owner brought in another partner, and decisions were unwisely made. Money was skimmed from the earnings, more LSD was shared, and the business went bankrupt.

Joan's investment of eighteen thousand dollars was lost, and Ellen was without moorings. Her mental state continued to oscillate, with low points moving from deep depression, to paranoia, to extreme agitation. She had severe mood swings and was volatile and threatening, but there were days, even weeks, when all was fine superficially. When Ellen was on an upswing, she and "Rasputin" accompanied Joan on an overnight train trip to Scottsdale to visit Norman. But good days for Ellen could turn sour. Norman found his mother ashen and distracted when she got off the train. Ellen and her cohort were stoned the entire visit, behaving inappropriately and laughing sardonically when nothing was funny. For the first time, Norman could see the struggle his sister was having with reality. Joan withdrew into silence. "It was an excruciating time, the weekend from hell," said Norman. "It was as ugly as anything I can remember."

Ellen's mental instability continued after returning to LA. She heard voices, had extreme ideas about reality, and acted out unreal personality distortions. After taking her clothes off at the Venice Beach, she was sent to Camarillo State Hospital, where she was diagnosed paranoid schizophrenic and a danger to herself and others. Joan said Ellen had four personalities, though it is not known if that was her observation or if she was repeating a professional opinion. When Joan sent Joanie to summer camp and did not tell Ellen her whereabouts, Ellen became suicidal. While at Edgemont Mental Hospital, she was fed anti-depressants, anti-psychotics, sleeping pills, pain pills, and muscle relaxants. The horrendous cocktail only made Ellen's condition worse. After a month of avoiding electroshock therapy, she escaped.

When eleven-year-old Joanie returned from camp, she was taken by her father, Chuck Hayward, to his family's cattle ranch in the Midwest.

Joan watched in horror as her family disintegrated, helpless to soothe Ellen's suffering or prevent Hayward from assuming care of his daughter. Joan had no reference points, no prior knowledge of medications or treatment for Ellen. For a long period, Joan did not even know that she was diagnosable. Joan was of a generation that saw mental illness, compounded with illegal drug use, as shameful and taboo for discussion. "You're just bewildered," Joan would say to Ellen in an attempt at maternal comfort. Her Christian Science faith helped Joan see Ellen as whole and complete, and kept her from affirming her daughter's illness. But her love and faith did not in themselves provide a remedy. Recriminations, an informal child-custody network, tears, avoidance, and denial arose in cyclical pattern. So did depression. Joan once confided to grandson Scotty, "Ellen's sick again and I want to die."

To generate cash and disassociate from memories, Joan sold Whitespeak and rented an apartment at the Sportsman's Lodge in Studio City. She was upbeat to a journalist when describing it as "a quite lovely hotel and a swinging one," near the Warner Bros. lot. "There's no need for a house when you're not married. It's just a bother," she explained. Her fastidiousness in earlier days slipped, and her small apartment was over-run. "I hang things on the floor," she confessed.

She chose Sportsman's Lodge because of work, and rarely was a pro-fessional distraction more welcome. Joan was again shooting at Warner's, playing the manager of a secretarial school in 1930s Los Angeles, in NBC's midseason private-eye replacement series *Banyon*. "I looked for the old dressing rooms at Warners . . . and there was nothing left," she noted wistfully. "I try, I really try not to gaze too far into the past. But then it all floods in: the grips and gaffers from the old days stop by and take me into a big bear hug and they say, 'Oh Joanie, it's good to have you back.' And I feel so ten-der I could cry. . . I keep getting memories. Not of all those pictures when I played stenographers and nurses and girl reporters and gang molls, but of what someone long dead said to me in front of Stage 27, and who I played mixed doubles with on the tennis court at the back. I look up, and hear a voice, and see a face, and there's no one there."

For all of Joan's miseries, there were times when the Blondell fortitude summoned forth a measure of joy. There were still great times with Ellen, Joanie, and the rest of her expanding family. Thanksgivings were always highly anticipated. Junie lived in the Valley, and Gloria and Victor ("Sissy Aunt" and "Uncle Vic" to the family) had a home in tony Pacific Palisades. When brothers and sisters reunited, the occasion was guaranteed to be therapeutically hysterical. "I think they were fabulous," said Junie's daughter Kathy. "Those three people—Joan, Junie, and Gloria— were resilient, funny, and found humor and love for each other and each other's families through everything that ever happened. Gretchen would cook on holidays, even after she and Junie were divorced. If everyone was in town, we felt so lucky." Pranks were common. Joan kept a life-sized dummy called "Mr. Dink" in the passenger seat of her car as a safety precaution when driving at night. Gloria kidnapped it, stuck it in the closet, then told Joan she had a present waiting there. When Joan opened the door, there was a piercing shriek, then tears of laughter.

While notching episodes of *Banyon*, Joan visited Richard Nixon's "Western White House" in the Southern California beach town of San Clemente. The occasion was a gathering of four hundred of Nixon's "friends." Joan told a reporter that she was happy in the company of self-chosen friends. Who does she see? "Joanie Bennett in New York. Barbara Stanwyck out here. I dearly love her, she's kind of like me; she enjoys being home more than going out. I like the kind of friends where two or three years pass, but you can pick up where you left off. Glenda Farrell [who died in 1971] was a dear, dear friend. . . . Every seven or eight years [Jimmy Cagney and I] exchange postcards." That same month, Joan was present to see a frail, eighty-three-year-old Frances Marion receive the honor of "the dean of Hollywood screenwriters" by the Los Angeles City Council.

In the fall of 1972, Joan's ten-year literary love child, *Center Door Fancy*, was published at last, its cover title in the popular barbell font of the day. Critics and friends were warm in their assessment. Joyce Haber wrote,

"To meet her—or read her—is to meet honesty, warmth, concern, and literacy (she spends $150 a month at Hunter's Bookstore, reads voraciously on all subjects)." The *New York Times* wrote, "Lively, warm, and funny." Ruby Keeler said, "*Center Door Fancy* took me on a trip I never thought I'd have again," while Patsy Kelly said, "I loved every minute of *Center Door Fancy*—it reminded me of the way the world used to be." Former brother-in-law Albert "Cubby" Broccoli sent Joan a check for ten thousand dollars to cover the film rights. Since divorcing Gloria, he had made a large fortune as the producer of James Bond movies, but he did not follow through on producing the film adaptation of Joan's book. Most likely he wanted to give more immediate help to Joan by offering financial support without appearing to give alms.

Joan had an inferiority complex for anyone who was lettered and/or published, so she was giddy from the positive response she received in her newly recognized identity as a writer. After her *Banyon* duties were complete, she readily submitted to a book tour in the fall. She offered a plot synopsis of *Center Door Fancy*. "It's about a man in the carnival world," she explained. "He starts out as a boy, becomes a barker, then becomes a tightrope walker in a circus, rises gradually, but all the time he doesn't have a real home; he's searching for one. . . . I've listened so often to show business stories that for many years that's all there was in the world. I guess my central figure, John Marten, is a composite of those great and lonely men. And there's something of my father in him." Although the published version of *Center Door Fancy* was a clear reflection of Joan's life, some details were missing. The Todd marriage is skimmed over in the last two pages, as though Joan could not bear to lay waste those feelings once again.

Though exhausted, Joan managed to have fun when the tour wound down in New York. Her unlikely friendship with Norman's college fraternity brother turned New York restauranteur Freddy Mohr was a salve against family troubles and public demands. Mohr adored Joan, felt for her loneliness and pain, nicknamed her "Moms," and became her travelling companion. He once took her to a Greenwich Village cabaret to see an aging comedian. The performer reverently approached Joan and said, "May I show you something?" He opened his jacket to reveal a photo of Ed Blondell stitched into the lining. Then they did a portion of *The Lost Boy* act together and the house went wild. Fred was fun, outrageous, a great cook, reliable, and loved by the family. He was so charming he could get away with anything, including marriage, fatherhood, and open homosexual love affairs simultaneously. He had a great ability to liberate people from their inhibitions. As Norman put it, Fred was the kind of guy who would pick you up at the airport sporting a bright purple Afro—just because.

By the time Joan was in New York, *Center Door Fancy* had become a Literary Guild selection and was selling well. But the traveling had exacerbated her health problems. In addition to arthritis, Joan suffered chronic back pain, a cold she could not shake, and a penicillin overload. "I looked at myself in the mirror this morning and I'm *puuuuur*-ple and green and I've got bags under my pleats," she told reporter Ronald L. Bowers. "You're just catching me at the tail end of a long promotion trip that didn't even give me time to go the ladies' room and I'm just about to take every piece of furniture in this room and break it." Bowers remembered exiting the elevator of Joan's sublet on East Sixty-fourth Street to find her waiting in the hallway outside her front door. He had brought an elegantly wrapped single yellow rose and a twenty-seven-dollar bottle of French red wine. She was "flabbergasted," telling him that these were the first gifts she had ever received for an interview. "In the old days, it was we movie stars who *had* to take gifts to Hedda or Louella when we would go to their homes to be interviewed," she said. The jovial interview was fueled with vodka and tonic and plenty of cigarettes. Bowers found Joan "a delight," and she followed up with a note letting him know that "the wine was divine."

Joan was so pleased at the reception for *Center Door Fancy* that it hardly mattered when *Banyon* executive producer Quinn Martin announced that the series was "999% sure not to be picked up." It lasted a mere thirteen episodes, but Joan did not mourn. She was having much more fun as a minor literary celebrity. "Everybody went to sleep," was her summary assessment of *Banyon*.

When Joan returned to Los Angeles in early 1973, she did not rent another room at the Sportsman's Lodge. Instead, she found a two-bedroom, two-bathroom apartment on the third floor of the Champagne Towers on Ocean Avenue in Santa Monica. The exterior of the Lawrence Welk–owned high rise had the bland features of a nameless conference hotel, but her flat came with some charm. It had a large terrace with a view over the esplanade and palm trees to the Pacific, an L-shaped dining room–living room, and a counter separating the kitchen. As was her custom wherever she lived, Joan displayed family photos on end tables and shelves. With time off, she occupied herself with preferred distractions: playing with the grandkids and cooking. She tried writing for children and came up with the delightful alliterative tale of a mother and her four look-alike daughters named "Poppy, Poony, Penny, and Peeny." When only three were about, Mother believed Poony to be missing, but it was Poppy, not Poony, said Penny. Roll call verified Peeny as absent, which sent mother and sisters scurrying in search of their misplaced loved one. She was found, merely asleep under her bed, and there was much rejoicing. Then mother announced a new one on the way. "This time you will see, a boy it will be," said Mother. But what shall be his name? "It took seconds and seconds and seconds galore till Mom got an answer from daughters four." They straightened their shoulders and called out their choice: "Pruney."

With her health improved, Joan wrote her will. She named friend and financial expert Flora Marks and Norman as executors. One-half of her estate was to go to Joanie for "her education and well-being." The other half was to be divided between her other three grandchildren: Sandra, Scott, and Stephanie Powell. Ellen was "to have whatever worldly goods (furniture, etc.) she needs to make a home for herself and Joan Ellen Hayward."

The unequal distribution speaks not to unequal affection, but to a recognition by Joan that one grandchild was in greater need. Her grandmotherly affection was otherwise fully democratic. "I love to take them for a while and spoil them to death," she once said, "and then when I'm through send them back to their parents!"

Joan's relations with her children were as complicated as ever. Ellen moved into the second bedroom of Joan's flat while Joanie was still with her father's family in Nebraska. When Ellen was home, genuine love was combined with routines of humor and deflections of harsh reality. She enrolled in a cosmetology program, earned her license, and was soon getting regular industry jobs as background hairdresser. But Ellen's condition remained volatile. Hollywood was awash in cocaine, and for her it acted as relief from the effects of the psychiatrists' anti-depressant and anti-psychotic drugs. Unfortunately, as often happens, she reacted with unpredictable and extreme behavior to the doctor's prescriptions. With her mental health history, she was judged "dangerous" by various state psychiatrists. The solution was woefully predictable: a stay in Metropolitan State Hospital.

As for Norman, *The New Dick Van Dyke Show* was still on the air, and Joan was hired for an episode that he directed. She played the widow of an old vaudevillian who left instructions to have a jolly funeral. Both mother and son found the experience to be discomforting, in part because Norman felt that he never pleased her. She withheld praise, saying he should be "another Francis Ford Coppola," not a director of TV sitcoms. But the quality of Joan's offerings hardly qualified her to stand in judgment of her son. Before taping *The New Dick Van Dyke Show*, she took a job on a Carroll O'Connor TV special, playing his mother (!) while he strained to be believably youngish with a dark toupee and high-pitched voice. *All in the Family* allowed O'Connor to flex his muscles as a writer, while Joan's scripts for *M*A*S*H* and *The Waltons*, written on the heels of *Center Door Fancy*, were never produced.

Encamped on her sofa, wreathed by smoke from her Benson and Hedges, Joan once said, "There is nothing in my life I would change if I could. The mistakes I made were made out of love. And who escapes heartaches? I loved too intensely for it not to be painful when things went wrong. You have to have gone through pain to end up with understanding and compassion for all people. I have that kind of compassion now. Tough as the going was then, I would have wanted to go through it, if I had a choice, in order to be able to sit here with the feeling I have inside of me. Why should I want to change anything that led to this moment?"

When the Hayward family returned Joanie, she lived with Ellen and Joan at Champagne Towers. She began to observe the small, telling moments of her grandmother's life. In preparing to go out, Joan would get a bowl of ice water, dunk a makeup pad in it, then pat her neck and face for a zesty wake-up. There was little need to pluck or shave, as Joan did not have much body hair. Using a little wooden suitcase with plug-in bulbs around the mirror that she had since the tour of *The Dark at the Top of the Stairs*, she could apply her face in quick time. Pancake, rouge, a little lipstick, eyebrows, with the eyelashes last, and her cosmetic mantle was complete. Sometimes Joanie would do her hair, and sometimes she wore a hair piece, but never a full wig. Neither was necessary; she had thick hair even as she got older. It was darker around the base of the neck, then grew lighter in front.

Joan's arthritis worsened. Her hands became gnarled, her fingers canting from swollen knuckles. She was terrified that the deformity would cost her employment. She medicated with eight to ten Percodan a day, flirting with addiction. She switched to aspirin, but continued to suffer horrible swelling. She often needed pills just to sit up in bed and bend her knees. There were the unhealed wounds of past abuses as well. Joan was prone to sleepwalking, and more than once Joanie woke up to hear her scream, "I hate you! I'm going to kill you!" Jumping out of bed, Joanie would find her grandmother sauntering down the hallway with eyes open, standing in the living room, or in the fetal position on the bathroom floor. Sometimes the nightmares would come without the sleepwalking. Joanie would enter her room, find Joan upright in bed, and touch her with one finger. With that, Joan would fall back and go to sleep. The next day she would prepare Joanie for school and prepare herself for the set, apparently without a memory of what happened during the night. "She never showed anger or rage like somebody owed her anything," said Joanie. "She was always thankful for what she had. Even during the worst troubles with Ellen, she would put on a happy face and go to work. She loved work, it was her escape."

Though suffering physically, Joan maintained her cast-iron constitution. "It takes all the talent you've got in your guts to play unimportant roles," she said. "It's not degrading, just tough to do. It's fine to start out as a curvy biz-whiz, but unfortunately, when you can't do those roles anymore, people think you're finished." But even in the 1970s, the rewards for work were not exclusively financial: "Even if you do have enough clams put away, your family's grown up, you're husbandless and after a week of reading day and night and fixing up the house real pretty, you want to get at it again. And I'm so used to work." Still, the mercurial world gave Joan pause. In March of 1974, she was in the company of Ronald Reagan, Frank Sinatra, and John Wayne, waxing nostalgic with American Film Institute Lifetime Achievement Award winner James Cagney. One week earlier, she and shock rocker Alice Cooper guest starred on NBC's *The Snoop Sisters* in an episode dedicated to Satan worshippers.

Joan was badly shaken when her brother, Junie, was admitted to the UCLA Hospital in July of 1974, where he died of a cerebral hemorrhage. The doctor spoke to the assembled family and apologized, explaining that he should have survived, but that he seemed indifferent to life. The words did not surprise anyone present. Junie had been unhappy in his last years; his most recent romance was not a good one. His professional reputation, however, was unassailable. At the time of his death, he had worked as electrician for seventy-six movies and television shows. The boy who hated the vaudeville life became as embedded in show business as his big sister.

The next month, a brokenhearted Joan went to Florida to do a dinner theater production of *Barefoot in the Park*. There was a slight upturn in her children's fortunes when Norman split from his second wife and returned to Los Angeles following the cancellation of *The New Dick Van Dyke Show*. Ellen was working steadily again while Joanie was in school, though Champagne Towers was beginning to seem too cozy for the three of them.

Joan's give-away habits kept her on the edge of solvency, so she was not in a position to be choosy about work. Paychecks had not grown with inflation, and on some gigs she was earning barely over Screen Actors Guild minimum. She and costar Ray Milland reported to the Fox set of the TV movie *The Dead Don't Die* in the fall of 1974. She had married dapper Milland in *Blonde Crazy*; now she was his loyal aide to an army of zombies. The director was young Curtis Harrington, who sought to re-create the B-horror genre of the 1930s, even down to the casting. Though Joan did not do horror films, she *was* a 1930s survivor. "I was thrilled to work with her," said Harrington. Ever professional, Joan approached him in search of clues to her character's motivation. "Curtis, why does she do this? Why does she hang around this man?" "Well, because she hopes to become a zombie and have eternal life," he answered with a straight face. Joan paused to absorb his response. "Ooooooooohh. *Now* I understand."

Her next foray into television was a notch above *The Dead Don't Die*. *Winner Take All* was a mild exposé on gambling addiction featuring a rueful, beleaguered Shirley Jones. Its first-time producer was actress Nancy Malone, who frankly adored Joan. She felt her as a kindred spirit, having starred as Aunt Sissy in a recent television remake of *A Tree Grows in Brooklyn*. "All I wanted to do was pay tribute to her," said Malone. "Then she called and was so complimentary. That makes a person fly high. That phone call did it." Years later, Malone recalled working with Blondell. "Like millions of people, I was a great fan," she said. "I spent a great deal of time as a young actress seeing old movies. She ranked way up there in terms of her genuine truth and her fantastic comedic timing. She could turn on a hair from being fabulously funny, blowzy, don't care personality to someone who could break your heart."

When casting *Winner Take All*, she fought to give Joan the role of a seasoned casino owner. "There was no one who could play this part but her," she said. "When production began, I alerted the crew that Joan Blondell and [costar] Sylvia Sidney were great stars with longevity and they were to be treated with respect. The crew was all young guys, but they were 'Oh Miss Blondell this' and 'Oh Miss Blondell that.' They adored her and couldn't do enough for her." As for Joan's performance, Malone noted that "she could take an ordinary line and make it a Shakespearean play. She filled it with everything she had. It was a thrill to walk on the set and there she was. She was a true professional—she came on the set, knew her lines, no muss, no fuss. 'Where do you want me?' She came with no entourage."

Malone was one of the few people who spoke of Blondell in degrees that were appropriate to her talent. "She had a wonderful improvisational quality about her," she said. "It was as though she had just popped into a scene and was part of the world that is being filmed. Brando had that as a young man. It was as though you had never seen a script before, yet it was technique that everyone strives for. Joan had it. 'Integrity' is the perfect word I would choose for her. There was no such thing as walking through it. She didn't have the major starring part, it was a supporting part. It was never approached that way and it was exquisitely performed. I also knew we needed to watch the hours, because she wasn't in great health. I was very cautious of not exhausting her. I just loved her, loved her, loved her."

Not all sets were as congenial as *Winner Take All*. In the summer of 1975, Joan filmed a cameo spot as a landlady in *Won Ton Ton, the Dog Who Saved Hollywood*. She didn't know what the movie was about or what her part was in the story. "I never know, even after I do them," she said. "I asked the director if it was okay if I didn't understand the script. You don't ask questions." The finished movie was a send up of 1920s Hollywood with dozens of old stars dropping in every few seconds. In Joan's one scene, she tells a naked young girl posing like kindergarten cheesecake to "get your clothes on, Norma Jean," implying that the junior coquette will grow up to become Marilyn Monroe. In *The Baron*, handsome Calvin Lockhart played an actor-producer-player with a mob debt. This was quintessential 1970s black action drama, dripping with attitude and edited with a scythe. At least Joan *looked* like she was having fun playing a filthy rich sugar mama to Lockhart, whom she affectionately called "hot dog."

When Ellen and Joanie lived with Joan, the threesome experienced as much pleasure as they did adversity. Joanie's school friends came over for pizza and swam in the rooftop pool of the Champagne Towers. They giggled over a handsome gray-haired gentleman they saw walking along the boardwalk, nicknaming him "Mr. Wonderful" and deciding that he and Matey should wed. After Shadow died, they delighted in spoiling Joan's next two cats. Flakey, the fat gray tabby, and OuiOui, the skinny Siamese who fetched, were fed the fanciest wet-food variety cans of beef, liver, shrimp, and sardines. Turtles Turt and Squirt were still in their aquarium, though the cats posed a constant threat to their safety.

Joanie has keen sense memories of her grandmother: the liberal use of Johnson's Baby Powder from the neck down, the eyelash glue that smelt like rubber cement, and the cold cream slathered on an aging face at bedtime. When she got angry, Joan had a habit of talking under her breath and walking away. She loved fresh cut flowers and had several bouquets around the apartment. Joan had a bit of a green thumb. She loved geraniums, azaleas, and pussy willows. If she was home at the right hour, she would gaze at sunsets from the balcony. She went to church off and on and continued her custom of writing biblical quotes to get through difficult times. Joan's deep spirituality never wavered. "I'm a great believer in God and His presence and help," she once said. "I'd never even be here without it."

The abundant love and humor made Ellen's breakdowns all the more agonizing. They came in waves, and by now Ellen had a patchwork history of diagnoses, first paranoid schizophrenia, then suicidal, then manic depressive, petit mal seizures, and convulsions. Each came with a different set of medications, and each misdiagnosis led to drugs that caused rather than cured symptoms. Over several years she was given Haldol, Artane,

Resterol, Lithium Citrate, Lithium Carbonate, Deprakot, Tegratol, Stelizine, Prolixin, Thorazine, Librium, and Xanax in various combinations.

Joan and Joanie were in the waiting area of yet another hospital when Ellen came shuffling down the hallway, her slippers never losing contact with the linoleum. She was on Thorazine this time and wearing a hospital gown open in the back. Though drooling and inaudible, she seemed glad to have company. "Those runs of insanity were long and excruciating," said Joanie. "We didn't talk about it. We lived through it."

CHAPTER 11

Predestiny

Life does not cease to be funny when people die any more than it ceases to be serious when people laugh.
—George Bernard Shaw, *The Doctor's Dilemma*

In mid-1976, Joan taped a two-hour season premiere of the popular cop series *Starsky & Hutch* with former *Here Come the Brides* regular David Soul. She played an emasculating drugstore manager whose hankering for he-men figures into both the whodunit and the why-do-it. "You take Clark Gable and Ty Power—those were *real* men," she said in her familiar timbre. "That's what's wrong with the world today—there are no real men around. Just sissy boys and perverts." Joan's line is spoken immediately before series costar Paul Michael Glaser inquires about panty hose.

Joan had a small role in the ABC-TV movie *Death at Love House*, directed by *Here Come the Brides'* director and friend E. W. Swackhamer ("Swacky" to Joan). Wearing one of her own Day-Glo caftans, Joan was the president of a movie-star fan club, and she was in pain. Her rheumatoid arthritis was not mollified by fistfuls of Percodan. When it became unendurable, she admitted herself to St. John's Hospital in Santa Monica. Doctors suspected something more sinister at work in Joan's body, and several blood tests were made. At the same time, Marlon Brando was there on a crash diet just before leaving for Manila to shoot *Apocalypse Now*.

When he found out Joan was in the hospital, he sent her a floral tower with a note: "To a woman I've always loved." Two days later, Joan was discharged, medicated for pain relief but uncertain of her condition. As a minor pick-me-up, she was moved to accept induction into the little-known Motion Picture Hall of Fame.

In early 1977, Joan was approached by loose-jointed director John Cassavetes to appear in one of his independent, highly personal films. She knew him by reputation but had never appeared in anything dedicated to such a uniquely modern aesthetic. The guerilla-style moviemaking initially put her off, with Cassavetes forever dodging unions and the City of Pasadena to shoot what he wanted. "You never know where the camera is," she said. "Cassavetes follows you around the corner, into the phone booth, under the bed, everywhere." He allowed actors to decide what they were going to do, which threw Joan further off-balance. She was used to unambiguous writing and directing, and here she had neither. And, to top off her bemusement, she was playing a writer! Joan's character, Sarah Goode, authored a play called *The Second Woman*, while the movie, *Opening Night*, followed the backstage turmoil just days before the premiere. "The play I've written is on the serious side," she explained as best she could, "but the girl [Cassavetes wife, Gena Rowlands] is putting in her own words and making a comedy out of what is not meant to be funny. And that irks me. But don't ask me if *Opening Night* is supposed to be a comedy or a drama. I'll have to see it before I can tell."

Lines that were spoken in one take were absent in the next. Blocking changed, moments leaning toward something comic would turn dramatic, and Joan was never sure why. After a half century of making movies, there was only so much flexibility available to her. "I could see she was terrified," said Cassavetes. "[Veteran costar] Paul Stewart said, 'Go talk to Joan. She doesn't know what she's doing. She's scared to death.' I'd go over to her—I couldn't help liking her, her warm, open face—and ask if she had a problem. 'No, not *at all*. I'm having the time of my life! Absolutely *not*.' And you could hear the hysteria in her voice." There was also her ill health to consider. The cortisone injections she took had a deleterious effect. "I blew up like a balloon, my wardrobe didn't fit me and I had no idea why I was so overweight," she said. "No one would believe that I was not overindulging. So I suffered in silence, though I was depressed."

Cassavetes was initially displeased with her performance. "Disagreement is *not* a bad thing," he said. "*Opening Night* was originally about the *writer*, and the integrity of the actor standing up to the writer. I wanted Bette Davis to play the Joan Blondell part. She would have been tougher. Gena can be grand. Intimidating. And Blondell was *too nice* to her—as a person and an actress. She didn't fight as hard as Bette would have."

To his credit, Cassavetes did not try to turn Joan Blondell into Bette Davis. "John puts such faith in his actors," said Joan. "When I'd ask him anything he'd just tweak my nose and giggle." He was avoiding specifics in the hopes that Blondell's reaction would inform her performance. His plan worked. After the early days of unease, her participation in *Opening Night* became an asset. She brought to Sarah Goode a compelling mix of womanly vulnerability, inveterate nerve, and muted rage at the desecration of her play. Camera operator Michael Ferris noted the transformation:

John knew he wanted a conflict between Gena and Joan's characters. There are several very arch conversations between them. . . . [Cassavetes] was never one to "direct" in the sense of giving specific or absolute instructions to an actor. My feeling was that he thought a gal in her character's position would be tough simply as a survivor of the theatrical wars. She would have come through as a professional writer with a storied career in the Lillian Hellman mold. Her talent, shrewdness, and extensive experience made her such a skilled and hard-nosed competitor that it rendered her gender moot. I think personally that Joan chose to present these aspects but in a somewhat more sympathetic manner than John had originally imagined. I remember thinking often as I watched her play this role that rather than explode her contempt for an actress playing her "creation" she let this vitriol seep out in little looks and manners and words with a few well chosen and perfectly timed barbs attached to them. She chose subtle over obvious.

Joan's awakening was felt throughout the cast and crew. "After she found out what she was supposed to do, she was lovely," said costar Ben Gazzara. "She was supposed to do nothing. Just be herself." Gena Rowlands simply loved her. "I don't know if the word 'endearing' is good enough for her," she said. When *Opening Night* ran out of money after six weeks of production, no one took another job. Cassavetes secured funding and the cast was back on the job after three weeks. "To me, John's the funniest man on earth," said Joan when it was all over, no longer the befuddled actor she was at the onset. "He's like a bad kid sometimes and he's got a double diesel engine. He doesn't bother with minor things like 'Action' or 'Cut.' You just do it and he's got it. It wouldn't surprise me if he'd push himself and his crew into a revolving door to get a shot. He sees things none of the rest of us do." By the last day, the set was aglow with goodwill. True to Cassavetes' vérité style, the movie's final scene was a party for the movie's extras, including granddaughter Joanie. Shot eleven times with hors d'oeuvres and plenty of champagne, most everyone got plastered. Underage Joanie did not, but Joan curled her hair and bought her a silk dress and platform heels for the occasion.

Opening Night is every bit the movie to expect from a stylistically uncompromising filmmaker. It is an exploration of age, of gender, of promise and remorse, and of *longueurs*, but that comes with Cassavetes. Janet Maslin of the *New York Times* astutely wrote that "the shifting-sands quality that colors Myrtle's [Gena Rowland's] performance on stage also extends to the actors in the film, but the cast has a vibrancy that is perhaps a byproduct of this kind of uncertainty." Reviews for Joan were generally rapturous. *Variety* called her "stunning." Her personal triumph was confirmed with a Golden Globe nomination.

The greatest gift of *Opening Night* was Joan's realization that she could still act and be stimulated by moviemaking. Physical, monetary, and familial woes had not destroyed her concentration, ability to imagine someone else's life, or adaptability to a new method of working. So many worthless movies and TV shows had not destroyed her talent. The gift came just in time.

More tests confirmed that Joan had both acute rheumatoid arthritis and pernicious anemia. But the worst of her medical news came with the diagnosis of leukemia. The arthritis and the stroke were known among family and friends, but she chose to keep this latest news a secret, referring to her malady vaguely as "my little blood problem." She accompanied Ellen to see the surprise hit *Rocky* and happily greeted the new wave of uplift that swept the movies in the mid to late 1970s. She believed that *Rocky* struck a chord because "people are yearning for optimism. You've got to have a whisper of it someplace or you'll go nuts."

Mobility was harder to maintain. Even with Ellen or Gloria's assistance, it would take Joan up to three hours to get ready to go out. As a result of the stroke, her eyesight was dimming. With so many personal heartaches, she needed the distraction of work. She found it with *Grease*, a lavish movie musical intended to take advantage of its stage predecessor's success. "I had to laugh when [producer] Allan Carr told me my role in *Grease* is that of a fast-talking waitress down at the local malt shop who is everyone's confidante with a heart-of-gold," she said. "Just like being back at Warners in the good old days."

Grease was a highly lucrative reinvention of the 1950s during an era of nostalgic glances backward. Not even *American Graffiti* and the TV series *Happy Days* tapped into the appetite for the '50s as did *Grease*, with its commitment to ducktails, bubble gum, poodle skirts, and rock and roll. Cameos by Eve Arden, Frankie Avalon, Sid Caesar, and Alice Ghostley, in addition to Blondell, contributed to the air of cross-generational sentimentality. With twenty-four-year-old John Travolta, twenty-nine-year-old Olivia Newton-John, and thirty-four-year-old Stockard Channing in starring roles, this was hardly an attempt at an honest portrayal of high school, even by the lenient standards of the genre.

After *The Phynx* and *Won Ton Ton, the Dog Who Saved Hollywood*, *Grease* became the first and last time Joan did a cameo in a hit movie. *Grease* was so big, in fact, that it became the highest-grossing movie of 1978 and for a time was the third-highest-grossing movie in film history. But for those following the travails of Joan Blondell, her appearance in a runaway success was bittersweet. Here was an enduring star of yesteryear reduced to serving malts to a pack of so-called teenagers. And her creeping ill health could not be hidden from the camera. When she carried a tray of dishes and reached with her right elbow for the light switch, she did not reach high enough, but the light went out anyway.

As she prepared to die, two unresolved issues preoccupied Joan: Ellen's continued health problems and Joanie's well-being. For all of Joan's efforts, teenaged Joanie had become a wild child—under-supervised, defiant, and too aware of her budding sexual appeal. When Joanie and boyfriend Dirk Evans brought a large flea-infested dog into Joan's apartment, she saw it as an opportunity to move. Hormonal teenagers were beyond her energy, so Joan informed Ellen in no uncertain terms that she must take Joanie. They moved to Santa Monica, while Joan settled into a smaller one-bedroom unit in Champagne Towers. Joan would not reveal her leukemia diagnosis, and she was reaching a stage of ill health where she often preferred being alone to preparing herself for company and companionship. The exodus of Ellen and Joanie was also the last, and perhaps most graphic, illustration of Joan's lifelong romanticism. After all the disasters she had witnessed, she still hoped that "Mr. Wonderful" would someday appear and take care of them. Only occasionally did she let reality intrude. "My grandchildren are in their teens and often I realize a sense of sadness in them," she said in 1977. "They are aware of so much I wasn't at their age, so much that is ugly and unacceptable. They belong to today's generation with its traumatic adult problems, problems they are really too young to cope with—and that makes me sad."

Joan was gladdened when Norman began dating Ellen Levine, who came from a "normal," middle-class Jewish family in Philadelphia. The damage caused by Norman's divorce from Ann and his unfortunate second marriage was eased with the arrival of "Ellen L," so nicknamed by Joan to distinguish her from her daughter. Norman and Joan were not close, and visits were sometimes onerous rather than pleasurable. But as Joan grew sicker, Norman pulled closer, inspired by urgings from Ellen L. He began softening and forgiving in the face of his mother's weakening grip on life. And Joan genuinely liked Ellen L. She once told Norman how happy she was that he had met someone undisturbed by the tumult of show business. Joan felt that Ellen L had a temperamental resemblance to Ann, which only elevated her in Joan's estimation.

Joan made the cheap television movie *Battered* in the spring of 1978, and her performance is hard to watch. Her knotted, arthritic hands are in plain view. Even more painful is the movie's topic, which must have brought back unwelcome memories of Mike Todd. Domestic violence is treated predictably in *Battered*: It runs in families, there's denial and appeasement, covering up, guilt, excuses, bureaucratic and legal ineffectiveness, and stark terror. Some die of it while others seek higher ground. Joan's character talks back to her brutal, hard-drinking husband and shows real backbone. Their sniping has a well-worn pattern to it, as though abuse becomes their primary method of communication. But their physical altercations, in light of Joan's frailty, are particularly disturbing.

Joan's television movies of the 1970s were not appreciably worse than the lowest of her Warner Bros. products of the 1930s. But they lacked any instinct for grace in storytelling, relying instead on attitude, topicality, and pop music. No reasonable viewer of most 1970s TV movies expected high quality, but their routine ponderousness might explain their limited shelf life even as historic curios. Age and infirmities left Joan's work less impeccable, but she still conducted herself with old school professionalism. She was always on time, knew her lines, and never spoke down to the crew, actors, or director who might have just sprung from the UCLA Film School. She knew better. In a list of suggestions she compiled for younger actors, called "Self-Preservation," she wrote, "Be considerate and nice to the entire crew. The prop man may be your producer someday. When you're exhausted, irritable, about to pass out from overwork, hot lights, confusion, SMILE BABY SMILE—the crew, never off their feet, were working steadily before you got there and will be the last to leave at night." She fulfilled her obligations as a bird builds a nest, with instinctive diligence and single-mindedness. But when it was done—a movie, radio appearance, costume fitting—it was *done*, forgotten as surely as last week's weather forecast. How else could she withstand the Sisyphean demands of her often uninspired assignments? How else could she keep that overworked smile looking sincere and those line readings so chipper? How else could she give her audiences their money's worth for seventy years?

Joan was called to work in Florida on *The Champ*, a big budget MGM remake of the weepy 1931 Wallace Beery boxing movie. She played salty horse owner and society matron Dolly Kenyon, whom she modeled after Liz Whitney Tippett, a wealthy friend from the New York Sutton Place days. Though the role had some teeth to it, Joan was unhappy on the set and appalled at her purple-tinged hairpiece. She was, however, grateful that her poor health had not scared off casting directors.

The most praiseworthy performance in *The Champ* came from scene-stealing eight-year-old Ricky Shroeder, who had the availability of emotions reminiscent of Peggy Ann Garner in *A Tree Grows in Brooklyn*. Much of the rest chafed: the too lovely photography, syrupy string and harp score, overacting of Jon Voight, and pedophiliac hints in a miscalculated performance from Faye Dunaway. Joan held some fondness for the story, as the original was written by Frances Marion, who had died in 1973 but was honored with a story credit in the remake. And the simple lesson of *The Champ*, that children will love their parents no matter what, was a poignant reminder to Joan of her own uneven history with motherhood.

Joan then went straight away to work on *The Rebels*, a four-hour television movie follow-up to *The Bastard*. Both were based on John Jakes's best-selling books of fictionalized stories of the American Revolution that capitalized on the recent Bicentennial. *The Rebels* was a sumptuous production by television standards, brimming with actorly imitations of Benjamin Franklin, George Washington, and John Adams. The 1970s are betrayed repeatedly, however, particularly in the starlets' generous décolletage and the young men's feathered hair. As midwife Mrs. Brumple, Joan was loving and kind, but her underwritten character did little more than register worry in close-up as the men rode off to battle. Twenty-year-old granddaughter Sandy Powell was on the set as Joan's personal assistant. As Joan's eyesight worsened, so did her depth perception, and Sandy was on hand to assist her navigating through the perils of an indoor-outdoor set full of electric cables, mud holes, and slated flooring.

Joan's next role was miniscule, hardly seen, and done strictly for a fast paycheck. *The Glove* had a sort of Bionic Man concept, as an escaped convict kills people with a custom-built steel glove. "A fistful of hate that's just lying in wait," as the title song informs us. *The Glove* was pure bilge water, with Joan showing up for a two and a half minute performance. As Mrs. Fitzgerald, a sweet old widow thief, she did a riff on Helen Hayes in *Airport*.

When CBS contacted Joan for an appearance on a *60 Minutes* segment on Bette Davis, she called her crusty old friend and asked what she ought to say. "Tell 'em whatever you want," said Davis. "So I can tell 'em what a bitch you are?" said Joan. "I don't care—tell 'em whatever you want." Joan's friendship with Davis was nothing if not plainspoken. When laughing over their combined seven failed marriages, Joan referred to Bette's quartet of Gentiles as "the Four Skins," no doubt bringing a blush to the somewhat prudish Davis. That bawdry did not get on television, and Joan once again disguised her illness to appear handsome and composed on *60 Minutes*. "Nothing stopped her, yet there was a soft quality about her that I loved," said Joan. Ever diplomatic, she let Bette discuss the private side of her own life—her virginity until age twenty-six, the divorces, and abortion. Bette indirectly commented on Joan's life as well: "A woman alone is a perfectly asinine way to live."

Joan had one more movie in her. *The Woman Inside*, a story of transsexualism, was the brainchild of novice writer-director Joseph Van Winkle.

Joan played Aunt Coll, aghast at her "faggot weirdo" nephew. Her character was a throwback to the Gorgon aunt she played in 1957's *Lizzie*. But where that film featured Eleanor Parker as a niece with multiple personalities, *The Woman Inside* featured actress Gloria Manon as a nephew with "severe sexual identity conflict" who will transform into a niece. On screen, an exhausted Joan appeared to have aged even since *The Champ*. Her double chin was lower, her hair predominantly gray, and her gait more halting. But the singsong line readings were intact, giving the languid movie some needed adrenaline. Manon said that "the experience was disastrous. There was no direction. Joe Van Winkle decided to just leave it to the actors."

Manon remembered that Van Winkle treated Blondell disrespectfully, ignoring her needs for comfort and rest. It was Manon who reminded the crew that Miss Blondell might appreciate a chair or a place to lie down during setups. On one occasion, Joan could not remember her lines. She and Manon did take after take, but the right words would not come. Everyone was tired and irritable and Van Winkle had long since left the shoot. Manon and Blondell kept going, logging in somewhere between twenty and thirty takes before the lines were delivered acceptably. "As many takes as she did, she fought to get that energy up," said Manon. "She never threw in the towel. Each take she would give it everything. I've never seen anyone try so hard to cover her illness and keep it to herself."

There is a humanity to *The Woman Inside*, hiding under its cheap veneer. It explores sexual needs, self-acceptance, employment, and medicine with sincerity if not artistic virtue. Any discomfort the audience may feel for transsexuality can be channeled through Joan's unsympathetic character, who is the symbol of pristine ignorance. When she caws, "You're having your *dong* cut off? What would your father say if he were alive? He played football for Stanford, you know that, don't you?" she is meant to be mocked. Manon was embarrassed by the whole enterprise and shocked that the low-budget indie was picked up by Fox for theatrical distribution. Her one happy memory was working with Joan. "I loved her," she said forthrightly. "And it had nothing to do with being an actor."

One last occasion of joy was left in Joan's life when, on 26 August 1979, granddaughter Sandy married Paul Espe at her mother's hillside home in Topanga Canyon. The small wedding allowed Joan to reflect on those attending. Gloria and Victor were there, the only others of her generation still alive. Ellen was there, her moods presently stabilized. The bride's siblings, Scott and Stephanie, were beaming with happiness for their sister. Joanie was there, too, with Dirk Evans. Soon they, too, would be married. Norman, accompanied by steady girlfriend Ellen Levine, gave away the bride. Joan, wearing a dress made by Gloria, came on the arm of Ted Hook. She looked tired and deathly pale and was barely able to walk.

Joan made numerous out-patient visits to St. John's in the next few months, quietly emptying the blood bank. She was trying to stay ahead of the leukemia, but the insults to her body kept coming. She was alone at Champagne Towers in mid-December 1979 when she turned the knobs in her tub to draw a bath. As she stepped over the rim, an angry pain blasted through her chest, causing her to clutch at her breasts. The heart attack sent her to St. John's for the last time. Gloria happened to be in Joan's hospital room when she had another stroke. As Joan was going blind, she told Gloria that there was "an explosion in [her] eye and it looked like *Star Wars*." The sisters became closer than ever as death neared for one of them. Gloria became Joan's constant companion at St. John's, summoning great strength and checking her own temper for the sake of Joan's serenity.

At her request, Joan received Christian Science treatment in the hospital in addition to standard medical care. Family and friends rotated in and out. Despite jackhammers destroying an adjacent parking lot, wrenching scenes were played out again and again, as the heart speaks openly when confronted with imminent loss. "Matey, I'm going to miss you," said Joanie. "I love you so much." When Scott visited his grandmother, she was listless and incoherent. She tried to speak, but she made no sound. He was inconsolable and left her room sobbing. All were shocked when they finally learned that Joan's "little blood problem" was leukemia diagnosed two years prior.

For Joan and Ellen, the fervent, indivisible mother-daughter relationship found its resolution. The worst of Ellen's mental illness was over as her diagnosis was downgraded by a compassionate and skilled doctor. "I sincerely believe that she held out her death until I was able to tell her that I had been diagnosed as manic-depressive and that lithium was the key to my stability," said Ellen. "I know that she horribly feared the words 'manic depression' or anything to do with a 'malpractice of the mind' from a Christian Science point of view. The reason manic-depression was so hard on her was because that's what she thought Mike Todd had. But it gave her some relief and helped her to go."

Norman pointed out that the most dramatic moments in a life are often silent. "We didn't talk about the inevitably of her death," he said. "Once we all knew she was dying, she couldn't communicate. Her death wasn't tidy or cinematic. There were no parting words. With her the apparatus for communication was gone. Her death was slow, slow, slow—then boom."

On Christmas Eve, the family was at her bedside talking as if she could no longer hear. They engaged in that peculiar type of impersonal chatting that can accompany a ghastly scene. "How will the hostage crisis be resolved?" "Do you think we'll have more rain?" "Did you hear that Darryl Zanuck died on Saturday?" When Ellen was alone with Joan, they established their final communication. With Ellen cupping her mother's arthritic right hand in hers, Joan was to squeeze once for "yes" and twice for "no." Ellen asked her, "Would [you] rather come home to die with your cats." Joan squeezed Ellen's hand once. Ellen excused herself and went to speak to the doctors about an ambulance ride to Champagne Towers. Joan's progression toward death was too advanced and they advised against it. "She would never make it," said one. "We'd have to bank her with sandbags." With nothing left to negotiate, Norman and Ellen requested that their mother be taken off life support. Ellen left the hospital at 10 p.m., went to a bar, had two drinks, and cried from relief that it would soon be over. Then she went home to write through her feelings.

Joan was still and unconscious. Her body was mercifully free of tubes. She lay extended on the bed, her eyes shut in readiness for a peaceful end, her breathing irregular and all but undetectable. The jackhammers had stopped, and there was near perfect silence. At 4:10 a.m. on Tuesday, Christmas morning 1979, Joan died. Daughter, Rosebud, sister, wife, mother, aunt, friend, actress, grandmother, Matey—her work was over.

Epilogue

Death leaves a heartache no one can heal, love leaves a memory no one can steal.

—Unknown headstone

Two services were planned for Joan, one in California and one in New York. Several hundred mourners packed the Forest Lawn Memorial Park's Wee Kirk O' the Heather in Glendale. The family arrived in limousines and sat in the front rows of the full chapel, with additional onlookers assembled outside. Family friend Alex Swan conducted the Christian Science Church ceremony. "Those of us here represent a microcosm of the love, respect, and admiration of moviegoers around the world who have been entertained and amused by Joan Blondell for over 65 years," he said. "The some 100 films in which she appeared show the endearing quality of her talent. Too frequently stars shoot to the top only to quickly fizzle out, but Joan displayed her ability to maintain her career." Ted Hook called her "one of the kindest, most wonderful people I have ever known." Costars from all major eras of her career were there, from the 1930s (Pat O'Brien), the 1950s (Theodore Bikel), the 1960s (Robert Brown and Bridget Hanley), and the 1970s (Gena Rowlands). They filed out to the strains of "Born Free," then made their way to a reception at Norman's beach house at Marina del Rey. Joan's body was cremated in the dress Gloria made for

Sandy's wedding. Her ashes were poured into an urn and vaulted in the Court of Freedom, in a privileged area known as the Garden of Honor, available only to those in possession of Forest Lawn's "Golden Key of Memory." Dick Powell preceded Joan to the sanctified realm.

In January of 1980, a New York memorial was held at St. Malachy's Roman Catholic Church on West Forty-ninth Street in the theater district. Norman spoke, along with Joan Bennett and Ted Hook. There was Art Carney, who was saved from the bottle numerous times by Joan's intervention. There were Warner Bros. brethren Frank McHugh and Ruth Donnelly, now antiques. James Cagney planned to attend, but ill health prevented him leaving his upstate farm. *The Village Voice* reported that the memorial tribute "was like a scene from *Footlight Parade* almost a half century after the fact," but it was "not a bit maudlin." Rex Reed read excerpts from *Center Door Fancy*, and Kay Armen sang her favorite song, "Danny Boy." Chita Rivera sang "I Only Have Eyes for You" from *Dames*. Columnist Arthur Bell lost all professional reserve: "For me, Blondell was one of the nicest women I've ever written about and one of the few people I continued to keep in touch with long after the profile appeared in print."

Flora Marks and Norman executed Joan's will. She wished that 50 percent of *Center Door Fancy* profits should go to grandchildren Stephanie, Scotty, and Sandy, divided equally between them, and that 50 percent should go to Joanie. Ellen was to have first choice of furnishings and effects and whatever "she needs to make a home for herself and Joan Ellen Hayward." Further choice of belongings was then to be offered to niece Kathy and former daughter-in-law Ann.

Joan's pals at Warner Bros. who outlived her—Pat O'Brien, Bette Davis, Barbara Stanwyck, James Cagney, Ruby Keeler, Mary Astor, Regis Toomey—are all gone now. Gone, too, are Joan Bennett, Art Carney, Melvyn Douglas, and her most flattering directors, including Elia Kazan and John Cassavetes. As for her family, the 1980s and beyond would see breakdowns, divorces, professional successes, estrangements, births, and deaths. For Joan Blondell's highly gifted and accomplished brood, life went on in all its disheveled magnificence:

Following Dick Powell's death, **June Allyson** twice married and divorced Powell's barber Glenn Maxwell. She married actor-dentist David Ashrow in 1976. She worked intermittently in movies and on stage, television, and cruise ships and published her autobiography in 1982. She found her greatest late-life fame as spokes-person for Depend protective underwear. Allyson died on 8 July 2006 at age eighty-eight.

Joan's sister, **Gloria Blondell**, was devastated twice in quick succession when husband **Victor Hunter** suffered a fatal heart attack in early 1980 only weeks after Joan's death. Her strength was further tested with a diagnosis of bladder cancer, treated without painkillers due to her many allergies. She died in Los Angeles on 25 March 1986.

Niece **Kathy Blondell**, often billed as Kathryn L. Blondell, became one of Hollywood's leading hairstylists. Her "heads" include Tom Hanks, Goldie Hawn, Jeff Bridges, Kate Hudson, and Jane Fonda. Her film credits include *Shampoo*, *Mommie Dearest*, *Prizzi's Honor*, *The American President*, and *The Aviator*.

Joan's granddaughter **Joan Hayward** has come through her stormy past to thrive in a happier life. She divorced **Dirk Evans**, earned a bachelor's degree in psychology, and became a certified day-care provider and preschool teacher. She is the mother of three great grandchildren of Joan Blondell and Dick Powell: **Joshua Scott Evans**, **Jessica Lee Matey Evans**, and **Kevin Lawrence Arnold II**. In 2004, she married **Arnold J. Krooms**, blacksmith and musician.

Before Joan's death, secretary-friend-confidant **Ted Hook** opened Ted Hook's Backstage, a lively nightclub in the heart of Broadway. Hook died of complications from AIDS-related pneumonia in 1995 at age sixty-five.

In 1980, former daughter-in-law **Ann McDowell** married engineer **Henry Traub**. They have enjoyed years of happy retirement in Pacific Palisades near two of her three children.

Joan's daughter, **Ellen Powell**, has made peace with her tumultuous past. She stopped cocaine use in 1984 but continued to have psychiatric episodes until 1993. Against medical advice, she stopped taking anti-psychotics and anti-depressants and the mental problems ended. Semi-retired in Northern California after working twenty-five years as a journeyman hairstylist in Local 706, she occasionally returns to Hollywood. She was on the Emmy-nominated team that hair-styled *Star Trek: Deep Space 9* and *Deadwood*. She practices Tibetan Buddhism and continues to write.

Joan's son, **Norman Powell**, was divorced in 1980 and married **Ellen Levine** in 1984. He has produced and/or directed hundreds of hours of primetime television as well as serving as senior vice president at CBS for many years. He has received a People's Choice Award and been nominated as producer for two Emmys and a Producers Guild Award. He is especially proud of the Telly Award–winning PBS documentary *American Valor*, which he directed, wife Ellen produced, and son Scott edited. Norman and Ellen's son, **Matthew Powell**, the only grandchild Joan never met, was born in 1986. Matthew is a talented bass player and composer, presently attending Canada's prestigious McGill University.

Joan's oldest grandchild, **Sandra Powell**, moved to Seattle soon after her 1979 marriage. In 2001, she returned to Southern California, where her husband, **Paul Espe**, cofounded a high-speed Internet business. They live with their teenage foster son in the high desert country of Anza Valley.

When visiting the *Here Come the Brides* set as a child, grandson **Scott Powell** knew he wanted to be a film editor or cameraman. Today he is both. He has operated a camera and edited a number of documentary films and was a multiple Emmy nominee for *24*, which won him the Eddy award from the American Cinema Editors. He lives in Pacific Palisades with his wife, Laurie. His stepson, David, and his wife, Juliet, are the parents of Zander and Dakota, making Scott a proud grandfather.

In 1995, Joan's granddaughter **Stephanie Powell** married Sean Murphy, owner and manager of a surf travel company. Dedicated world travelers, they own property in Samoa and Indonesia. She inherited Joan's love of pets and at this writing has three cats, a pug, a lab, and two exotic African turtles.

Stepson **Mike Todd Jr**. was seventy-two and living in Ireland at the time of his death in 2002 from lung cancer. His foray into film producing was marked by the short-lived gimmick "Smell-O-Vision," which combined odors with movie projection. In 1983, he published *A Valuable Property: The Life Story of Michael Todd* for Arbor House. He is survived by eight children by two wives.

Joan was never afraid to express the love that she felt for places, animals, and people. Her open emotions can be found in "Beauty Secret," a poem she wrote in her customary longhand. If it cloys, no matter. She would never apologize for anything that was sincerely rendered:

> *You are beautiful when you yearn to love and be loved. When optimism is your warmth. When you hold back the tears.*
> *It's a thing of beauty when you fondle a puppy and love him even more when he is old.*
> *It is beautiful when you can say, "I was wrong and you were right."*
> *Beautiful are you when you can see swaying trees, the color of mountains, a child's point of view.*
> *There is beauty in getting up after a fall, in breaking someone else's fall.*
> *Your eyes are beautiful when they catch another eye in understanding.*
> *Beautiful are your arms when they're around stooped shoulders.*
> *Your feet and legs are beautiful when they're running to help someone.*
> *Hands that have scrubbed, tended, labored and provided are beautiful.*
> *A stomach that can't stomach injustice, intolerance, a stomach stretched in childbearing—beautiful.*
> *A straight back, upturned lips, head held high, a twinkle in your eye, a heart of compassion, a heart who feels God—then beauty is yours.*

FILMOGRAPHY

The films of Joan Blondell are listed in order of their release in the United States.

1930

The Office Wife. Warner Bros.
Director: Lloyd Bacon.
Producer: Darryl F. Zanuck.
Cast: Dorothy Mackaill, Lewis Stone, Natalie Moorhead, Hobart Bosworth, Joan Blondell.

Sinners' Holiday. Warner Bros.
Director: John Adolfi.
Producer: Darryl F. Zanuck.
Cast: Grant Withers, Evalyn Knapp, James Cagney, Lucille La Verne, Joan Blondell.

1931

Other Men's Women. Warner Bros.
Director: William A. Wellman.
Producer: Darryl F. Zanuck.
Cast: Grant Withers, Mary Astor, Regis Toomey, James Cagney, Fred Kohler, J. Farrell MacDonald, Joan Blondell.

Millie. RKO Radio.
Director: John Francis Dillon.
Producer: Charles R. Rogers.
Cast: Helen Twelvetrees, Robert Ames, Lilyan Tashman, Joan Blondell, John Halliday, Anita Louise.

Illicit. Warner Bros.
Director: Archie Mayo.
Producer: Darryl F. Zanuck.
Cast: Barbara Stanwyck, James Rennie, Ricardo Cortez, Charles Butterworth, Joan Blondell, Natalie Moorhead.

God's Gift to Women. Warner Bros.
Director: Michael Curtiz.
Producer: Darryl F. Zanuck.
Cast: Frank Fay, Laura La Plante, Joan Blondell, Charles Winninger, Alan Mowbray, Yola d'Avril, Louise Brooks.

The Public Enemy. Warner Bros.
Director: William A. Wellman.
Producer: Darryl F. Zanuck.
Cast: James Cagney, Jean Harlow, Edward Woods, Joan Blondell, Mae Clarke.

My Past. Warner Bros.
Director: Roy Del Ruth.
Producer: Darryl F. Zanuck.
Cast: Bebe Daniels, Ben Lyon, Lewis Stone, Joan Blondell, Natalie Moorhead.

Big Business Girl. Warner Bros.
Director: William A. Seiter.
Producer: William A. Seiter.
Cast: Loretta Young, Frank Albertson, Ricardo Cortez, Joan Blondell, Frank Darien.

Night Nurse. Warner Bros.
Director: William A. Wellman.
Producer: Darryl F. Zanuck.
Cast: Barbara Stanwyck, Ben Lyon, Joan Blondell, Charles Winninger, Clark Gable.

The Reckless Hour. Warner Bros.
Director: John Francis Dillon.
Producer: Darryl F. Zanuck.
Cast: Dorothy Mackaill, Conrad Nagel, Joan Blondell, H. B. Warner, Helen Ware.

Blonde Crazy. Warner Bros.
Director: Roy Del Ruth.
Producer: Darryl F. Zanuck.
Cast: James Cagney, Joan Blondell, Louis Calhern, Noel Francis, Guy Kibbee, Ray Milland.

1932

Union Depot. Warner Bros.
Director: Alfred E. Green.
Producer: Darryl F. Zanuck.
Cast: Douglas Fairbanks Jr., Joan Blondell, Guy Kibbee, Alan Hale, George Rosener, Dickie Moore.

The Greeks Had a Word for Them. Goldwyn-United Artists.
Director: Lowell Sherman.
Producer: Samuel Goldwyn.
Cast: Madge Evans, Joan Blondell, Ina Claire, David Manners, Lowell Sherman, Betty Grable.

The Crowd Roars. Warner Bros.
Director: Howard Hawks.
Producer: Darryl F. Zanuck.
Cast: James Cagney, Joan Blondell, Ann Dvorak, Eric Linden, Guy Kibbee.

The Famous Ferguson Case. Warner Bros.
Director: Lloyd Bacon.
Producer: Darryl F. Zanuck.
Cast: Joan Blondell, Grant Mitchell, Tom Brown, Adrienne Dore, Vivienne Osborne.

Make Me a Star. Paramount.
Director: William Beaudine.
Producer: B. P. Schulberg.
Cast: Joan Blondell, Stuart Erwin, ZaSu Pitts, Ben Turpin, Charles Sellon.

Miss Pinkerton. Warner Bros.
Director: Lloyd Bacon.
Producer: Hal B. Wallis.
Cast: Joan Blondell, George Brent, Mae Madison, John Wray, Ruth Hall.

Big City Blues. Warner Bros.
Director: Mervyn LeRoy.
Producer: Darryl F. Zanuck.
Cast: Joan Blondell, Eric Linden, Jobyna Howland, Ned Sparks, Guy Kibbee.

Three on a Match. Warner Bros.
Director: Mervyn LeRoy.
Producers: Samuel Bischoff, Raymond Griffith, Darryl F. Zanuck.
Cast: Joan Blondell, Ann Dvorak, Bette Davis, Warren William, Lyle Talbot, Humphrey Bogart, Glenda Farrell.

Central Park. Warner Bros.
Director: John Adolfi.
Producer: Darryl F. Zanuck.
Cast: Joan Blondell, Wallace Ford, Guy Kibbee, Henry B. Walthall.

Lawyer Man. Warner Bros.
Director: William Dieterle.
Producer: Hal B. Wallis.
Cast: William Powell, Joan Blondell, David Landau, Helen Vinson, Claire Dodd, Alan
 Dinehart.

1933

Broadway Bad. Fox.
Director: Sidney Lanfield.
Producer: Uncredited.
Cast: Joan Blondell, Ricardo Cortez, Ginger Rogers, Adrienne Ames, Donald Crisp.

Blondie Johnson. Warner Bros.
Director: Ray Enright.
Producer: Lucien Hubbard.
Cast: Joan Blondell, Chester Morris, Allen Jenkins, Claire Dodd, Earle Foxe.

Gold Diggers of 1933. Warner Bros.
Director: Mervyn LeRoy.
Producers: Robert Lord, Jack L. Warner.
Cast: Joan Blondell, Ruby Keeler, Aline MacMahon, Dick Powell, Ginger Rogers, Warren
 William, Guy Kibbee, Ned Sparks.

Goodbye Again. Warner Bros.
Director: Michael Curtiz.
Producer: Henry Blanke.
Cast: Warren William, Joan Blondell, Genevieve Tobin, Helen Chandler, Hugh Herbert,
 Ruth Donnelly.

Footlight Parade. Warner Bros.
Director: Lloyd Bacon.
Producer: Robert Lord.
Cast: James Cagney, Joan Blondell, Ruby Keeler, Dick Powell, Guy Kibbee, Ruth
 Donnelly, Claire Dodd.

Havana Widows. Warner Bros.
Director: Ray Enright.
Producer: Robert Lord.
Cast: Joan Blondell, Glenda Farrell, Guy Kibbee, Lyle Talbot, Allen Jenkins.

Convention City. Warner Bros.
Director: Archie Mayo.
Producer: Henry Blanke.
Cast: Joan Blondell, Adolphe Menjou, Dick Powell, Mary Astor, Guy Kibbee, Frank McHugh.

1934

I've Got Your Number. Warner Bros.
Director: Ray Enright.
Producer: Samuel Bischoff.
Cast: Joan Blondell, Pat O'Brien, Glenda Farrell, Allen Jenkins, Eugene Pallette.

He Was Her Man. Warner Bros.
Director: Lloyd Bacon.
Producer: Robert Lord.
Cast: James Cagney, Joan Blondell, Victor Jory, Frank Craven, Harold Huber, Russell Hopton.

Smarty. Warner Bros.
Director: Robert Florey.
Producer: Robert Presnell.
Cast: Joan Blondell, Warren William, Edward Everett Horton, Frank McHugh, Claire Dodd.

Dames. Warner Bros.
Director: Ray Enright.
Producer: Hal B. Wallis.
Cast: Joan Blondell, Dick Powell, Ruby Keeler, ZaSu Pitts, Hugh Herbert, Guy Kibbee.

Kansas City Princess. Warner Bros.
Director: William Keighley.
Producer: Louis F. Edelman.
Cast: Joan Blondell, Glenda Farrell, Robert Armstrong, Hugh Herbert, Osgood Perkins.

1935

The Traveling Saleslady. Warner Bros
Director: Ray Enright.

Producer: Samuel Bischoff.

Cast: Joan Blondell, Glenda Farrell, William Gargan, Hugh Herbert, Grant Mitchell, Ruth Donnelly.

Broadway Gondolier. Warner Bros.

Director: Lloyd Bacon.

Producer: Samuel Bischoff.

Cast: Dick Powell, Joan Blondell, Adolphe Menjou, Louise Fazenda, William Gargan, Grant Mitchell.

We're in the Money. Warner Bros.

Director: Ray Enright.

Producer: Harry Joe Brown.

Cast: Joan Blondell, Glenda Farrell, Hugh Herbert, Ross Alexander.

Miss Pacific Fleet. Warner Bros.

Director: Ray Enright.

Producers: Hal B. Wallis, Jack L. Warner.

Cast: Joan Blondell, Glenda Farrell, Hugh Herbert, Allen Jenkins, Warren Hull.

1936

Colleen. Warner Bros.

Director: Alfred E. Green.

Producers: Hal B. Wallis, Jack L. Warner.

Cast: Dick Powell, Ruby Keeler, Jack Oakie, Joan Blondell, Hugh Herbert, Louise Fazenda, Paul Draper.

Sons o' Guns. Warner Bros.

Director: Lloyd Bacon.

Producer: Harry Joe Brown.

Cast: Joe E. Brown, Joan Blondell, Beverly Roberts, Winifred Shaw, Eric Blore.

Bullets or Ballots. Warner Bros.

Director: William Keighley.

Producer: Louis F. Edelman.

Cast: Edward G. Robinson, Joan Blondell, Barton MacLane, Humphrey Bogart, Frank McHugh.

Stage Struck. Warner Bros.

Director: Busby Berkeley.

Producer: Robert Lord.
Cast: Dick Powell, Joan Blondell, Warren William, Frank McHugh, Jeanne Madden, the
   Yacht Club Boys.

Three Men on a Horse. Warner Bros.
Director: Mervyn LeRoy.
Producer: Mervyn LeRoy.
Cast: Frank McHugh, Joan Blondell, Carol Hughes, Allen Jenkins, Guy Kibbee, Sam Levene.

Gold Diggers of 1937. Warner Bros.
Directors: Lloyd Bacon, Busby Berkeley.
Producers: Hal B. Wallis, Jack L. Warner.
Cast: Dick Powell, Joan Blondell, Glenda Farrell, Victor Moore, Lee Dixon, Osgood Perkins.

1937

The King and the Chorus Girl. Warner Bros.
Director: Mervyn LeRoy.
Producer: Mervyn LeRoy.
Cast: Fernand Gravet, Joan Blondell, Edward Everett Horton, Alan Mowbray, Jane Wyman.

Back in Circulation. Warner Bros.
Director: Ray Enright.
Producers: Samuel Bischoff, Hal B. Wallis, Jack L. Warner.
Cast: Pat O'Brien, Joan Blondell, Margaret Lindsay, John Litel.

The Perfect Specimen. Warner Bros.
Director: Michael Curtiz.
Producer: Hal B. Wallis.
Cast: Errol Flynn, Joan Blondell, Hugh Herbert, Edward Everett Horton, Dick Foran,
   May Robson, Allen Jenkins.

Stand-In. United Artists.
Director: Tay Garnett.
Producer: Walter Wanger.
Cast: Leslie Howard, Joan Blondell, Humphrey Bogart, Alan Mowbray, Maria Shelton.

1938

There's Always a Woman. Columbia.
Director: Alexander Hall.

Producer: William Perlberg.
Cast: Joan Blondell, Melvyn Douglas, Mary Astor, Frances Drake, Jerome Cowan.

1939

Off the Record. Warner Bros.
Director: James Flood.
Producer: Samuel Bischoff.
Cast: Pat O'Brien, Joan Blondell, Bobby Jordan, Alan Baxter, William K. Davidson.

East Side of Heaven. Universal.
Director: David Butler.
Producer: Herbert Polesie.
Cast: Bing Crosby, Joan Blondell, Mischa Auer, Irene Hervey, Jerome Cowan, C. Aubrey
   Smith.

The Kid from Kokomo. Warner Bros.
Director: Lewis Seiler.
Producer: Samuel Bischoff.
Cast: Pat O'Brien, Wayne Morris, Joan Blondell, Jane Wyman, May Robson.

Good Girls Go to Paris. Columbia.
Director: Alexander Hall.
Producer: William Perlberg.
Cast: Melvyn Douglas, Joan Blondell, Walter Connolly, Alan Curtis, Joan Perry, Isabel Jeans.

The Amazing Mr. Williams. Columbia.
Director: Alexander Hall.
Producer: Everett Riskin.
Cast: Melvyn Douglas, Joan Blondell, Clarence Kolb, Ruth Donnelly.

1940

Two Girls on Broadway. Metro-Goldwyn-Mayer.
Director: S. Sylvan Simon.
Producer: Jack Cummings.
Cast: Lana Turner, Joan Blondell, George Murphy, Kent Taylor, Richard Lane.

I Want a Divorce. Paramount.
Director: Ralph Murphy.

Producer: George M. Arthur.
Cast: Joan Blondell, Dick Powell, Gloria Dickson, Frank Fay, Jessie Ralph, Conrad Nagel.

1941

Topper Returns. United Artists.
Director: Roy Del Ruth.
Producer: Hal Roach.
Cast: Joan Blondell, Roland Young, Carole Landis, Billie Burke, Dennis O'Keefe, Patsy
Kelly, Eddie "Rochester" Anderson.

Model Wife. Universal.
Director: Leigh Jason.
Producer: Leigh Jason.
Cast: Dick Powell, Joan Blondell, Ruth Donnelly, Charles Ruggles, Lucile Watson, Lee
Bowman, Gloria Blondell.

Three Girls about Town. Columbia.
Director: Leigh Jason.
Producer: Samuel Bischoff.
Cast: Joan Blondell, Robert Benchley, Binnie Barnes, Janet Blair, John Howard, Eric
Blore, Una O'Connor.

1942

Lady for a Night. Republic.
Director: Leigh Jason.
Producer: Albert J. Cohen.
Cast: Joan Blondell, John Wayne, Ray Middleton, Blanche Yurka, Edith Barrett, Hattie Noel.

1943

Cry "Havoc." Metro-Goldwyn-Mayer.
Director: Richard Thorpe.
Producer: Edwin Knopf.
Cast: Margaret Sullavan, Ann Sothern, Joan Blondell, Fay Bainter, Marsha Hunt, Ella
Raines.

1945

A Tree Grows in Brooklyn. Twentieth Century-Fox.
Director: Elia Kazan.
Producer: Louis D. Lighton.
Cast: Dorothy McGuire, Joan Blondell, James Dunn, Peggy Ann Garner, Lloyd Nolan.

Don Juan Quilligan. Twentieth Century-Fox.
Director: Frank Tuttle.
Producer: William LeBaron.
Cast: William Bendix, Joan Blondell, Phil Silvers, Anne Revere, B. S. Pully.

Adventure. Metro-Goldwyn-Mayer.
Director: Victor Fleming.
Producer: Sam Zimbalist.
Cast: Clark Gable, Greer Garson, Joan Blondell, Thomas Mitchell, Tom Tully.

1947

The Corpse Came C.O.D. Columbia.
Director: Henry Levin.
Producer: Samuel Bischoff.
Cast: George Brent, Joan Blondell, Adele Jergens, Jim Bannon, Leslie Brooks.

Nightmare Alley. Twentieth Century-Fox.
Director: Edmund Goulding.
Producer: George Jessel.
Cast: Tyrone Power, Joan Blondell, Coleen Gray, Helen Walker, Taylor Holmes, Ian Keith.

Christmas Eve. United Artists.
Director: Edwin L. Marin.
Producer: Benedict Bogeaus.
Cast: George Brent, George Raft, Randolph Scott, Joan Blondell, Virginia Field, Ann Harding.

1950

For Heaven's Sake. Twentieth Century-Fox.
Director: George Seaton.

Producer: William Perlberg.
Cast: Clifton Webb, Joan Bennett, Robert Cummings, Edmund Gwenn, Joan Blondell,
    Gigi Perreau.

1951

The Blue Veil. RKO Radio.
Director: Curtis Bernhardt.
Producers: Norman Krasna, Jerry Wald.
Cast: Jane Wyman, Charles Laughton, Joan Blondell, Richard Carlson, Agnes Moorehead,
    Audrey Totter, Natalie Wood, Vivian Vance.

1956

The Opposite Sex. Metro-Goldwyn-Mayer.
Director: David Miller.
Producer: Joe Pasternak.
Cast: June Allyson, Joan Collins, Dolores Gray, Ann Sheridan, Ann Miller, Leslie Nielsen,
    Jeff Richards, Agnes Moorehead, Charlotte Greenwood, Joan Blondell, Alice Pearce.

1957

Lizzie. Metro-Goldwyn-Mayer/Bryna.
Director: Hugo Haas.
Producer: Jerry Bresler.
Cast: Eleanor Parker, Richard Boone, Joan Blondell, Hugo Haas, Johnny Mathis.

Desk Set. Twentieth Century-Fox.
Director: Walter Lang.
Producer: Henry Ephron.
Cast: Spencer Tracy, Katharine Hepburn, Gig Young, Joan Blondell, Dina Merrill, Sue Randall.

This Could Be the Night. Metro-Goldwyn-Mayer.
Director: Robert Wise.
Producer: Joe Pasternak.
Cast: Jean Simmons, Paul Douglas, Anthony Franciosa, Julie Wilson, Neile Adams, Joan
    Blondell, J. Carrol Naish, ZaSu Pitts.

Will Success Spoil Rock Hunter? Twentieth Century-Fox.
Director: Frank Tashlin.
Producer: Frank Tashlin.
Cast: Tony Randall, Jayne Mansfield, Betsy Drake, Joan Blondell, Henry Jones.

1961

Angel Baby. Allied Artists.
Director: Paul Wendkos.
Producer: Thomas F. Woods.
Cast: George Hamilton, Mercedes McCambridge, Salome Jens, Joan Blondell, Henry Jones, Burt Reynolds.

1964

Advance to the Rear. Metro-Goldwyn-Mayer.
Director: George Marshall.
Producer: Ted Richmond.
Cast: Glenn Ford, Stella Stevens, Melvyn Douglas, Jim Backus, Joan Blondell, Jesse Pearson.

1965

The Cincinnati Kid. Metro-Goldwyn-Mayer.
Director: Norman Jewison.
Producer: Martin Ransohoff.
Cast: Steve McQueen, Edward G. Robinson, Tuesday Weld, Karl Malden, Ann-Margret, Joan Blondell, Rip Torn, Jack Weston, Cab Calloway.

1966

Ride beyond Vengeance. Tiger-Sentinal-Fenady/Columbia.
Director: Bernard McEveety.
Producer: Andrew J. Fenady.

Cast: Chuck Connors, Michael Rennie, Kathryn Hays, Joan Blondell, Gloria Grahame, Gary Merrill, Bill Bixby.

The Spy in the Green Hat. Metro-Goldwyn-Mayer.
Director: Joseph Sargent.
Producers: David Victor, Boris Ingster.
Cast: Robert Vaughn, David McCallum, Jack Palance, Janet Leigh, Leticia Roman, Eduardo Ciannelli, Allen Jenkins, Leo G. Carroll, Ludwig Donath, Joan Blondell.

1967

Waterhole #3. Blake Edwards-Geoffrey/Paramount.
Director: William Graham.
Producer: Joseph T. Steck.
Cast: James Coburn, Carroll O'Connor, Margaret Blye, Claude Akins, Timothy Carey, Bruce Dern, Joan Blondell, James Whitmore.

1968

Stay Away, Joe. Metro-Goldwyn-Mayer.
Director: Peter Tewksbury.
Producer: Douglas Laurence.
Cast: Elvis Presley, Burgess Meredith, Joan Blondell, Katy Jurado, Thomas Gomez, Henry Jones.

Kona Coast. Warner Bros.
Director: Lamont Johnson.
Producers: Richard Boone, Lamont Johnson.
Cast: Richard Boone, Vera Miles, Joan Blondell, Steve Ihnat, Chips Rafferty, Kent Smith.

1969

Big Daddy. Syzygy/United.
Director: Carl K. Hittleman.
Producer: Carl K. Hittleman.
Cast: Victor Buono, Joan Blondell, Chill Wills, Tisha Sterling, Reed Sherman.

1970

The Phynx. Warner Bros.—Seven Arts.
Director: Lee H. Katzin.
Producers: Bob Booker, George Foster.
Cast: A. Michael Miller, Ray Chippeway, Dennis Larden, Lonny Stevens, Lou Antonio, Michael Ansara with Joan Blondell, Xavier Cugat, Andy Devine, Louis Hayward, Ruby Keeler, Butterfly McQueen, Maureen O'Sullivan, Johnny Weissmuller, Richard Pryor, et al. in cameo roles.

1971

Support Your Local Gunfighter. Cherokee-Brigrade/United Artists.
Director: Burt Kennedy.
Producer: William Finnegan.
Cast: James Garner, Suzanne Pleshette, Jack Elam, Joan Blondell, Harry Morgan, Marie Windsor.

1976

Won Ton Ton, the Dog Who Saved Hollywood. Paramount.
Director: Michael Winner.
Producers: David V. Picker, Arnold Schulman, Michael Winner.
Cast: Bruce Dern, Madeline Kahn, Art Carney, Phil Silvers, Teri Garr with Joan Blondell, Ann Miller, Cyd Charisse, Edgar Bergen, Regis Toomey, Alice Faye, Tab Hunter, Stepin Fetchit, Ethel Merman, et al. in cameo roles.

1977

The Baron. Tripps Production Corporation.
Director: Phillip Fenty.
Producer: Chiz Schultz.
Cast: Calvin Lockhart, Richard Lynch, Charles McGregor, Marlene Clark, Joan Blondell.

Opening Night. Faces.
Director: John Cassavetes.
Producer: Al Ruban.
Cast: Gena Rowlands, John Cassavetes, Ben Gazzara, Joan Blondell, Paul Stewart.

1978

Grease. Paramount.
Director: Randal Kleiser.
Producers: Allan Carr, Robert Stigwood.
Cast: John Travolta, Olivia Newton-John, Stockard Channing, Jeff Conaway, Didi Conn, Eve Arden, Sid Caesar, Joan Blondell.

1979

The Champ. United Artists/Metro-Goldwyn-Mayer.
Director: Franco Zeffirelli.
Producer: Dyson Lovell.
Cast: Jon Voight, Faye Dunaway, Ricky Schroder, Jack Warden, Joan Blondell, Arthur Hill, Strother Martin.

The Glove. J./Pro International.
Director: Ross Hagen.
Producer: Julian Roffman.
Cast: John Saxon, Roosevelt Grier, Joanna Cassidy, Jack Carter, Keenan Wynn, Joan Blondell.

1981

The Woman Inside. Twentieth Century-Fox.
Director: Joseph Van Winkle.
Producer: Sidney H. Levine.
Cast: Gloria Manon, Dane Clark, Joan Blondell, Michael Champion, Marlene Tracy.

STAGE APPEARANCES

Tarnish by Gilbert Emery. Opened 1 Oct. 1923 at the Belmont Theatre, New York.

The Miracle staged by Max Reinhardt. Opened 15 Jan. 1924 at the Century Theatre, New York.

The Trial of Mary Dugan by Bayard Veiller. National tour, Jun. 1928.

Maggie the Magnificent by George Kelly. Opened 21 Oct. 1929 at the Cort Theatre, New York.

Penny Arcade by Marie Baumer. Opened 24 Mar. 1930 at the Fulton Theatre, New York.

Goodbye to Love by Sheldon Davis. California tour, Jun. 1940.

The Naked Genius by Gypsy Rose Lee. Opened 21 Oct. 1943 at the Plymouth Theatre, New York.

Something for the Boys by Cole Porter and Herbert and Dorothy Fields. National tour, Feb. 1944.

Happy Birthday by Anita Loos. Northeastern tour, Jun. 1949. Subsequent tours in 1951, 1954, and 1955.

Come Back, Little Sheba by William Inge. National tour, Nov. 1949. Subsequent tours in 1951, 1952, and 1967.

A Tree Grows in Brooklyn by Arthur Schwartz, Dorothy Fields, George Abbott, and Betty Smith. National tour, Sep. 1952.

A Palm Grows in a Rose Garden by Meade Roberts. Pre-Broadway tour, Jun. 1955.

The Time of the Cuckoo by Arthur Laurents. National tour, Aug. 1956.

Copper and Brass by David Craig. Pre-Broadway tour, Sep. 1957.

The Rope Dancers by Morton Wishengrad. Opened 20 Nov. 1957 at the Cort Theatre, New York.

New Girl in Town by George Abbott and Bob Merrill. Northeastern tour, Jun. 1958.

Crazy October by James Leo Herlihy. National tour, Sep. 1958.

The Dark at the Top of the Stairs by William Inge. National tour, Sep. 1959.

Bye Bye Birdie by Michael Stewart, Lee Adams, and Charles Strouse. National tour, Mar. 1961.

The Effect of Gamma Rays on Man-in-the-Moon Marigolds by Paul Zindel. Opened 27 Sep. 1971 at the New Theatre, New York.

260

RADIO APPEARANCES

Hollywood Hotel. "The Traveling Saleslady" with Glenda Farrell. 29 Mar. 1935, CBS.

Shell Chateau with Al Jolson. 13 Jul. 1935, CBS.

Hollywood Hotel. "Bullets or Ballots" with Edward G. Robinson. 8 May 1936, CBS.

The Royal Gelatin Hour with Rudy Vallee. 8 Oct. 1936, CBS

Hollywood Hotel. "Three Men on a Horse" with Frank McHugh. 6 Nov. 1936, CBS.

Lux Radio Theatre. "The Gold Diggers" with Dick Powell. 21 Dec. 1936, CBS.

The Chase and Sanborn Hour with Edgar Bergen and Charlie McCarthy. 13 Jun. 1937, NBC.

Lux Radio Theatre. "She Loves Me Not" with Bing Crosby. 8 Nov. 1937, CBS.

Lux Radio Theatre. "The Perfect Specimen" with Errol Flynn. 2 Jan. 1939, CBS.

Federal Theatre Special with Walter Abel. 26 Jun. 1939, NBC.

The Chase and Sanborn Hour with Edgar Bergen and Charlie McCarthy. 13 Aug. 1939, NBC.

The Gulf Screen Guild Theater. "Variety" with Eddie Cantor. 31 Dec. 1939, CBS.

The Campbell Playhouse. "Only Angles Have Wings" with Orson Welles. 25 Feb. 1940, CBS.

I Want a Divorce with Dick Powell. Oct. 1940–Apr. 1941, NBC.

The Gulf Screen Guild Theater. "Hired Wife" with Melvyn Douglas. 20 Apr. 1941, CBS.

Lux Radio Theatre. "Model Wife" with Dick Powell. 19 May 1941, CBS.

Miss Pinkerton with Dick Powell. Jun. 1941, NBC.

The Eddie Cantor Show. 10 Dec. 1941, NBC.

Stage Door Canteen with Charles Laughton and Pat O'Brien. 1 Oct. 1942, CBS.

Command Performance. 10 Jan. 1943, AFRS.

Lux Radio Theatre. "This Gun for Hire" with Alan Ladd. 25 Jan. 1943, CBS.

Frank Sinatra in Person. 6 May 1944, CBS.

GI Journal. 17 Nov. 1944, AFRS.

Duffy's Tavern. 2 Mar. 1945, CBS.

The Chase and Sanborn Hour with Edgar Bergen and Charlie McCarthy. 11 Mar. 1945, NBC.

GI Journal. 8 Jun. 1945, AFRS.

Lux Radio Theatre. "Destry Rides Again" with James Stewart. 5 Nov. 1945, CBS.

Theatre of Romance. "Next Time We Love" with Howard Duff. 12 Mar. 1946, NBC.

Lux Radio Theatre. "Deadline at Dawn" with Paul Lukas. 20 May 1946, NBC.

Studio One. "So Big." 30 Dec. 1947, CBS.

The Ford Theater. "Page Miss Glory" with Macdonald Carey. 10 Dec. 1948, CBS.

Theatre USA with Mel Torme. 2 Jun. 1949, ABC.

TELEVISION APPEARANCES

Who Said That? 20 Mar. 1949, NBC.

Penthouse Party with Betty Furness. 1950, ABC.

This Is Show Business with Rudy Vallee. 1950, CBS.

The Colgate Comedy Hour. Episode #4. 1 Oct. 1950, NBC.

What's My Line? Episode #22, mystery guest. 29 Oct. 1950, CBS.

Kollege of Musical Knowledge with Kay Kyser. 14 Dec. 1950, NBC.

Versatile Varieties. 15 Dec. 1950, NBC.

Bert Parks Show. 22 Dec. 1950, NBC.

Leave It to the Girls. 24 Dec. 1950, NBC.

Inside USA with Chevrolet. 1951, CBS.

Nash Airflyte Theatre. "Pot o' Gold." 18 Jan. 1951, CBS.

Don McNeill's TV Club. 24 Jan. 1951, ABC.

The Frank Sinatra Show. 3 Mar. 1951, CBS.

All Star Revue with Perry Como. 22 Sep. 1951, NBC.

Footlights and Kleighlights. 24 Sep. 1951, NBC.

Tales of Tomorrow. "The Little Black Bag." 30 May 1952, ABC.

Schlitz Playhouse of Stars. "The Pussyfootin' Rocks." 21 Nov. 1952, CBS.

Suspense. "Vacancy for Death." 20 Jan. 1953, CBS.

Texaco Star Theatre with Milton Berle. 3 Feb. 1953, NBC.

All Star Revue with Perry Como. 14 Feb. 1953, NBC.

Lux Video Theatre. "Tango." 9 Jul. 1953, CBS.

The Colgate Comedy Hour. "Let's Face It." 21 Nov. 1954, NBC.

Fireside Theatre. "Sergeant Sullivan Speaking." 11 Jan. 1955, NBC.

Shower of Stars. "Burlesque." 17 Mar. 1955, CBS.

The General Electric Theater Parade of Stars. "Star in the House." 5 Jun. 1955, CBS.

Buick-Berle Show. 14 Jun. 1955, NBC.

Eddie Cantor Comedy Theatre. "Bombshell Goes to College." 20 Jun. 1955, SYN.

Playwrights '56. "Snow Job." 8 Nov. 1955, NBC.

The United States Steel Hour. "White Gloves." 21 Dec. 1955, ABC.

Playhouse 90. "Child in Trouble." 2 May 1957, CBS.

Studio One. "A Funny-Looking Kid." 19 May 1958, CBS.

Today. Guest interview. 19 Sep. 1958, NBC.

The Jacksons. Unaired pilot. 1959, NBC.

Person to Person with Edward R. Murrow. Guest interview. 10 Apr. 1959, CBS.

Playhouse 90. "A Marriage of Strangers." 14 May 1959, CBS.

Masquerade Party. Guest. 25 Jun. 1959, NBC.

About Faces. 1960, ABC.

Adventures in Paradise. "The Forbidden Sea." 4 Apr. 1960, ABC.

Witness. "Ma Barker." 12 Jan. 1961, CBS.

The Untouchables. "The Underground Court." 16 Feb. 1961, ABC.

The Barbara Stanwyck Show. "Sign of the Zodiac." 3 Apr. 1961, NBC.

Your First Impression. Mystery celebrity. 31 Aug. 1962, NBC.

The Dick Powell Show. "The Big Day." 25 Dec. 1962, NBC.

Death Valley Days. "The Train and Lucy Tutaine." 22 Feb. 1963, SYN.

The Real McCoys. Series regular. 10 Mar.–22 Sep. 1963, CBS.

Your First Impression. Guest. 10 Sep. 1963, NBC.

The Virginian. "To Make This Place Remember." 25 Sep. 1963, NBC.

Burke's Law. "Who Killed Harris Crown?" 11 Oct. 1963, ABC.

Wagon Train. "The Bleecker Story." 9 Dec. 1963, ABC.

The Twilight Zone. "What's in the Box." 13 Mar. 1964, CBS.

The Greatest Show on Earth. "You're All Right, Ivy." 28 Apr. 1964, ABC.

Burke's Law. "Who Killed Half of Glory Lee?" 8 May 1964, ABC.

Bonanza. "The Pressure Game." 10 May 1964, NBC.

The Steve Allen Show. Guest. 15 May 1964, SYN.

Dr. Kildare. "Dolly's Dilemma." 21 May 1964, NBC.

Vacation Playhouse. "Hooray for Hollywood." 22 Jun. 1964, CBS.

Walt Disney's Wonderful World of Color. "Kilroy, Part IV." 4 Apr. 1965, NBC.

The Lucy Show. "Lucy and Joan." 11 Oct. 1965, CBS.

The Lucy Show. "Lucy the Stunt Man." 18 Oct. 1965, CBS.

My Three Sons. "Office Mother." 22 Oct. 1965, CBS.

Slattery's People. "The Last Commuter." 19 Nov. 1965, CBS.

Ace of the Mounties. Unsold pilot. 1966, ABC.

Baby Crazy, aka *Baby Makes Three*. Unsold pilot. 1966, ABC.

Bob Hope Presents the Chrysler Theatre. "The Blue-Eyed Horse." 23 Nov. 1966, NBC.

The Man from U.N.C.L.E. "The Concrete Overcoat Affair, Parts I and II." 25 Nov.–2 Dec. 1966, NBC.

Mrs. Thursday. Unsold pilot. 1967, ABC.

The Girl from U.N.C.L.E. "The U.F.O. Affair." 3 Jan. 1967, NBC.

Winchester '73. Television movie. 14 Mar. 1967, CBS.

Family Affair. "Somebody Upstairs." 11 Dec. 1967, CBS.

The Guns of Will Sonnett. "A Sunday in Paradise." 15 Dec. 1967, ABC.

Petticoat Junction. "Girl of Our Dreams." 3 Feb. 1968, CBS.

Dear Mr. Gable. Guest interview. 5 Mar. 1968, NBC.

That Girl. "Just Spell the Name Right." 28 Mar. 1968, ABC.

Here Come the Brides. Series regular. 25 Sep. 1968–18 Sep. 1970, ABC.

The Dating Game. 19 Oct. 1968, ABC.

The Outsider. "There Was a Little Girl." 25 Dec. 1968, NBC.

The Name of the Game. "Battle at Gannon's Bridge." 9 Oct. 1970, NBC.

The Movie Game. Panelist. 5 Nov. 1970, SYN.

The Tonight Show Starring Johnny Carson. Guest interview. 12 Aug. 1971, NBC.

Love, American Style. "Love and the Lovesick Sailor." 29 Oct. 1971, ABC.

McCloud. "Top of the World, Ma!" 3 Nov. 1971, NBC.

Today. Guest interview. 16 Nov. 1971, NBC.

Banyon. Series regular. 15 Sep. 1972–12 Jan. 1973, NBC.

Love, American Style. "Love and the Swinging Surgeon." 14 Sep. 1973, ABC.

The Rookies. "Cry Wolf." 15 Oct. 1973, ABC.

Medical Center. "Stranger in Two Worlds." 29 Oct. 1973, CBS.

Carroll O'Connor Special: Three for the Girls. 5 Nov. 1973, CBS.

Sonny Boy. Pilot episode. 5 Nov. 1973, CBS.

The New Dick Van Dyke Show. "Exit Laughing." 26 Nov. 1973, CBS.

The Snoop Sisters. "The Devil Made Me Do It." 5 Mar. 1974, NBC.

Bobby Parker and Company. Unsold pilot. 22 Apr. 1974, NBC.

The Dead Don't Die. Television movie. 14 Jan. 1975, NBC.

Winner Take All. Television movie. 3 Mar. 1975, NBC.

Police Story. "Little Boy Lost." 28 Nov. 1975, NBC.

Switch. "One of Our Zeppelins Is Missing." 10 Feb. 1976, CBS.

Death at Love House. Television movie. 3 Sep. 1976, ABC.

Starsky & Hutch. "The Las Vegas Strangler." 25 Sep. 1976, ABC.

Rosetti and Ryan. "The Ten-Second Client." 13 Oct. 1977, NBC.

Battered. Television movie. 26 Sep. 1978, NBC.

The Love Boat. "Ship of Ghouls." 28 Oct. 1978, ABC.

$weepstake$. "Dewey and Harold and Sarah and Maggie." 2 Feb. 1979, NBC.

Fantasy Island. "Bowling/Command Performances." 19 May 1979, ABC.

The Rebels. Television miniseries. 14–21 May 1979, OPT.

60 Minutes. "Bette Davis." 20 Jan. 1980, CBS.

SOURCE NOTES

Joan Blondell: A Life between Takes is the result of research in film libraries and archives and numerous interviews with her friends, colleagues, and family. Screening Blondell's film and television work was also critical to research. I was able to see all but two of Blondell's ninety-two feature films. *Convention City* (1933) is lost, while *Big Daddy* (shot in 1965, released in 1969) has never been released to the home market and is apparently too obscure for ebay or private collectors. Through private collectors, the Museum of Television and Radio in New York, and the UCLA Film and Television Archive, I saw Blondell's television appearances on drama series (*Burke's Law*), comedy (*Vacation Playhouse*), unsold pilots (*Bobby Parker and Company*), anthologies (*The Barbara Stanwyck Show, The Dick Powell Show*), variety (*All Star Revue, Don McNeill's TV Club*), game shows (*The Movie Game*), commercials (*Butter-Nut Coffee*), and many others. Many more of her films and television appearances are available on DVD and via Turner Classic Movies, which televises films from the Warner Bros. library.

Many newspaper and magazine clippings on Blondell at various archives have no date or source ascription. Available information on printed sources is in the notes that follow. A bibliography also follows, listing books as well as significant articles on Blondell that are cited in this book.

The following abbreviations are used in the notes:

AMPAS: Margaret Herrick Library, Academy of Motion Picture Arts and Sciences, Beverly Hills
CKF: Charles K. Feldman Special Collection of the Louis B. Mayer Library, American Film Institute, Los Angeles
EP: Ellen Powell
JB: Joan Blondell
JHK: Joan Hayward Krooms
JJ: Jill Jackson
KB: Kathryn L. Blondell
MK: Matthew Kennedy
NP: Norman Powell

NYPL: New York Public Library for the Performing Arts
PCA: Production Code Administration
RB: Ronald L. Bowers's private clipping collection
SA: Shubert Archive, New York
UCLA: Twentieth Century Fox Special Collection, Arts Library Special Collections, University of California, Los Angeles
USC: Cinema-Television Library, University of Southern California, Los Angeles
WB: Warner Bros. Archives, School of Cinema-Television, University of Southern California

Introduction

Quotations

3   "Without work": Kobal 182.
4   "Her voice": Parish and Stanke 19.
4   "martini olive green": JHK interview with MK, 29 May 2005.
4   "always sparkled": Tolsky interview with MK, 1 Aug. 2006.
6   "Ann Sothern": Kobal 181.
6   "She made everybody's job easy": Anzures interview with MK, 19 Jul. 2006.
7   "impulsive, passionate": Marion (*Off with Their Heads!*) 303–304.
7   "The most generous": JJ interview with MK, 29 Aug. 2005.
7   "I don't know how": Hanley interview with MK, 11 Jul. 2006.
8   "an incredible history": *Village Voice*, 18 Nov. 1971.

Chapter 1: The Next Town

Family, particularly EP, provided much of the background on JB's parents and childhood. Additional vital statistics were found in the census records at www.ancestry.com. *The Lost Boy* characters come from Ann McDowell Traub's private collection of family ephemera. Written accounts of JB's early years come from Parish and Stanke, *The Leading Ladies*; Munter, "Joan Blondell: Heart of Gold" from *Films of the Golden Age* (fall 2002); *Movie Mirror* (Jun. 1934); *Hollywood Citizen News* (2 Jun. 1937); and various clippings in the JB file of the NYPL. I found the *New York Times* accounts of *The Miracle* on 20 Jan. and 3 Feb. 1924 most revealing. The Atlantic City beauty contest is covered in Van Meter's *The Last Good Time*. The Dempsey-Tunney bet is in *Silver Screen*, Aug. 1937.

Quotations

12   "streams of laughter": *Brooklyn Eagle*, 10 Mar. 1901.
13   "This is a nice": *Variety*, 25 Dec. 1909.
13   "In Australia": Johnson 38.
14   "The Americanisms": *New York Telegraph*, 10 Jul. 1910.
14   "Kind audience": *Variety*, 31 Dec. 1910.
15   "Life on the boat": JB file, NYPL.
15   "I became educated": Kobal 187.
16   "When vaudeville was going": *TV Guide*, 19 Apr. 1969.
16   "Just go out there": AMPAS Special Collections, 22 May 1972.
17   "There is a lot": *Los Angeles Times*, 24 Jul. 1918.
17   "I always thought": JB file, NYPL, 1938.
17   "I got a serious disease": ibid.
18   "With me protesting": JB file, AMPAS, 1945.
19   "We gave her vast tureens": JB file, NYPL.
19   "I have seen": ibid.
20   "It's a party": EP interview with MK, 28 Jul. 2004.
20   "I couldn't take it": Bowers 193–194.
20   "It produced an effect": *New York Times*, 16 Jan. 1924.
21   "It was a screwy thing": *New York World-Telegram*, 27 Apr. 1935.
22   "It was a dirty trick": *Silver Screen*, Jan. 1942.
22   "Mom—Ah'm Miss Dallas": ibid., Aug. 1937.
22   "a pretty Texas lassie": *Boardwalk Illustrated News*, 13 Sep. 1926.
23   "an awfully nice old guy": Kobal 194–195.
24   "Miss Manhattan Transfer!": RB, 1976.

Chapter 2: Starlight

The rape was recounted to me by EP during a marathon taped interview on 14 May 2004. A thinly fictionalized account is also found in JB's *Center Door Fancy*. An additional source on JB's life in the early 1930s comes from RB and Bowers's "Joan Blondell." The details of JB's Warner Bros. salary and contract are found in the JB legal file of the WB. Another account of Warner Bros. in the 1930s is found in Tornabene, *Long Live the King*.

Quotations

25   "was a good clerk": Parish and Stanke 25.

28   "The first day": *Silver Screen*, Jan. 1942.

28   "I've known what it is": Parish and Stanke 25.

29   "Every actor and actress": *Los Angeles Times*, 20 Jul. 1969.

29   "He sat me down": ibid.

29   "Now, boys and girls": Cagney 48–49.

30   "Jimmy Cagney made": Kobal 191.

30   "make good [her] my family": Parish and Stanke 26.

30   "I believe it was": Kobal 186.

31   "Manna from heaven": McCabe 69.

32   "Cagney and I": Kobal 186.

33   "Compliment my mother": Marion (*Off with Their Heads!*) 217–218.

34   "is what some": *Los Angeles Examiner*, 20 Sep. 1930.

34   "We were getting paid": Kobal 186.

35   "Grandma": Munter 17.

35   "as smart as": *Los Angeles Examiner*, 21 Feb. 1931.

36   "God, the weather here": McCabe 78.

37   "When he showed up": Wayne 73.

38   "When I first got into pictures": Kobal 187.

38   "The shyness only leaves": Parish and Stanke 28.

38   "Miss Blondell has a way": *Los Angeles Evening Express*, 7 Aug. 1931.

38   "nearly steals things": *Variety*, 4 Aug. 1931.

40   "Blondell's beauty": McCabe 88.

41   "I would get endless fan mail": Kobal 187.

41   "I can't play a neurotic": McCarthy 161.

42   "hard, hard labor": Munter 19.

42   "were put on the payroll": Higham 88–89.

43   "We started work at 5": *New York Times*, 20 Aug. 1972.

43   "They'd even pan us": Michael Frank 232.

43   "Writers were pressed": Cagney 103.

44   "Nobody believed she was sick": Berg 216.

45   "I had been one of those kid fans": Parish and Stanke 34.

Chapter 3: Hammer and Tongs

The *Miss Pinkerton* set was described in the *Los Angeles Evening Herald Express* of 12 Mar. 1932. The working conditions at Warner Bros. are described in Lumet, *Making Movies*; Balio, *History of the American Cinema*; and *Screenbook* of Jan. 1934. David Martin interviewed actor Lyle

Talbot in 1996 and choreographer-director Busby Berkeley in 1963 on life at Warner Bros. in the 1930s. Studio production costs and box-office earnings are found in the Warner Bros. ledger sheet in the William Schaefer Collection at USC. The virginity certificate is from EP and is mentioned in Blondell, *Center Door Fancy*. JB's life on Lookout Mountain is described in Parish and Stanke, *The Leading Ladies*. Issues of salary, suspension, production assignments, scheduling, and contracts are kept in the JB legal file and in film production files at the WB. JB's social life and personal life were frequently mentioned in the gossip columns and feature articles of the *Los Angeles Examiner*, *Los Angeles Evening Herald Express*, *Modern Screen*, and *Silver Screen*, among others. The Seamen's Church honor was reported in *New York Times*, 17 Sep. 1933. The house fire was reported in *New York Times*, 22 Oct. 1933. The wedding ring incident is from *Hollywood Citizen News*, 21 May 1934. The baby shower was reported in *Los Angeles Examiner*, 2 Aug. 1934. *Dames* production information is found in the PCA files of AMPAS. JB's first labor was recounted by EP as told to her by JB.

Quotations

46	"Here was a young woman": EP to author, 14 May 2004.
47	"I'm so sick of that": *Movie Mirror*, Apr. 1932.
48	"tedious and distasteful": *New York Times*, 29 Oct. 1932.
48	"*Whee*—am I jealous!": *Movie Mirror*, Apr. 1932.
49	"I didn't say I was married": *Los Angeles Examiner*, 18 Aug. 1932.
50	"It's the same script": Maltin 3.
50	"You had to sell a lot of tickets": Sperling, Millner, and Warner Jr. 159.
51	"Guys like Lloyd Bacon": Bowers 195–196.
51	"We seldom said hello": Maltin 3.
51	"Warners never made": Finler 243.
52	"It's great what love can do": *Modern Screen*, Apr. 1933.
53	"I could be happy": Kobal 184.
53	"winding up the road": *Louisville Courier*, 26 Dec. 1971.
55	"It was a spectacle": David Martin 34.
56	"Smash girl-and-music special": *Film Daily*, 25 May 1933.
57	" 'The Forgotten Man' number": *Village Voice*, 18 Nov. 1971.
58	"You will see the most extravagant": *Los Angeles Post Record*, 9 Nov. 1933.
58	"Those musicals were tough": Kobal 190.
59	"a helter-skelter lark": *New York Times*, 23 Nov. 1933.
59	"Please be advised": JB legal file, WB, 31 Aug. 1933.
59	"please replace [her]": ibid., 11 Sep. 1933.
60	"seemed to indicate": PCA file, AMPAS, 14 Sep. 1933.
60	"Me. I was the one": Vieira 151.
60	"We must put brassieres": *Convention City* file, WB, 5 Oct. 1933.

60   "We were forever doing things": Kobal 193.

61   "We were all brothers and sisters": ibid. 191.

61   "until such incapacity": JB legal file, WB, 19 Dec. 1933.

62   "I'm stuttering": Maltin 5.

63   "was just a case of nerves": Munter 20.

63   "my poor baby": EP interview with MK, 14 May 2004.

63   "I made six pictures": Kobal 188.

64   "come up and see": *Dames* file, WB, 19 Mar. 1934.

65   "never was there": *Los Angeles Examiner*, 9 Oct. 1934.

66   "To my baby": *Modern Screen*, Aug. 1935.

66   "We're all ready": *Los Angeles Examiner*, 2 Oct. 1934.

66   "You see, this is the first": *Los Angeles Examiner*, 21 Nov. 1934.

67   "cutest little fellow": ibid.

Chapter 4: Nearer to Heaven

I found information on JB's home and work life in *Hollywood Citizen News*, *Los Angeles Examiner*, *New York Times*, *Modern Screen*, *Los Angeles Times*, and *Los Angeles Evening Herald Express*. Additional information comes from family history as passed down to NP and EP. Studio production costs and box-office earnings are found in the Warner Bros. ledger sheet in the William Schaefer Collection at USC. Details of her divorce from George Barnes appeared in the *New York Times*, 13 Aug. and 5 Sep. 1935. Betty Wood was reported in the *Los Angeles Times*, 6 Aug. 1935. Ed Blondell's move to California and divorce was shared by his daughter KB in an interview with MK, 18 Aug. 2004. The JB-Sherman-Warner business is recounted in JB legal file, WB, 27 Sep. and 8 Oct. 1935. For reporting on the Blondell-Powell marriage, see the *Los Angeles Times*, 12 and 15 Sep. 1936. The boat honeymoon and New York visit were reported in the *New York Times*, 7 and 11 Oct. 1936. The casting and making of *The Perfect Specimen* is recorded in that film's production file at WB. JB's commercial endorsements and radio appearances are noted in JB legal file, WB. JB's announced departure from Warner Bros. is in the *New York Times*, 25 Dec. 1937. JB was declared "Public Gold Digger #1" in the *Los Angeles Times*, 28 Apr. 1938. The Academy Awards mishap is recounted in Wiley and Bona, *Inside Oscar*.

Quotations

69   "That was when": Johnson 40.

69   "I do not know": JB file, WB, 21 and 22 Feb. 1935.

70 "utters comedy lines": *Hollywood Citizen News*, 2 Aug. 1935.

70 "You made one good movie": Considine 41.

70 "I never saw rushes": *Village Voice*, 18 Nov. 1971.

71 "I've been thinking!": JB legal file, WB, 23 Aug. 1935.

72 "My body belongs to Warner Bros.": ibid., 28 Aug. 1935.

73 "This business of a baby": *Modern Screen*, Aug. 1935.

74 "one of the funniest things": Cagney 113.

74 "I started out with two assets": *New York Times*, 4 Jan. 1963.

75 "From this day on": JB legal file, WB, 17 Sep. 1935.

76 "No one would be able": www.classicimages.com/1998/may98/glendafarrell.html 24.

76 "Joan and my mother": ibid. 27.

76 "Although Joan has been hard hit": *Modern Screen*, Mar. 1936.

76 "It looks very much to us": PCA file, AMPAS, 30 Nov. 1935.

77 "Now that I dress": *Modern Screen*, Mar. 1936.

78 "a lovely girl": *Los Angeles Examiner*, 19 Sep. 1936.

80 "I'm deliriously happy": *New York Times*, 11 Oct. 1936.

81 "People took all that love stuff": Kobal 189.

81 "no intention of letting": *Los Angeles Evening Herald Express*, 24 May 1936.

81 "I'll never forget": Koch 28.

82 "is at her best": *Los Angeles Evening Herald Express*, 27 Feb. 1937.

82 "Dorothy in *The King and the Chorus Girl*": *Saturday Evening Post*, 26 Apr. 1947.

82 "What was foremost": Kobal 184.

83 "I'm 32": RB.

85 "He wasn't a man": *TV Guide*, 19 Apr. 1969.

86 "had no intention of reporting": JB legal file, WB, 11 Sep. 1937.

87 "This is something": *Los Angeles Examiner*, 16 Jan. 1938.

87 "Sometimes I wish": ibid., 25 Jan. 1938.

88 "my baby": *Modern Screen*, Dec. 1938.

Chapter 5: Freelancing

Studio production costs and box-office earnings are found in the Warner Bros. ledger sheet in the William Schaefer Collection at USC. JB's announced departure from Warner Bros. is in the *New York Times*, 12 Dec. 1938. JB's Warner Bros. salary history is found in the WB. The *Gone with the Wind* casting was noted in the *Los Angeles Evening Herald Express*, 20 Feb. 1939. For an understanding of JB's domestic leanings, Todd Jr.'s *A Valuable Property* proved to be instructive. *I Want a Divorce* production information (13 Feb. 1940) is at

AMPAS Special Collections. *Goodbye to Love* production was reported in the *New York Times*, 8 and 11 Jun. 1940 and in the *San Francisco Chronicle*, 10 and 18 Jun. 1940. The Blondell-Broccoli marriage is in the *Los Angeles Times*, 27 Jul. 1940. Background on Dussell is from KB in an interview with the author on 18 Aug. 2004. Newport Beach was recalled by NP and EP to MK in multiple interviews from 2004 to 2006. *The Model Wife* contract terms, costs, and income are in the CKF. The *Three Girls on a Man* joke was found in the *New York Post*, 4 Nov. 1972. The Memphis Belle story is from Ethell, *Aircraft Nose Art*. Pearl Harbor is remembered as told to EP and NP by JB.

Quotations

89	"How's the baby?": *Los Angeles Examiner*, 8 Sep. 1938.
90	"because, after all, under your modern contract": JB legal file, WB, 16 Sep. 1938.
91	"Warners coined money": Thomas 7.
91	"He hated to sing": *Los Angeles Times*, 20 Jul. 1969.
91	"I have found sanity": *Screenland*, Jun. 1939.
91	"I suppose I was a fool": Munter 23.
91	"All the others on the lot": Kobal 188.
91	"None of the pictures stand out": ibid. 191.
92	"There was a pattern": *Life*, 19 Feb. 1971.
92	"I've had more than enough": *Film Weekly*, 23 Dec. 1938.
94	"Skip it": *Screenland*, Jun. 1939.
95	"After having cracked": *New York Times*, 30 Mar. 1941.
95	"I'm a daancer": Edgar Bergen Collection, USC, 13 Aug. 1939.
97	"The Most Glamorous Mother": Parish and Stanke 51.
98	"Miss Joan Blondell of Hollywood": *New York Times*, 3 Oct. 1940.
98	"These 22 weeks": *New York Times*, 30 Mar. 1941.
101	"The story is wonderful": *Silver Screen*, Jan. 1942.
102	"Now, Dick, don't drive too fast": Powell ("A Pony in the Pile") 33.

Chapter 6: The Interrupted Family

Accounts of home life during the war, the Todd romance, and the Powell divorce and its aftermath come from NP and EP in multiple interviews and conversations with MK, 2004–2006. A description of the Powell's home on Selma is in M. Frank, "Joan Blondell and Dick Powell." A recap of Todd's career is in Todd Jr., *A Valuable Property*. The condition of JB's film career in 1943 is suggested by contemporary correspondence in the CKF. Information on Ed Blondell's death is from NP, EP, and *Los Angeles Times*, 15 Aug. 1942. Todd's deal with Fox to film *The Naked Genius* is in *New York Times*, 7 Nov. 1943. JB's breakdown is noted in *Movieland*, Sep. 1944, and in interviews with NP and EP by MK. The terms of JB's Fox contract are spelled out in papers at UCLA. The Blondell-Powell divorce appeared in *New York Times*, 10 Jun. 1944. Accounts of the making of *A Tree Grows in Brooklyn* appear in the JB file, AMPAS. Junie and Gretchen Blondell information is supplied by KB in an interview with MK, 18 Aug. 2004.

Quotations

105	"Being a truck horse": *New York Times*, 20 Jun. 1943.
106	"Miss Blondell is deserving": SA collection, 5 Dec. 1942.
106	"Well, he's hep": ibid.
107	"the favorite date": ibid.
107	"some godforsaken place": Todd Jr. 173.
107	"If I don't get [a furlough]": SA collection, 1942.
109	"It's time I told you": Powell ("A Pony in the Pile") 52–53.
110	"early English on the outside": *Look*, 5 Sep. 1944.
110	"She would get so much attention": EP to author, 14 May 2004.
111	"We'd all sit": ibid.
111	"He may parlay himself": *Variety*, 26 Mar. 1958.
113	"There were daily dialogue changes": Todd Jr. 106.
114	"Joan forgot about trying": ibid. 107.
114	"There are sad and dreary tidings": *New York Times*, 22 Oct. 1943.
115	"You won't leave this": Preminger 64.
115	"wanted to own the world": *Los Angeles Times*, 20 Jul. 1969.
115	"Oh, did I want to get out": Johnson 40.
115	"To pay $3.30 instead": *New York Times*, 31 Oct. 1943.
115	"In show business you can't please everyone": ibid., 17 Nov. 1943.
116	"I'll make it up": Marion ("Hollywood") 557.
117	"a certain young lady": ibid.
118	"Joan Blondell, one of the best-loved actresses": Munter 24.
118	"What good am I?": EP to MK, 14 May 2004.
118	"I am going to file": *Los Angeles Times*, 8 Jan. 1944.
119	"Exclusive!": Cohn 152.
119	"Do you have to sit in the *first* row?": ibid. 142–143.
119	"Was a beautiful, delightful minx": ibid. 143.
120	"The West Coast radio announcement": ibid. 152–153.

120   "I didn't think I was taking": Allyson 216.
120   "I actually lost my breath": *Look*, 5 Sep. 1944.
121   "is too young to understand": *Movieland*, Sep. 1944.
122   "The lack of information": NP interview with MK, 29 May 2004.
123   "He kept his office in our home": *Los Angeles Examiner*, 15 Jul. 1944.
123   "It's only a spat": *Movieland*, Sep. 1944.
123   "like a brother": *Los Angeles Times*, 20 Jul. 1969.
124   "the bigamous characterization of Sissy": PCA file, AMPAS, 26 Apr. 1944.
124   "There were no big meetings": Maltin 7.
125   "Producer Louis Lighton": *New York Times*, 24 Dec. 1944.
125   "I'm operating on the theory": JB file, Fox publicity biography, AMPAS.
125   "Where Miss Smith": *New York Times*, 1 Mar. 1945.
126   "Joan Blondell is little short": *New York Daily News*, 1 Mar. 1945.
126   "You'll be crazy": *A Tree Grows in Brooklyn* file, USC, 2 Mar. 1945.
126   "Thank God censorship has improved": *New York Times*, 20 Aug. 1972.
126   "Joan Blondell's performance": ibid., 1 Mar. 1945.
127   "She always felt": Bowers interview with MK, 18 Jun. 2004.
127   "Kazan let me have a moment": *Life*, 19 Feb. 1971.
127   "Yeah! Well, here's one star": Edgar Bergen Collection, USC, 11 Mar. 1945.
128   "I wouldn't know what to do": Fox publicity release, AMPAS Special Collection.

Chapter 7: Gulag-on-the-Hudson

The house fire is recounted in *Los Angeles Examiner*, 9 Jul. 1946, and by EP and NP in interviews with MK. The affair with Todd is told in Cohn, *The Nine Lives of Mike Todd*. The UFO event is in Todd Jr., *A Valuable Property*, and was retold by EP to MK, 26 Aug. 2005. Marriage to Todd is in Cohn, *The Nine Lives of Mike Todd*, and in Todd Jr., *A Valuable Property*. *Nightmare Alley* records are in the PCA files at AMPAS, 13 Mar. 1947. The purchase of Irvington is detailed in Todd Jr., *A Valuable Property*. Todd's financial woes are in Bowers, "Joan Blondell," and Todd Jr., *A Valuable Property*. Irvington home life and Todd's domestic abuse is detailed in Todd Jr., *A Valuable Property*, and Powell, "A Pony in the Pile." The *Our Miss Brooks* opportunity is in Sanders, *Desilu*. JB's reaction to the Louis-Walcott fight is noted in the JB file at AMPAS. The creation of *As the Girls Go* is in Todd Jr., *A Valuable Property*. Ed Blondell and family at Irvington is recalled by KB to MK, 17 Aug. 2004. The story of cufflinks in the city dump comes from an EP interview with MK, 26 Aug. 2005. The Princeton incident is in H. Kennedy, *No Pickle, No Performance*. The European trip was mentioned in *New York Times*, 10 Feb. 1950. Information on the end of the Todd marriage comes from an EP interview with MK, 26 Aug. 2005.

Quotations

130   "Clark adored women": Harris 282.
131   "He'd go get some steaks": Tornabene 325.
131   "a swell job": *Los Angeles Times*, 14 Jun. 1945.
131   "almost a reborn actress": *Variety*, 19 Dec. 1945.
131   "one for you, one for me": Parish and Stanke 61.
132   "There was no particular catalyst": Broccoli 72–73.
133   "Without referring to his unhappy life": Todd Jr. 156–157.
134   "a short, chunky, dark, dynamic fellow": *Los Angeles Examiner*, 26 Oct. 1947.
134   "I've been broke": *Variety*, 26 Mar. 1958.
134   "He was a psychopathic loser": Cohn 219.
134   "I was once described": *Saturday Evening Post*, 26 Apr. 1947.
135   "Don't rush into this marriage": NP private collection.
136   "It felt a little rushed": EP interview with MK, 26 Aug. 2005.
138   "reveals herself as a dramatic actress": *Hollywood Reporter*, 9 Oct. 1947.
138   "Mom didn't talk about her work": NP interview with MK, 29 May 2004.
139   "Joan generated tremendous enthusiasm": Todd Jr. 173.
139   "Joan didn't spend extravagant sums": ibid. 75.
141   "She remodeled him completely": Cohn 240.
141   "She tried to keep us protected": EP interview with MK, 14 May 2004.
143   "What's the matter, Mike?": Todd Jr. 187.
144   "Ed Blondell was a goodhearted extrovert": ibid. 191.
144   "What's wrong with those two guys?": McClelland 191.
144   "He would hear Joan laughing": Todd Jr. 191.
145   "I am sure": Todd Jr. 191–192
145   "Michael had another nightmare": Powell ("A Pony") 93.
145   "She seemed to spend a lot of time": ibid. 92.
145   "[it] went into the hall": NP interview with MK, 29 May 2004.
146   "In my book each gave": Todd Jr. 192–193.
146   "clap trap bedlam": Marion ("Hollywood") 608–609.
146   "Joan was whizzing": ibid.
147   "Joan was kinder": Cohn 245–246.
147   "I'll show you": NP interview with MK, 29 May 2004.
148   "If I had a man like Victor": EP interview with MK, 14 May 2004.
149   "The original story": *New York Times*, 19 Jul. 1949.
149   "Miss Blondell used foul and abusive language": Cohn 257.
150   "You're the only woman": *Village Voice*, 21 Jan. 1980.
150   "She never gave the same performance twice": EP interview with MK, 18 Jul. 2006.

150   "Mike was the most driven": Marion (*Off with Their Heads!*) 304.
151   "did not open even one big blue eye": EP private collection.
151   "peed over, interviewed": ibid.
152   "Ellen and I both loved our mother": NP interview with MK, 29 May 2004.

Chapter 8: Solo Rites

The Blondell-Todd separation and divorce is covered in *Los Angeles Examiner*, 24 Apr. 1950, and *New York Times*, 9 Jun. 1950, while details were recalled to MK by EP in a letter dated 17 Jul. 2006. Terms of employment in *For Heaven's Sake* are at UCLA. The sale of the Irvington mansion and subsequent auction is in *New York Times*, 22 Oct. 1950. Reference Librarian Anne Coco of AMPAS supplied information on the 1952 Academy Awards ceremony. The spirit of George Barnes is in RB. The Vicksburg, Mississippi, trip is mentioned in a letter from JB to Gloria Blondell in EP's private collection, dated 19 Dec. 1953. Family gifts and loans are in a letter from JB to Gloria Blondell in EP's private collection, dated 3 Apr. 1954. The evenings with Vanderbilt, Sinatra, and Cannon are mentioned in Vanderbilt, *It Seemed Important at the Time*. Remembrances of JB's social life in New York are recalled by NP and EP in multiple interviews with MK. Dorothy Ponedel is referenced in Parish and Stanke, *The Leading Ladies*. *A Palm Tree in a Rose Garden* is remembered by cast member Alice Ghostley in an interview with MK on 5 Jul. 2005 and in Parish and Stanke, *The Leading Ladies*. JB's *This Could be the Night* salary is on file at UCLA. *New Girl in Town* crew member Eleanor Knowles Dugan shared her memories with MK in 23 May 2004.

Quotations

154   "Let's go": EP interview with MK, 14 May 2004.
154   "The things that hurt": Parish and Stanke 76.
155   "I like a trailer": *Hollywood Citizen News*, 24 Jul. 1950.
155   "It took a long while": Elkins interview with MK, 5 Oct. 2004.
155   "A lot of people believe": Fisher 110.
156   "the former and future Mrs. Todd": Cohn 276.
156   "The whole situation struck me": ibid. 208–209.
157   "When I saw the word": *Los Angeles Herald-Examiner*, 24 Jul. 1972.
157   "The only right thing I ever did": *New York Post*, 4 Nov. 1972.
157   "Miss Blondell dazzles": *Variety*, 7 Sep. 1951.
157   "Miss Blondell wows the audience": *Hollywood Reporter*, 7 Sep. 1951.

159   "You've got to decide": NP interview with MK, 29 May 2004.

159   "They grew up in Hollywood": Bikel 146.

159   "had come the familiar route": Cohn 246.

159   "Nothing pleased us more": Jerry Wald Collection, USC, 12 Feb. 1952.

160   "My life was locked": EP interview with MK, 11 Oct. 2004.

160   "I later realized": EP letter to MK, 17 Jul. 2006.

160   "They can sit in the living room": *New York Times*, 21 Jun. 1953.

161   "Home is where": EP letter to MK, 17 Jul. 2006.

161   "it's beautiful and I'm going to be happy": KB interview with MK, 6 Feb. 2006.

162   "That kind of entertainment": JB file, NYPL, 3 Oct. 1953.

163   "she was the milk cow of the family": EP interview with MK, 29 Sep. 2004.

164   "Jimmy Cannon has a big crush": EP private collection, 19 Dec. 1953.

164   "Judy Garland and Joan Blondell": Marion (*Off with Their Heads!*) 304–305.

164   "wonderfully kind and generous": *TV Guide*, 19 Apr. 1969.

165   "Home is not merely a house": EP private collection.

167   "Ann and Norm": *New York Daily Mirror*, 23 Jul. 1956.

168   "I grew up with Joan Blondell": Franciosa interview with MK, 30 Sep. 2004.

168   "I loved working with the two of them": Maltin 7.

168   "I really don't have envy": Bowers 200.

169   "shines": *Variety*, 15 May 1957.

169   "fine and earthy counterpart": *Hollywood Reporter*, 10 May 1957.

169   "I don't remember ever taking one": JB file, AMPAS, 1957.

170   "I have to show them my wares": Munter 27.

170   "She didn't take Mike away from me": JB file, NYPL, 1968.

171   "You know that there's something wrong": Kreuger interview with MK, 10 Jul. 2004.

172   "She expresses the sentiment of the part": *New York Times*, 1 Dec. 1957.

172   "[It is] a wonderfully exhilarating": ibid., 21 Nov. 1957.

172   "She was very good, utterly professional": Bikel interview with MK, 1 Dec. 2004.

172   "I went backstage to see Siobhan": Kreuger interview with MK, 10 Jul. 2004.

174   "It was beautifully written": Johnson 40.

174   "Dear Joan": EP private collection, 3 May 1958.

175   "Mother Earth": Lobenthal 477.

175   "My part was better": Bowers 200-201.

175   "chased by saddened reviewers": Lobenthal 483.

176   "It was Sunday": Blondell ("A Tale of Two Dogs") 10.

176   "I itched": ibid.

176   "Actress Joan Blondell": Murrow, *Person to Person*, 10 Apr. 1959.

177   "The pugs received more fan mail": Blondell ("A Tale of Two Dogs") 25.

178   "serious about acting": *Los Angeles Times*, 23 Sep. 1956.

Chapter 9: Love, Matey

Accounts of *The Dark at the Top of the Stairs* tour are in letters from JB to Gloria Blondell, EP private collection. "Do's and Don'ts for the Bride-to-Be" is in EP's private collection. The Colonial House crowd is recounted in Beauchamp, *Without Lying Down*. The relationship between JB and EP was recalled in a letter from EP to MK, 19 Jul. 2006. JB's last visit with Dick Powell was shared with MK by JJ, 29 Aug. 2005. The Powell funeral and estate business was reported in the *Los Angeles Times* (5 Jan. 1963) and in the *New York Times* (11 Jan. 1963). For Castle's intentions to cast JB in *Strait-Jacket*, see the *Los Angeles Times*, 22 Feb. 1963. JB's fee for TV is in the *Los Angeles Times*, 20 Jul. 1969. The *Big Daddy* set was recalled by Sterling in an email to MK on 29 Aug. 2005. NP's second marriage was recalled by NP in an interview with MK on 29 May 2004. Whitespeak was described to MK by EP. Bridey and Fresh's accommodations are mentioned in AMPAS Special Collection, 22 May 1972. Stephanie Powell Murphy's memories were shared in an interview with MK on 19 Jul. 2005. JHK discussed the *Here Come the Brides* set with MK on 25 Oct. 2004. Rich memories of the series were shared with MK in interviews with actors Robert Brown (24 May 2006), Bridget Hanley (11 Jul. 2006), and Susan Tolsky (11 Jul. and 1 Aug. 2006), and story consultant William Blinn (12 Jul. 2006).

Quotations

179   "It's the kind of role I love": *Los Angeles Times*, 24 Jan. 1960.
179   "[I] had a night out with Merman": EP private collection, 3 Aug. 1959.
180   "This is the way to see the country": *Los Angeles Times*, 24 Jan. 1960.
180   "They tell you the road is dead": ibid.
182   "had slung that marvelous ass": *Soho Weekly News*, 3 Jan. 1980.
183   "Her life was those two ugly dogs!": JJ interview with MK, 29 Aug. 2005.
184   "In New York, the mother was played": *Los Angeles Times*, 4 Jun. 1961.
184   "I wouldn't have been half as good": ibid., 7 Oct. 1962.
184   "I did it for seven months": Johnson 40.
185   "I'm going to try desperately": Hedda Hopper Collection, AMPAS, 18 Feb. 1963.
186   "Dear Joan: Loved your card": EP private collection.
186   "It was a thoughtful thing": Allyson 218.
187   "They were different types": Munter 29.
188   "It's a fantastic acting role": Hedda Hopper Collection, AMPAS, 18 Feb. 1963.
188   "then proceed[ed] to turn his picture upside down": Considine 334.

188   "I stepped through a glass": ibid.

188   "The sets are depressing": *Los Angeles Times*, 5 Mar. 1963.

189   "It isn't ambition": Munter 28.

189   "So you're in the picture, too?": *Los Angeles Times*, 18 Aug. 1963.

190   "through back lots": Blondell ("A Tale of Two Dogs") 33–34.

191   "When she entered and had a few lines": Jewison interview with MK, 15 Oct. 2004.

192   "The sad thing": Kobal 195.

192   "I loved Eddie Robinson in *The Cincinnati Kid*": *Los Angeles Times*, 5 Nov. 1972.

192   "Hal Ashby and I had so much fun": Jewison interview with MK, 15 Oct. 2004.

192   "Unfortunately these plays were done": *Los Angeles Times*, 9 May 1965.

192   "one of life's biggest heart aches": JB file, AMPAS.

193   "That's when Ellen": Lundin interview with MK, 25 Oct. 2004.

193   "You haven't tried it": *New York Post*, 4 Nov. 1972.

193   "Lucille was intimidated by Joan Blondell": Fidelman 199–200.

194   "to offer moral support": ibid.

194   "I've *never* been treated so badly": JJ interview with MK, 29 Aug. 2005.

195   "Comedy is as elusive as a waiter's eye": *Hollywood Citizen News*, 25 Nov. 1966.

195   "I still like motion pictures best": Parish and Stanke 72.

195   "After thousands of miles of travel": Blondell ("A Tale of Two Dogs") 5.

196   "crude, impolite, and cruel": EP interview with MK, 25 Oct. 2004.

196   "a dear, dear woman": Miles letter to MK, 27 Sep. 2004.

197   "I loved working with her": KB interview with MK, 17 Aug. 2004.

198   "Are you kidding?": *Newark Sunday News*, 16 Jun. 1968.

199   "The show is the opposite of hip": *TV Guide*, 4 Jan. 1969.

199   "It's a marvelous part": JB file, AMPAS, 1968.

199   "When we came to talk": Blinn interview with MK, 12 Jul. 2006.

199   "homey, poolish, bookish with a view": JB file, NYPL.

200   "Sometimes I'd like to bathe": Blondell ("A Tale of Two Dogs") 32.

200   "We've never been apart": *TV Guide*, 19 Apr. 1969.

200   "The best thing I'm good at": ibid.

201   "the most generous person": JHK interview with MK, 25 Oct. 2004.

201   "She was so easy": Brown interview with MK, 24 May 2006.

202   "it was the coup": Hanley interview with MK, 11 Jul. 2006.

202   "Based on time in service and grade": *TV Guide*, 19 Apr. 1969.

202   "In a world of plastic flowers": ibid.

202   "beautiful new vulva!": Brown interview with MK, 24 May 2006.

202   "I read a little first": *Los Angeles Times*, 20 Jul. 1969.

202   "Funny thing about a series": *TV Guide*, 4 Jan. 1969.

203   "I don't know why": *Los Angeles Times*, 20 Jul. 1969.

Chapter 10: I Hear Voices

Life with JB in the 1970s was shared with MK by JHK, 25 Oct. 2004. The Academy Award appearance is recounted in Wiley and Bona, *Inside Oscar*. JB's departure from Whitespeak is in Koch, "Joan Blondell." Opening night of *Marigolds* was reported in the *Los Angeles Times*, 8 Mar. 1978. The rabbit at the curtain call was mentioned to MK by EP. The JB-EP-JHK relationship was recalled by JHK to MK, 25 Oct. 2004 and 11 Nov. 2004 and by EP on 20 Aug. 2006. The story of "Mr. Dink" was told to MK by Stephanie Powell Murphy, 19 Jul. 2005, and by Robert Brown, 24 May 2006. The Marion honor is in Beauchamp, *Without Lying Down*. The Nixon event is reported in the *New York Times*, 28 Aug. 1972. Freddy Mohr was remembered by NP and Ellen Levine to MK, 29 May 2004. JB's will was shared with MK by family members.

Quotations

205	"I feel if my heart lifts": Parish and Stanke 73.
205	"They cut my scenes out of it": Johnson 42.
205	"For the first time": *Life*, 19 Feb. 1971.
206	"it was an uphill thing": ibid.
206	"I think a series is a dangerous thing to do.": Johnson 42.
206	"Joan, you're late": Hanley interview with MK, 11 Jul. 2006.
206	"It began as a comedy": Blinn interview with MK, 12 Jul. 2006.
207	"it is very unfortunate for everyone": www.bobbysherman.com/hctbmain.htm/.
207	"I want you to cry, too": Powell interview with MK, 19 Jul. 2005.
208	"They went everywhere with me": *New York Times*, 20 Aug. 1972.
209	"Oh, God. Who was that with": Johnson 42.
209	"I thought [it] was beautiful.": Koch 26.
209	"I'm sane enough to know": Kobal 183–184.
211	"I called my agent": *Playfare* 3.11 (Nov. 1971).
211	"I wanted to make a quick change": Johnson 38.
211	"rich and complex": *Village Voice*, 18 Nov. 1971.
211	"It was very, very painful to do": *New York Times*, 20 Aug. 1972.
212	"One day the little fellows' eyes suddenly reopened": Koch 26.
212	"I was never so grateful": *New York Times*, 20 Aug. 1972.
212	"That woman would never": *Village Voice*, 18 Nov. 1971.
212	"The entire audience rocked": Koch 26.
212	"All of that stuff is painful": *Village Voice*, 18 Nov. 1971.
213	"I'm not a night person anymore": *New York News*, 26 Nov. 1972.

213 "Uhhhh. Ohhh": Johnson 42.

213 "I write at night": RB, 1976.

214 "My life had no anchor": EP letter to MK, 27 Jul. 2006.

214 "It was an excruciating time": NP interview with MK, 29 May 2004.

215 "You're just bewildered": EP private collection, 1994.

215 "Ellen's sick again": Powell interview with MK, 19 Jul. 2005.

215 "a quite lovely hotel": Koch 25.

215 "I looked for the old dressing rooms": *New York Times*, 20 Aug. 1972.

216 "I think they were fabulous": KB interview with MK, 17 Aug. 2004.

216 "Joanie Bennett in New York": *Los Angeles Times*, 5 Nov. 1972.

217 "To meet her—or read her": ibid.

217 "Lively, warm, and funny": *New York Times*, 22 Oct. 1972.

217 "*Center Door Fancy* took me on a trip": *New York Times*, 20 Nov. 1972.

217 "It's about a man in the carnival world": ibid., 20 Aug. 1972.

218 "I looked at myself in the mirror": Bowers interview with MK, 18 Jun. 2004.

218 "999% sure not to be picked up": *Los Angeles Times*, 5 Nov. 1972.

218 "Everybody went to sleep": *New York Post*, 4 Nov. 1972.

219 "Poppy": EP private collection.

220 "I love to take them for a while": Koch 25.

220 "another Francis Ford Coppola": NP interview with MK, 29 May 2004.

220 "There is nothing in my life": JB file, NYPL, 1968.

221 "I hate you!": JHK interview with MK, 25 Oct. 2004.

222 "It takes all the talent you've got": *New York Post*, 4 Nov. 1972.

223 "I was thrilled to work with her": Harrington interview with MK, 28 Sep. 2004.

223 "All I wanted to do was pay tribute": Malone interview with MK, 3 Mar. 2005.

224 "I never know, even after I do them": *Los Angeles Herald-Examiner*, 13 Sep. 1975.

225 "I'm a great believer in God": Parish and Stanke 76.

226 "Those runs": JHK interview with MK, 11 Nov. 2004.

Chapter 11: Predestiny

The last years of JB's life were recalled by family members in multiple interviews and informal conversations with MK. JHK remembered the *Opening Night* set in an interview with MK, 11 Nov. 2004. The dynamics of the JB-NP-Ellen L relationship were told to MK by NP and Levine, 29 May 2004. *The Rebels* set and the Powell-Espe wedding were recalled by Sandra Powell Espe to MK, 26 Jul. 2005. The circumstances of JB's last hospital stay were shared with MK by NP, EP, KB, JHK, Scott Powell, Ellen Levine, and Ann McDowell Traub in multiple interviews and conversations from 2004 to 2006.

Quotations

228   "To a woman I've always loved": JB file, AMPAS, 14 Oct. 1976.
228   "You never know where the camera is": *Los Angeles Herald-Examiner*, 2 Mar. 1977.
228   "I could see she was terrified": Carney 420–421.
229   "I blew up like a balloon": *Los Angeles Times*, 25 Jul. 1977.
229   "Disagreement is *not* a bad thing": Carney 420.
229   "John puts such faith in his actors": *Los Angeles Times*, 8 Mar. 1978.
229   "John knew he wanted a conflict": Ferris e-mail to MK, 18 Aug. 2004.
230   "After she found out": Gazzara-Rowlands interview, *Opening Night* DVD, www.criterionco.com/.
230   "To me, John's the funniest man": *Los Angeles Times*, 8 Mar. 1978.
230   "the shifting-sands quality": *New York Times*, 1 Oct. 1988.
230   "stunning": *Variety*, 28 Dec. 1977.
231   "people are yearning for optimism": *Los Angeles Times*, 17 Apr. 1977.
231   "I had to laugh": *Los Angeles Herald-Examiner*, 26 Jun. 1977.
232   "My grandchildren are in their teens": ibid.
233   "Self-Preservation": EP private collection.
235   "Tell 'em whatever you want": Sandra Powell Espe interview with MK, 26 Jul. 2005.
236   "the experience was disastrous": Manon interview with MK, 5 Dec. 2005.
236   "I loved her": ibid., 14 Dec. 2005.
237   "an explosion in [her] eye": EP private collection, 1994.
237   "Matey, I'm going to miss you": JHK interview with MK, 11 Nov. 2004.
238   "I sincerely believe that she held out": EP interview with MK, 16 Aug. 2004.
238   "We didn't talk about": NP interview with MK, 29 May 2004.
238   "Would [you] rather come home": Powell ("Tracings of an Ordinary Mind") 26.
238   "She would never make it": interview with MK, 16 Aug. 2004.

Epilogue

Memories of JB's California service were shared with MK by JHK, 14 Nov. 2004. JB's will, dated 28 Feb. 1973, is in the family's private collection. Internet and interviews provided updated information on lives that closely touched JB's. Hook's obituary appeared in the *New York Times*, 29 Jul. 1995.

Quotations

240   "Those of us here": *Los Angeles Herald-Examiner,* 29 Dec. 1979.

241   "was like a scene from *Footlight Parade*": *Village Voice,* 21 Jan. 1980.

241   "For me, Blondell was one of the nicest": ibid.

244   "You are beautiful when you yearn": EP private collection.

BIBLIOGRAPHY

Allyson, June. *June Allyson*. New York: Putnam's Sons, 1982.

Bachardy, Don. *Stars in My Eyes*. Madison: U of Wisconsin P, 2000.

Balio, Tina. *History of the American Cinema*. Vol. 5: *Grand Design, 1930–1939*. New York: Scribner, 1993.

Beauchamp, Cari. *Without Lying Down: Frances Marion and the Powerful Women of Early Hollywood*. New York: Scribner, 1997.

Berg, A. Scott. *Goldwyn*. New York: Knopf, 1989.

Bikel, Theodore. *Theo*. New York: HarperCollins, 1994.

Billips, Connie, and Arthur Pierce. *Lux Presents Hollywood*. Jefferson: McFarland, 1995.

Blondell, Joan. *Center Door Fancy*. New York: Delacorte, 1972.

———. "A Tale of Two Dogs." Unpublished short story, 1966.

———. "Tick Tock, an Actor's Life" Unpublished article, undated.

Bona, Damien, and Mason Wiley, *Inside Oscar: The Unofficial History of the Academy Awards*. 10th ed. New York: Ballantine, 1996.

Bowers, Ronald L. "Joan Blondell Epitomized the Tough Gal with a Warm Heart." *Films in Review* 23.4 (Apr. 1972): 193–211.

Broccoli, Cubby, with Donald Zec. *When the Snow Melts: The Autobiography of Cubby Broccoli*. London: Boxtree, 1998.

Cagney, James. *Cagney by Cagney*. Garden City: Doubleday, 1976.

Carney, Ray. *Cassavetes on Cassavetes*. London: Faber & Faber, 2001.

Cohn, Art. *The Nine Lives of Michael Todd*. New York: Cardinal, 1959.

Considine, Shaun. *Bette & Joan*. New York: E. P. Dutton, 1989.

Crosby, Bing. *Call Me Lucky*. New York: Simon and Schuster, 1953.

Doherty, Thomas. *Pre-Code Hollywood*. New York: Columbia UP, 1999.

Ethell, Jeffrey L. *Aircraft Nose Art from World War I to Today*. Osceola: Motorbooks International, 2003.

Fidelman, Geoffrey Mark. *The Lucy Book*. Los Angeles: Renaissance, 1999.

Finch, Christopher, and Linda Rosenkrantz. *Gone Hollywood*. New York: Doubleday, 1979.

Finler, Joel W. *The Hollywood Story*. New York: Crown, 1988.

Fisher, Eddie. *Been There, Done That*. New York: St. Martin's, 1999.

Frank, Gerold. *Judy.* New York: Harper & Row, 1975.

Frank, Michael. "Joan Blondell and Dick Powell: The Versatile Musical Comedy Actors off Sunset Boulevard." *Architectural Digest* (Apr. 1998): 230–235, 310.

Giddins, Gary. *Bing Crosby: A Pocketful of Dreams.* New York: Little, Brown and Company, 2001.

Hagen, Ray, and Laura Wagner. *Killer Tomatoes: Fifteen Tough Film Dames.* Jefferson: McFarland, 2004.

Halberstam, David. *Summer of '49.* New York: William Morrow, 1989.

Hamann, G. D., ed. *Joan Blondell in the '30s.* Hollywood: Filming Today, 2004.

Harris, Warren G. *Clark Gable.* New York: Harmony, 2002.

Harvey, James. *Romantic Comedy in Hollywood, from Lubitsch to Sturges.* New York: Knopf, 1987.

Higham, Charles. *Warner Brothers.* New York: Scribner's, 1975.

Hirschhorn, Clive. *The Warner Bros. Story.* New York: Crown, 1979.

Israel, Betsy. *Bachelor Girl: 100 Years of Breaking Down Rules—a Social History of Single Living.* New York: William Morrow, 2002.

Jerome, Stuart. *Those Crazy Wonderful Years When We Ran Warner Bros.* Secaucus: Lyle Stuart, 1983.

Johnson, David. "The Original Miss Show Biz." *After Dark* (Dec. 1971): 38–42.

Kazan, Elia. *Elia Kazan.* New York: Knopf, 1988.

Kennedy, Harold J. *No Pickle, No Performance.* Garden City: Doubleday, 1978.

Kennedy, Matthew. *Edmund Goulding's Dark Victory: Hollywood's Genius Bad Boy.* Madison: U of Wisconsin P, 2004.

Kobal, John, ed. *People Will Talk.* New York: Knopf, 1985.

Koch, Maureen. "Joan Blondell — The Great Golddigger Still Digging Hollywood." *Andy Warhol's Interview* (Aug. 1972): 24–29.

LeRoy, Mervyn. *Mervyn LeRoy: Take One.* New York: Hawthorn, 1974.

Liebman, Roy. *Vitaphone Films.* Jefferson: McFarland, 2003.

Lobenthal, Joel. *Tallulah!* New York: Regan, 2004.

Lumet, Sidney. *Making Movies.* New York: Vintage, 1996.

Maltin, Leonard. "*FFM* interviews Joan Blondell." *Film Fan Monthly* 99 (Sep. 1969): 3–7.

Marion, Frances. "Hollywood." Unpublished memoirs, Special Collections, USC Cinema-Television Library, Los Angeles, California.

———. *Off with Their Heads!* New York: Macmillan, 1972.

Martin, David. *The Films of Busby Berkeley.* San Francisco: Dave Martin, 2000.

Martin, Mart. *Did She or Didn't She?* New York: Citadel, 1996.

McCabe, John. *Cagney.* New York: Knopf, 1997.

McCarthy, Todd. *Howard Hawks: The Grey Fox of Hollywood.* New York: Grove, 1997.

McClelland, Doug. *Forties Film Talk.* Jefferson: McFarland, 1992.

Merritt, Greg. *Celluloid Mavericks: A History of American Independent Film.* New York: Thunder's Mouth, 2000.

Munter, Pam. "Joan Blondell: Heart of Gold." *Films of the Golden Age* (fall 2002): 14–31.

Nash, Jay Robert, and Stanley Ralph Ross. *The Motion Picture Guide*. Chicago: Cinebooks, 1986.

O'Brien, Pat. *The Wind at My Back*. Garden City: Doubleday, 1964.

Parish, James Robert. *The Complete Actors' Television Credits, 1948–1988*. Vol. 2: *Actresses*. Metuchen: Scarecrow, 1991.

———, and Michael Pitts. *Hollywood Songsters: Singers Who Act and Actors Who Sing*. New York: Routledge, 2003.

Parish, James Robert, and Don E. Stanke. *The Leading Ladies*. New York: Arlington House, 1977.

Powell, Ellen. "A Pony in the Pile." Unpublished memoirs, 1985.

———. "Tracings of an Ordinary Mind." Library of Congress, 1982.

Preminger, Erik Lee. *My G-String Mother: At Home and Backstage with Gypsy Rose Lee*. Berkeley: North Atlantic, 2004.

Sanders, Coyne S. *Desilu: The Story of Lucille Ball and Desi Arnaz*. New York: Harper Paperbacks, 1994.

Schatz, Thomas. *The Genius of the System*. New York: Henry Holt, 1988.

Sennett, Ted. *Warner Brothers Presents*. New Rochelle: Arlington, 1972.

Sheppard, Dick. *Elizabeth*. Garden City: Doubleday, 1974.

Smith, Ella. *Starring Miss Barbara Stanwyck*. New York: Crown, 1974.

Sperling, Cass Warner, and Cork Millner, with Jack Warner Jr. *Hollywood Be Thy Name*. Rocklin: Prima, 1994.

Starr, Michael Seth. *Art Carney*. New York: Fromm International, 1997.

Thomas, Tony. *The Dick Powell Story*. Burbank: Riverwood Press, 1993.

Todd, Mike, Jr. *A Valuable Property*. New York: Arbor, 1983.

Tornabene, Lyn. *Long Live the King*. New York: Putnam's Sons, 1976.

Troyan, Michael. *A Rose for Mrs. Miniver*. Lexington: UP of Kentucky, 1999.

Van Meter, Jonathan. *The Last Good Time*. New York: Crown, 2003.

Vanderbilt, Gloria. *It Seemed Important at the Time*. New York: Simon & Schuster, 2004.

Vieira, Mark. *Sin in Soft Focus*. New York: Abrams, 1999.

Wayne, Jane Ellen. *Gable's Women*. New York: Prentice Hall, 1987.

Young, Jeff. *Kazan*. New York: Newmarket, 1999.

INDEX